Sanjay Sharma represented In[illegible]n badminton, and also served as coach for the national badminton squad. He is now a commentator on the game and a writer. Sanjay penned *The World Beneath His Feet*, the critically acclaimed biography of Pullela Gopi Chand, the iconic shuttler.

Medini Sharma, a former tennis international and sports producer on television, now works as senior producer with STAR Sports.

COURAGE *beyond* COMPARE

HOW TEN ATHLETES **OVERCAME DISABILITY** AND **ADVERSITY** TO BECOME **CHAMPIONS**

Sanjay Sharma ⋆ Medini Sharma

RUPA

First published by
Rupa Publications India Pvt. Ltd 2014
7/16, Ansari Road, Daryaganj
New Delhi 110002

Sales Centres:

Allahabad Bengaluru Chennai
Hyderabad Jaipur Kathmandu
Kolkata Mumbai

ISBN: 978-81-291-3119-5

First impression 2014

10 9 8 7 6 5 4 3 2 1

Printed by Thomson Press India Ltd, Faridabad

Contents

Foreword *vii*

Preface *xi*

Rajeev Bagga
Magician on the Badminton Court 1

Satya Prakash Tewari
The Lion Hearted 27

Nir Bahadur Gurung
The Quintessential Street Fighter 54

Murlikant Petkar
Hero Extraordinaire 77

Taranath Shenoy
A Genius in Every Way 107

Mansoor Ali Khan Pataudi
A New Dimension to Courage 125

Farman Basha
Pocket-sized Hurricane 153

Rajaram Ghag
Conqueror of the Seas 179

Devendra Jhajharia
A Real Indian Hero 209

Malathi Holla
Queen of Her Chariot 233

Acknowledgements 253

A Word of Gratitude 255

Dedication 257

FOREWORD

I am truly overwhelmed by this incredible book which tells us the stories of the extraordinary struggles and trauma faced by some of the highly accomplished para athletes of India, who overcame unbelievable physical and mental challenges to become world beaters in their chosen sports disciplines. It is great to read that sports became the vehicle that catapulted them from traumatic lives to become true legends of India.

This was an emotional roller-coaster ride for me as I thumbed the pages. And I realized that what we, the so-called 'able-bodied' have achieved, simply cannot be compared with the achievements of the ten athletes profiled here. Our successes pale in comparison when compared to the courage and devotion of these selected names. Sanjay Sharma, my old friend and colleague in the Indian badminton squad, and his charming daughter Medini, have written this with great passion, and they have very rightly said that for all 'differently abled' people, every minute of their life is a trauma, riddled with obstacles that we cannot even begin to understand.

Simple things like boarding a train, a bus, or just walking down a street brings challenges to them which we cannot comprehend. The authors are right in saying that we as a society are mentally dysfunctional when it comes to understanding the lives the 'differently abled' in our country lead. Do we ever give a thought to the problems they face every day, every hour? And are we not guilty as a people of not giving them simple dignity in life by trying to bring about changes that can make their lives more meaningful? And have we become so callous that we cannot even give the para athletes their dues after they have brought huge honours to India? We begrudge them even a well-achieved Arjuna Award or other state awards.

Imagine the super-athlete and former soldier Nir Bahadur Gurung, who has three silvers in the Asian Games, and also the elusive gold medal, and who does not even have a state award for excelling in sport. He brought tears to my eyes when he asks in his simple but very penetrating way, 'When they ask me to shed blood for the country, they do not ask which state of India I come from. But for getting a simple award, which I deserve, my statehood comes into question.' Is this not a shame or a 'national embarrassment' as the authors rightly say, that should shock our combined consciences?

I was stunned to read that Farman Basha defeated able-bodied athletes in powerlifting and that the federation passed a rule which then prohibited the differently abled from competing against so-called 'normal' lifters. I would have thought that vice versa would have been the rule. And this pint-sized Hercules has never lost in the Indian Nationals in the last twenty years, has been ranked fourth and fifth in two Paralympics, is the Asian champion and has been awarded the Arjuna Award—but our society could not even offer him a job!

And what a great story the 'Queen of her Chariot', Malathi Holla's life makes. A fellow Banglorean, she defeated her male counterparts in wheelchair racing.

Each and every chapter gives us some lesson to learn from.

It is well chronicled that Mansoor Ali Khan Pataudi and Rajeev Bagga played, competed and then excelled against normal players not only in 'open' events in India, but took on the world and showed off their memorable talent which brought laurels to the country. They were indeed superhumans and I can only salute them. But how many know that Murlikant Petkar is the first Indian to win an Olympic gold way back in 1972? This brave soldier, wounded in war and with one bullet still lodged in his spine, made gigantic leaps by not only winning the Paralympics gold—setting a record in the process—but also won the gold in the Asian and Commonwealth Para Games. He makes us all look like pygmies.

Devendra Jhajharia is the only Indian ever to have the national flag unfurled in his honour at the main Olympic stadium when he won gold in the one-armed javelin throw at the 2004 Athens Paralympics. He repeated this feat at the 2013 world para athletics championships in France. He is a world champion with a world record, an Olympic champion with an an Olympic record and an Asian champion with an Asian record. In what way can I, or so many peers of mine, even think of comparing ourselves to this man?

This book is a treasure. I recommend it whole-heartedly and hope the entire country reads and learns something from the legends who are chronicled here. I, for one, felt humbled after reading every story. I hope that I have learnt something from each one of these heroes. If I imbibe even an iota of their greatness, I will become a better person. And so will each and every reader who lays his or her hands on this incredible book.

Prakash Padukone

PREFACE

It is believed that the word 'courage' was coined in or around 1300 AD and was derived from the Middle English word *corage*. The word courage is a noun and, in modern layman terms, it is defined as 'the quality of mind or spirit that enables a person to face danger, difficulty, pain, etc. without fear; bravery'.

So what does courage actually mean? Does it mean a state of mind that makes ordinary people perform extraordinary acts? Or does it make the common man—the aam admi—fight daily battles in our country, to live a life of respect? The essence of this word is something we see in many shades in our daily lives.

History also offers us many examples of courage that went beyond the realms of ordinary life: whether it was our own Bapu who, singlehandedly and with his sheer belief and conviction, took on the might of the Raj and threw the British out from India; or the venerable Anna Hazare who recently exhorted his countrymen to throw out the corrupt and venal politicians who have plundered the country and save the future for a new generation of Indians.

Of course it is in wars and natural calamities that we see courage of yet another kind where soldiers and even simple ordinary people rise above expectations and perform heroic deeds to save their motherland or just to save human lives and property from destruction.

However, it is in mainstream and adventure sports that we see examples of raw courage globally and on an almost daily basis. Sport, by its very definition, means that one has to compete with the other. In adventure sports, one tries to conquer obstacles placed by nature which are almost always extremely difficult, dangerous and hazardous.

In the world of sports, we can see many instances which have made everyone sit up and take notice. The 1976 Olympics will be synonymous with Shun Fujimoto, a twenty-six-year old Japanese athlete, who stretched the boundaries of pain as he went on to help Japan win the men's team gold in gymnastics, despite shattering his kneecap.

Even India's original Little Master, Sunil Gavaskar faced the famed West Indies armada, which included Andy Roberts, Michael Holding, Joel Garner, Colin Croft and the invincible Malcolm Marshall. Unperturbed, the batting maestro faced the furious onslaught in the most audacious manner and scored some of his most well-known centuries against the mighty West Indies, without wearing a helmet. Can we even imagine a single batsman of today facing fast bowlers in such a fashion?

And did not Nari Contractor, the first southpaw captain of the Indian cricket team, add a new dimension of courage? He came back on to the field after being hit on the head by a vicious bouncer from Charlie Griffith, which had knocked him unconscious. After regaining consciousness, and despite nursing a concussion, Contractor walked back on to the field to finish the task that had remained incomplete.

Even the eleven-year-old Kearan Tongue-Gibbs, the wonder cricketer from London, has defined his own brand of courage. Tongue-Gibbs does not possess hands or forearms due to a birth defect. Nonetheless, he bats eloquently and imparts vicious spin to his bowling, much to the astonishment of all who watch him.

Only recently, courage of a different kind was exhibited by Nik Wallenda who became the first human being to walk on a tightrope, unassisted, over the Niagara Falls. After achieving this remarkable feat, he said very humbly, 'The impossible is not quite the impossible if you set your mind to it.'

And what about double amputee Mark Inglis who shocked one and all when he conquered his final frontier by scaling the summit of the tallest and the mightiest peak in the world, Everest. His inspiring story has led many to achieve heroic feats despite having faced tremendous setbacks in their lives. For example, Canada's Spencer West made it to the top of Africa's highest peak, the 19,341-feet-high Kilimanjaro, despite being a double amputee.

The world is certainly rife with millions of examples of ordinary able-bodied individuals exhibiting extraordinary courage just to survive and conquer insurmountable obstacles put in their way. But there are certain special individuals who have given a new meaning to courage by facing unfathomable odds every minute of their lives, especially in India, where society as a whole suffers with infrastructural disability.

Indian sportsmen and sportswomen have never had it easy to win the right to wear the Indian colours. Shamefully, there are enough true stories of the trials and turbulences of such individuals who have brought glory to India in their own way by conquering all the odds that were stacked against them, be it their disability, their fight for their right to play sports, even financial problems which threatened to cripple their dreams, and last, but not the least, petty politics.

Our 'differently abled' brethren, however, face many more problems and prejudices. While we, the so called 'able-bodied' take things for granted, for the handicapped, every minute of existence is a trauma. We cannot even imagine the scale of the problems they must face. Yet, despite such odds stacked against them, there are many 'differently abled' Indian athletes who have conquered their fears and have gone on to become legends in sports of their choice. They may not be known to the rest of the country but, nonetheless, they have brought glory to India we can only dream of. Some are soldiers who were struck down during wars, some are amputees who lost limbs to accidents and some are afflicted with polio. Some tried to commit suicide to escape the miseries of their lives. Yet somehow, through the glory of sports, they found a reason to live. And yes, to ensure dignity for themselves and their families.

This book is an ode to the indomitable human spirit, a profile that redefines courage, a story of sheer guts, determination and fortitude of just ten such individuals—a microscopic number, really—but people who are, in their own way, the 'jewels of India'. Their courage is beyond compare.

Murlikant Rajaram Petkar survived a lynching mob when he was just twelve years old. He then survived seven bullets at the precocious age of eighteen, as soldier of the Indian Army fighting on the Sialkot front in the 1971 war. He survived umpteen operations, survived a suicide attempt and then took to the water like a proverbial fish to win India's first Olympic gold medal. Yes, you heard it right, it is Murlikant Petkar who won first individual gold at any Olympics for India. Petkar, who still has a bullet lodged in his spine, won the 1972 freestyle swimming gold at the Heidelburg Paralympics—India's first ever foray into para sports. Petkar, a true legend of Indian sports, also won gold at 1970 CWG Para Games and gold at the 1982 Asian Para Games. Can any 'abled' athlete even approach the scale of what Petkar has achieved? Yet he is unknown and was not even honoured with the Arjuna Award, let alone the Rajiv Gandhi Khel Ratna, which he so richly deserved. Petkar is the quintessential Indian hero.

Rajeev Bagga, born deaf and mute, was a natural at

badminton. A four-time national champion in the open category, he represented India with distinction, playing in many tournaments, including the Thomas Cup, the CWG 1990, the Asian Championships and the All England, in a highly illustrious career. But what made him legendary was the fact that the World Federation of the Deaf conferred on him the title of the 'world deaf athlete of the century'. For winning sixteen gold medals in four Deaf Olympiads over some sixteen years, Rajeev was also awarded the Arjuna Award by a grateful nation.

West Indian pace bowlers such as Wesley Hall and Charles Griffith used to bowl at speeds of up to 100 mph. But Mansoor Ali Khan Pataudi, blind in one eye, toyed with such fearsome bowling and scored centuries at will. He was also one of the best fielders of his era. Aptly nicknamed 'Tiger', Pataudi, despite his major handicap, went on to captain the Indian cricket team with distinction and élan.

Rajaram Ghag is the swimming legend of Mumbai. Afflicted with polio, the heroic Rajaram developed such powerful arms and shoulders that he went on to to cross the English Channel and the treacherous Strait of Gibraltar using just his arms. He was the first Asian to do so.

Despite being visually and hearing impaired, legendary swimmer Taranath Shenoy has many firsts to his name. On 8 August 1988, this powerhouse became the first deaf and mute person to swim across the Strait of Gibraltar. He has also crossed the English Channel thrice and has set many national records, which still remain unbeaten even today. Shenoy received the prestigious Arjuna Award and the Padma Shri, amongst many other awards.

Rajasthan's Devendra Jhajharia has earned the distinction of being India's first medallist at any World Paralympic Games in

2013. The one-armed javelin thrower won the gold medal and also set a new world record in the process. He also won the gold medal at the 2002 Paralympics and also at the eighth Far East and South Pacific Games for the Disabled in Korea in 2002. In 2012, Jhajharia also became the first Paralympian to receive the prestigious Padma Shree Award.

Not only do we ignore the feats of such icons, we pay no heed to the needs of close to the 7 per cent of our population that is physically challenged, and requires special help? Seven per cent is a huge number. As Devendra Jhajharia says in his story—'We are ignored by government and politicians because we have not become a vote-bank. But we should not forget that all citizens over seventy years of age also belong to the "differently abled" category. They also have special needs as senior citizens, but they too are ignored.' He is absolutely right.

The purpose of writing this book is also to highlight a bigger question, to which Indian society must find answers if we are to be called a civilized nation.

How many differently abled people do we see on our roads, in malls, or in cinemas? Most public places do not have ramps for entry and egress, cannot be negotiated by them. Given the despicable condition of our roads, most differently abled people cannot negotiate potholes without risking serious injury. Can differently abled people climb on to most of the buses which ply on our streets? Can they enter our railway stations or our passenger-unfriendly trains? Can they use any of the public conveniences that operate in our cities? Do we so-called 'abled' spare even a passing to the suffering of such people? How many of us help a visually impaired person cross a road. Have we fought for the right to have footpaths for such citizens? We all are going to be, as Jhajharia says, differently abled some day. But we do not even think of our own future.

In a way, therefore, there is a forced ostracization by the society at large of such Indian citizens. They are forced to remain at home, caged, which poses problems for their families. There is hardly any social life and yes, it is for this precise reason that the handicapped feel angry with the rest society.

It is not just the financial stress and strains that families of such people face, which break their backs, something that society must appreciate and find ways of helping in. But we forget the roles the care-giver plays in giving a life to our handicapped brethren. These people have to be applauded, as they spend their entire lives looking after such people. The care-giver, which are mostly spouses or parents, are forced to lead lives of as much difficulty and hardships, as those of the person in their care. We must also give a thought to their selfless service.

In the end we as authors, want this book to motivate all of us, through the real-life stories of our 'true' sporting legends. We feel that if society can help and provide a level playing field to all differently abled, they can contribute to the well being of India as much as rest of us. They will manage magnificently, all they need is initial push. As one of our ten subjects says, 'Do not lift a wheel-chair bound, up the steps and then abandon him/her there to his/her own device. What will happen tomorrow when no one is there to help? How will he/she manage with no one around? Instead, build a ramp so that he can negotiate the heights and thereby become self-sufficient to walk the path to self-help. That will be the best contribution that can be made to our lives. We do not need sympathy. We need understanding.'

RAJEEV BAGGA
Magician on the Badminton Court

We never know how tall we are
Until we are asked to rise
And then if we are true to plan
Our statures touch the sky

~EMILY DICKINSON~

On 6 April 1967 the Bagga family welcomed a third child, a son, and named him Rajeev. Little did they anticipate the heights of glory this young infant was to one day touch. Indeed how could they, when his path appeared to be so fraught—within eleven months of his birth, Rajeev was diagnosed as being deaf and mute. As Rajeev's father, Brigadier S.R. Bagga recalls, the family was thunderstruck. The ensuing flurry of visits to army hospitals and various other doctors was of no avail and the gloomy diagnosis began to sink in.

Rajeev, unaware of all the hullabaloo and commotion he was inadvertently causing to the family, was happy within himself and his fast enveloping world of silence. He had a typical army childhood, with a change of address and school almost every two to three years, as his father was transferred across the country. Rajeev attended some schools where all the children were deaf, and also a couple of schools where the other children did not have a hearing impairment.

'There was a Hindi-medium school in Delhi where he was studying first, and we employed the principal to come home and teach Rajeev with charts, drawings etc. But a leading army surgeon told us that, worldwide, the deaf language—the sign language—uses English denotations. And that a really good school was located in Mumbai. So I requested a transfer to Mumbai and the army kindly agreed,' reminisces Brigadier Bagga. This school was exclusively for deaf-mute children.

During this posting to Bombay, another aspect of Rajeev's nature came to the fore. It reflected something that the family as a whole really enjoyed—sports. Says his elder sister Sangeeta, 'Both our parents were very keen on sports, both played different sports, and swam whenever they could. Our mother, in fact, was a swimming champion right from her childhood days in Jamshedpur. She won many events and father was also the sports administrator at most of his army postings. He used to just love sports. I remember when we came back from school, mother used to be in a hurry to get us out of the house. We changed clothes and were out playing various outdoor games. My father firmly believed, military style if I may add, that running, jumping, skipping, swimming, etc., helped us become stronger, healthier and more focused in life.'

Rajeev was a good student according to Sangeeta and was always in the top five in his class exams. 'He always sat in the front bench, absorbed all that his teachers taught him and often studied till midnight to ensure success in his studies.'

In Bombay, Rajeev was lucky to be living right next to the Armed services-dominated United Services Club, right in the heart of Colaba's Navy Nagar area. The popular golf course at this club, its tennis courts, running track, and badminton and squash facilities were superb and enticed young Rajeev, who was growing up fast. Rajeev tried his hand at every game available and the coach or marker of each discipline wanted Rajeev to pick up their sport seriously. Then his father was transferred and Rajeev moved with the family to a new posting and a new school. Brigadier Bagga was transferred to Pune as Deputy Commandant of the College of Military Engineering (CME) and also given charge of sports at CME.

There was so much emphasis on sports in the family that the three kids had only their school uniforms and sports kits as far as clothing was concerned. They had hardly any other clothes, as they simply had no time for socializing or for any other activity. In fact, Sangeeta recalls that though Rajeev was confirmed as hearing-impaired, he was so popular at each posting that a gang of young boys would always be waiting for him to join them after school to start playing whatever the choice of sport was that day. In fact, it may be correct to mention here that in all the running he did in football, hockey, cricket, or whenever he went cycling or swimming with his friends, young Rajeev was always at the front. This also helped in building stamina and in making him stronger.

'Almost all the coaches that we interacted with in those days told us that he had fantastic hand-eye co-ordination,' remembers Brigadier Bagga. 'He was very good at racquet sports. They said he was a natural sportsman and this gladdened us in many ways as we were not sure what his life would be when he grew up. But sports as a career did occur to us in those early days.'

Of course, since all the three siblings kept up to date in studies, kept up their grades, the parents never pressurized them on this aspect. By the time Rajeev was about twelve years old, he had already started playing local squash tournaments. This sport was very much a real 'military' sport, as squash courts had mushroomed in all cantonment areas. Cantonments had badminton and tennis courts, too, but not in such abundance as squash courts. In fact, going down the list of past national squash champions one can see total domination by the armed forces, as most champions at senior levels came from the defence services. Squash, therefore, initially became the natural outlet to consume all young Rajeev's energies.

The sport is fast and technical, where correct footwork and movements, coupled with razor-sharp reflexes, are the main ingredients. The hours he put in at the squash courts had toned Rajeev's body and he was lithe and fast, yet economical in movement. The effort also helped in developing a well-trained, sharp eye, which was to help him right through his sports career. And most importantly, practising with the heavy squash racquet ensured that he developed a very strong backhand, which was to become his most important stroke in badminton—and it was in badminton that this future world champion was to eventually find his calling.

Meanwhile, young Rajeev progressed quickly and won many sub-junior level events in squash across the country along with winning a well-fought place in the finals of the Sub-junior National Championships (under-15 age group), in 1981 at Jaipur. Rajeev lost the finals, but questions on the exact age of the winner complicated the situation. It was later found that the winner had already passed the tenth standard Secondary School Certificate (SSC) board examination and, therefore, should not have played in the under-15, category. A month later Rajeev was rightly declared the Sub-junior National Squash Champion. Incidentally, he was also a finalist at the Maharashtra State Tennis Championships in the same age category in the same year. However, despite his excellent on-court performances, Rajeev had a problem competing in both squash and tennis.

In squash, he could not follow the scores as the match referee sat outside the court and Rajeev could not lip-read through the thick glass partition. 'I was present at Jaipur,' says Brigadier Bagga, 'and I had to repeat the scores to him standing close to the rear of the court glass area where he could see me. I used to mumble the score and hope that he understood. I realized that this was going to be a problem and that his handicap would come in way of his progress in squash. After all, I could not go everywhere, and the opponent could also object.'

Despite this handicap, his performance was so good that the president of the Squash Federation of India (SFI) said, 'Brigadier, the way Rajeev is playing, moving on the court and contacting the ball, he is going to play for India in two years time. You just make sure he continues to play, and we will find a way out of this score-reading problem which puts him at a disadvantage.' Some other senior SFI officials present at Jaipur also beseeched Brigadier Bagga to ensure that Rajeev did not give up squash.

However Rajeev, who liked this sport a lot, had another far more serious problem with it. Many a time in rallies, the opponent comes up behind you and hits the ball off the back wall. At such times Rajeev could neither see the ball nor his opponent unless he turned around to look, and that could be very dangerous as he risked injury—nor could he hear the ball making contact with his opponent's racquet. Thus, neither being able to track the ball visually at all times, nor being able to mark its position through sound, Rajeev had to depend on his instinct to gauge where the ball would go, which direction it would take. Along with the fact that he could not track the scores during the game, this created a major handicap.

Another favourite sport was tennis, which Rajeev loved. In

fact he had the ideal physique for most sports, especially racquet games. In tennis, however, the length of the court and the various strokes that could be imparted on the ball, in terms of slicing under the ball, topspin, side spin or just a straight hit, posed a problem. Obviously, he could not hear the stroke at all and this was a slight handicap in the long run. Rajeev also felt that the length of the tennis court posed a problem because as he says, 'I wanted the opponent to be close by so I could look him in the eye,' to better predict and control the game.

Now it was up to the hearing-impaired teenager to decide which sport would suit him most. Finally, when he was just about to turn fifteen, after being crowned the Sub-junior National Squash Champion, the family decided that Rajeev was not going to play either tennis or squash, it was badminton that all of them would focus their energies on. Rajeev would have their unstinted support in fulfilling his dream of playing for India one day—a thought that had germinated in his mind after winning the squash nationals.

'In long run, therefore, I opted for badminton,' says Rajeev, elucidating the benefits as he then saw them. 'As the court is not very big, I could see the opponent clearly and look him in the eye and all strokes were played in front of me. Plus the match referee sat close by, so keeping count of score was not much of a problem. And I used to love badminton the most after squash, which in any case was not destined for me.' So badminton it was, that was to become his all-consuming passion. Though later, after he migrated to England and received British citizenship, this outstanding sportsman also played beach volleyball internationally in the senior-age-group category for the UK team!

Meanwhile Brigadier Bagga, who had been again posted to Bombay, decided to find out how Rajeev could get some professional coaching in badminton. 'Once we decided that Rajeev was to play badminton competitively, the hunt for proper and professional coaching started. I went around to the clubs close to Colaba area, [where the family lived] and was told to meet one Mr K.K. Cheema, a former international player, who used to coach at the P.J. Hindu Gymkhana on Marine Drive. I met Cheema and Secretary of the Badminton Department, Shyam Bashishta, and both said I should contact Sanjay Sharma* who was playing for India at that time and was a prominent player.'

Both as author, and as Rajeev's newly selected coach at the time, I would like to digress slightly before I present to the reader how Rajeev was actually introduced to top-standard badminton at the junior level. I had written an article in the *Hindustan Times* many years ago, when the popular film *Iqbal* directed by Nagesh Kukunoor had become a runaway hit. The film was about a deaf-mute boy Iqbal, who dreamt of playing cricket for India and actually went on to realize his dream. Rajeev Bagga, however, was the real and not reel Iqbal who, despite his hearing impairment, went on not only to win the national championships multiple times and represent India internationally in what he charmingly calls the 'hearing' category and what we term the 'normal' or 'abled' category, but also went on to become one of the best sportsmen ever seen in the world, measured by any parameter possible.

To return to my initial meeting with Rajeev, Brigadier Bagga and he came to the P.J. Hindu Gymkhana one morning late in 1982 and sought me out. They had been told by Cheema and Shyam Bashishta that I used to train at the gym from early in the morning and that I also used to give physical training to some players. This was not entirely correct. I used to train and

---

*One of the authors of this book.

practice, and many other senior players did the same along with me. That particular day I was practising for the forthcoming Senior National Championships, hardly a month away, with Leroy D'sa, a formidable doubles player.

Father and son came and stood by the court. I thought they were some guests who were just seeing the facilities at the Gymkhana. However, when they stood there for almost ten minutes, I asked them what they wanted. The Brigadier said he wanted to talk to me about coaching and training for his son. I requested them to wait. Later, when Leroy and I were resting, the duo came to me again. That I told them I was not coaching at all and they should find some professional coach. Brigadier Bagga, however, said, 'We have been advised to talk to you and request you to coach Rajeev.'

I was getting a bit irritated by then and said, 'I am trying to explain to you that I do not coach and that your son should get a membership here and play with the Marker [club-appointed coach or helper]. He is big enough to take care of himself.' But the Brigadier again said that Rajeev was keen to learn from me and that I should take up the assignment. 'You will not be disappointed,' he added.

So I turned to Rajeev who seemed to be smiling all the while, and asked him why he wanted to play badminton. He, of course, could not reply and kept smiling. I asked him again and since he was not forthcoming I asked the father in an exasperated tone, making a cardinal mistake that most of us make, 'Is he deaf and dumb?'

I was highly embarrassed and turned crimson with shame when the Brigadier replied, 'No, he is not dumb. He is deaf-mute. Actually he is very intelligent. If you talk slowly, looking at him, he can lip-read you and also reply in his own way.' I did not know where to look, but then realized that since they had shown so much patience and decency, I had to do something about it.

I then slowly got into a sort of conversation with Rajeev and he explained to me that he was a National Squash Champion but that his impairment came in the way of actually executing the types of strokes he wanted to, as he saw the ball late when it was hot off the back wall.

He told me why he liked badminton and said I should try him out that same moment. Since my practice session was almost over we did try him out and I found that he had excellent contact with the shuttle, sweet-timed his strokes, and that his long legs carried him around quiet well. In short, it appeared to me that here was a boy with great potential and if we could find somehow a way to communicate with him, he was a champion in making.

I told the duo that though I was not coaching professionally, I would still take him under my wing and that as a first step he should try coming out and training with us early in the morning, so that I could gauge his fitness level. I must add here that though he looked fit, we still had to work hard together and I also found him a bit lazy in the beginning. But once he got the hang of things, there was no stopping Rajeev.

He progressed very fast and though the sport was not the one he played regularly or competitively prior to coming to me, he still went on to become the top Maharashtra State Under-18 Player of Maharashtra two years in a row, and narrowly missed becoming the National Junior Under-18 Champion due to a quirk of fate. All this within two years of taking up the sport seriously.

The finals of the Junior Nationals were scheduled for 1 November 1984 at Kota in Rajasthan. Most unfortunately for the entire country, then prime minister Indira Gandhi was shot dead early in the morning by her bodyguards at her residence, on 31 October 1984. The nation was shell-shocked and anti-Sikh riots erupted in many states nationwide, including the city of Kota where Rajeev was due to play in three semi-finals: the singles, doubles and the mixed doubles.

The organizers were in a hurry to wind up the championships. They had received reports that riots had begun in Kota city, and that the situation was going to worsen by the next day. They asked Rajeev to grant a walkover in both the doubles events. Brigadier Bagga, who was there in Kota with Rajeev, also felt that his son should back out and play only the singles. But Rajeev refused. He told his father, 'My partners are depending on me. How can I let them down? I am going to play all three events. I have to be true to myself.' It is another matter that he lost both, the doubles and the mixed doubles, and won the singles which qualified him for the finals the next morning. However, the riot situation had worsened as predicted and it was decided that the finals would comprise only one game of 21 points, instead of the usual best of three games of 15 points each. But no one thought to inform Rajeev of this before he came out to face Aritra Nandi of Bengal.

Now, from the time he had started playing, there was one weakness in his approach to the game, for which he was personally responsible. Rajeev was a slow starter and always took his time to gain momentum. This meant that the opponent was always ahead at the start of the first game and slowly but surely, once warmed up, Rajeev would start unleashing his amazingly comprehensive game.

In Kota, too, the same thing happened. Rajeev was way down at the start but caught up at the 10-10 scoreline and warmed up now, raced ahead to 'claim' the first game 15-12. At least that is what he thought, but with Nandi not coming forward to change courts, and the Chair Umpire asking the game to be continued, Rajeev was very confused. He tried to understand what was happening, but no one—not a single soul—came forward to explain to this finalist that the match was to be of one game only. Nandi, sensing the confusion, got quick points from the deaf-mute champion and sealed the one game match at 21-18 and was 'crowned' the new National Under-18 Champion.

When we—Sanjay Sharma and Rajeev Bagga—were playing the Commonwealth Games Championships at Auckland in January 1990, Rajeev explained what had happened that day. 'I was shocked and stunned. Perhaps for the first time I realized that my handicap had come in my way. This was unjust. Someone from the Badminton Association of India (BAI) should have sat me down and patiently explained what was going to happen. They did not bother. In fact the BAI never helped me in any way right through my career. Still, I have no anger or malice towards anyone. I know I will have many more opportunities to prove that on the badminton court I can be as good as the "hearing" people.'

Brigadier Bagga has another really interesting anecdote to tell us about Rajeev's huge effort at Kota, where he reached the semi-finals in all three events, and also the finals of the singles. Says the father, 'Rajeev had so many matches till the semis that he was on court for at least two matches per event, making a total of six matches daily, in the first four days. This effort, and the fact that he played the singles finals also, dehydrated him so much that once he crashed on to bed after the finals he would not get up. We had a train to catch and with a lot of difficulty I tried to drag him to the station, but he collapsed on the way. I immediately took him to a doctor near the station and he said to take Rajeev to where some roadside stalls were selling food. The doctor said, "Let him smell some pakodas [fritters] frying in oil, and the aroma of the frying pakodas will ensure that he fully revives!" '

No sooner did the aroma hit Rajeev that he woke up and, according to his father, ate almost a kilogram and a half of the hot and tasty pakodas. Only after eating the whole lot bought for him did Rajeev feel strong enough again to walk down to the station where they boarded the train to Bombay.

From 1984, till he started playing for India in the senior team in 1988, Rajeev had stamped his class as a player, both in singles and doubles matches. In fact when he was just about twenty years old, the deaf-mute shuttler stunned the world of Indian sports by securing a victory of epic proportions, a victory that catapulted Rajeev Bagga's name into the national consciousness and made him a hero, someone to watch out for.

There is no name bigger in Indian sports in general, and in Indian badminton in particular, than the legendary Prakash Padukone. The nine-time former national champion also won the biggest trophy in the game—the All England singles crown in 1980—and the inaugural World Cup in 1981 at Kuala Lumpur. A hugely successful international career, which started with the fantastic gold medal win at the 1978 Commonwealth Games, saw a Padukone blitzkrieg around the world, netting him, amongst others, the British Masters at Albert Hall in 1979, the Danish Open and the Swedish Open in 1980, the Indian Masters in 1981 and a whole lot of other major titles including the Hong Kong Open, the German Open and the Penang Open. Suffice it to say that Prakash Padukone was the most revered name in world badminton.

After the All England victory in March 1980, Padukone shifted base to Denmark for professional reasons, coming to India occasionally to lead the country in international events. He was still in the top-ten world rankings when pressure from the BAI ensured that he came to participate in the 1987 Senior National

Championships held at Jammu.

During those days locally made shuttlecocks were used in the country as the Government of India did not allow imported shuttles for any event other than internationals held in the country, but these were few and far between. For example, after the 1982 Asiad meet in Delhi, the only international championships held in the country were South Asian Championships—organized under the aegis of the South Asian Association for Regional Cooperation or SAARC—and the Asian Confederation Championships in Kolkata in 1983. Prakash, who was living in Copenhagen, was not used to the inferior quality shuttles, and since he had not played in any domestic championships since the 1980 Nationals at Vijaywada, was not at all used to the funny flight and brittleness of local brands.

Be that as it may, given his stature and enormous experience, it was expected that he would simply walk over any opponent, leave alone an almost unknown player called Rajeev Bagga. After all, if anyone could have been capable of putting up a fight against the great man it only could be the reigning champion Syed Modi, or any of the other seasoned campaigners such as Partho Ganguly, Sanat Mishra, Vimal Kumar or Harjeet Singh.

Rajeev, living in his own cocoon, an isolated world where communication with other players was not very frequent, was obviously aware of the name Padukone but, as was typical of him, was not overawed or bothered by the legend. And yes, Rajeev, to his advantage, was very much in practice with local brands of shuttlecocks being used in the nationals. And by this time the twenty-year-old had grown into a lean, mean player who knew how to exploit situations.

When the two clashed in the third round match, Rajeev came out a surprising winner, much to the shock of an astounded nation.

No one could believe that he had defeated Padukone. Of course the media blamed the shuttles and other things. But whichever way one looked at it, the eventual winner, creating history of sorts, was the Maharashtra player, who was not considered to have even a ghost of a chance before the match.

This really was the turning point in his career, a moment of time from which he milked great amount of self-confidence and an innate understanding of his own qualities and abilities. Though he lost in the next round, he knew he could build upon this momentous victory.

On the return journey to Bombay, in communication with me, he explained, 'I now realize that if I can beat Prakash sir, I can beat anyone on the court. The shuttles were one thing, but I was matching his movements and I could read his game. Furthermore your training to help me reach and contact the shuttle early at the net helped immensely. There is more work to be done but I think I can get into the national team soon.' Clearly, he was also an analyst who could work out his own weaknesses and his strong points. This was a revelation to me as his coach. Later, even a player like Pullella Gopi Chand, who was to win the All England in 2001, but who lost out to Rajeev in the National Championships of 1992 and 1993, told me that he found Rajeev a very ferocious and intelligent player on court.

'I have great respect for Rajeev Bagga, both as a player and as a person. He played fair and square, no hanky-panky about him. He was a very shrewd player who would immediately exploit your weakness if he found any. He hardly had any weak points. The only area I can now think of is that in very long-lasting matches, he was found wanting in stamina. But he hardly ever allowed matches to go long. And he had the strongest wrist I have encountered. He could hit the shuttle hard from any area of the court, be it backhand or forehand. He had a wonderful touch at the net and his defence was hard to breach. In my early years, I know I could have won more national titles but for him. I was defeating everyone else, but for the three years that Rajeev dominated the singles game, he was a real stumbling block for me. I sometimes wonder where he would have reached had he played with the shuttles we use today, or the new racquets and string that make your game effortless. He would have been really demonic on court had he played in this era. And I learnt a lot watching him,' says Gopi.

It was not long before Rajeev made his debut for India in the senior team. As a junior he had gone to Kuala Lumpur in Malaysia to play a junior international. In 1988 he was selected to play the Far East tour and the SAARC games. In 1989 he was again selected to play in the Malaysian and Singapore Opens and, of course, the big break came when, in a period of just six months, he was selected to play the Asian Championships in Indonesia at the end of 1989, the 1990 Commonwealth Games at New Zealand in January, and the Asian Zone Thomas Cup matches at Kuala Lumpur in February of the same year. He had arrived, and now really cemented his place in the national senior squad.

His fame as a deaf-mute player, the only one playing top-grade international badminton, reached far and wide as local media in all countries where he went to play highlighted his impairment, not in any way offering sympathy, but more as something wondrous that he had achieved. There was a curiosity attached to him. And, more importantly, the local deaf-mute community came in droves to cheer him on. He was their own—a gifted shuttler who was taking on the 'hearing' players and making many of them bite the dust. It was in a way cocking a snook at the 'hearing' world. Rajeev Bagga was becoming a worldwide sensation, garnering as much print and television coverage as eventual winners, sometimes more.

One journey that was to change the destiny of Rajeev, in a way, was the trip to the Junior Championships in Kuala Lumpur in 1985. It was here that Brigadier Bagga learnt of the Deaflympics (formerly called the World Games for the Deaf) held every four years, under the banner of the International Olympic Committee. The Brigadier read in a local newspaper that the 1985 Games were being held at Lausanne in Switzerland. On coming back to India he got in touch with the National Association for the Deaf, which could send a badminton team for the next games. The officials were not aware of Rajeev and, in fact, told his father that there was no deaf player in the country.

Brigadier Bagga chased the concerned sports association and got them to organize the National Deaf Championships in Mumbai in 1987, which Rajeev won hands down. In 1988 and 1989 he again won the title with hardly any opposition. And, by this time, another deaf-mute player, Sandeep Dhillon, who was representing Maharashtra at the senior level in 'hearing' games, had also joined in. Luckily he too trained with me, and these two formed a formidable doubles combination. And playing in the 'hearing' category open events, their skill and game had also become sharp and lethal. The hard work of Brigadier Bagga and the two players paid off, and a badminton squad comprising Rajeev and Sandeep was selected to represent the country for the 1989 World Games for the Deaf in New Zealand. Brigadier Bagga was selected to manage the affairs of the two players in terms of travel, local communication and any other sort of help they would need. And the rest, as the cliché goes, is history.

Top deaf players at the world level in those years came from the UK and the Scandinavian countries. In the matches draw, made up of sixty-four players from forty-five countries, the two

Indians were kept in separate halves and, after much persuasion, the tournament committee agreed that Rajeev, given the fact that he was already representing India in the 'hearing' national team, should be seeded at least at the eighth position.

As the matches began, Rajeev went through his opponents with surgical precision right up to the finals. Such was his class and depth that no one could even with 10 points in any game, leave alone win a game. Sandeep was troubled in the semi-final, which he won in three fiercely fought games and the two clashed then in the finals, where Rajeev won the gold and Sandeep the silver. The two combined to win gold in the doubles division as well, thus bringing Rajeev's haul to two gold medals, and India's tally to three. This was a class act. No one individually, or as a team, from India, at any world-level sports championships had ever achieved this phenomenal success. In the deaf-mute community worldwide, Rajeev was already being perceived as a legend in the making and he got lots of press attention in Europe, from where many badminton players had come to play. And the fact that he was also playing for his country in the 'hearing' national squad, further cemented his reputation as a very formidable athlete.

The All India Sports Council for the Deaf made a recommendation to the International Committee of Sports for the Deaf to start a team event at the next world games, comprising all five badminton events. This was accepted and at Sofia, Bulgaria where the next games took place in 1993, Rajeev Bagga led a strong Indian contingent, but this time he did not allow his father to accompany him, even though the Government had given Brigadier Bagga a ticket to accompany the squad.

'I had to prove to myself that I could take care of myself anywhere in the world. I had to overcome my disability and had to conquer all obstacles in my way if I had to make a mark in my life. I had already travelled abroad before, but now I was going as team leader and in that role I had to be strong. So I told my father to return the ticket and other things given to him. My family was not prepared for this, but I was clear in my mind I was not going to be dependent on any one in future. The outside world is not very helpful or caring, especially in India, and therefore I must have the mental strength to face all problems,' says Rajeev about that decision. In his mind he was clear that he had to live alone sometime or the other, and that he had to lead his own life on his own terms. So a beginning had to be made.

The team led by this champion shuttler won the team gold, with him playing the singles, the doubles with Sandeep Dhillon, and the mixed doubles with another Mumbai-based player. After the exhausting team championships, he was motivated enough to snatch the triple crown in the 1993 Sofia games, winning individual gold medals in the singles, the doubles and the mixed doubles—all the three events he had entered in. The world deaf community was stunned by this heroic effort and he was hailed as the Athlete of the Games.

By this time Rajeev had also already won two Senior National Singles titles, hammering away the likes of Deepankar Bhattacharya, Pullella Gopi Chand, Srikant Bakshi, Harjeet Singh and others—all big names on the domestic scene. He became the first player in twenty-seven years from Maharashtra, after Nandu Natekar, to win the Senior National Championship.

But in the year 1993, one event occurred which hurt Rajeev a lot, scarring him for good. He was the national champion, ranked number one in the country and was scheduled to lead the Indian challenge at the 1993 World Cup, which was being held in Delhi. This was a showcase event and almost all top players in the world were participating in the championships. There was a training camp which the BAI had organized for the squad, which unfortunately clashed with the World Games for the Deaf being held at Bulgaria. However the World Cup was to be held almost fifteen days after the World Games for the Deaf.

This posed a dilemma for Rajeev, but he then opted to play the World Games for the Deaf as this came every four years and he was emotionally attached to the event. He requested the BAI to exempt him from the training camp, adding that he would be back a week before the World Cup and would join the squad. He even suggested to the BAI that a trial be conducted before the World Cup and, if he won, to select him, and if he lost to leave him out.

The BAI in its wisdom refused him permission, insisting that he join the training camp. A former top player in the national selection committee was even quoted as saying that if he were Rajeev, he would have sacrificed the World Games for the Deaf and played the World Cup. To this quote in the national press, Brigadier Bagga replied, 'It is fine to say this, but he is not deaf. If he was deaf like Rajeev, he would not have made this statement.'

Rajeev was to explain to me later, 'I am very hurt. They have taken advantage of my being deaf. I have never felt more helpless. I am India's best player and that has accounted for nothing. I am prepared to play trial matches, but they will not listen to me. What wrong have I done? Is playing in the Deaflympics and getting gold medals not important? In a way this is an insult—as neither my status as top player nor the world's best deaf player has meant anything. Sure, I will try to forget this, but I will carry this thought for a long time.'

The 1997 World Games for the Deaf were held in Denmark and Rajeev cleared three golds, including the team title, but missed out on the mixed doubles finals as there was some confusion on the timing of the match in his mind. His team managers had gone away for a party and did not inform Rajeev of the exact timing of his mixed doubles finals. This was shocking but, for most disabled athletes playing for India, this is a regular phenomenon as team officials and managers hardly ever do their work; they are more interested in sightseeing, shopping and partying whenever they are abroad.

Rajeev got married in 2000 and in the 2001 Deaflympics, held in Italy, his wife went as team manager and Rajeev went on to win three more gold medals, bringing his tally to twelve gold medals from four Deaflympics. This was a feat never seen in any arena in the world, if one considers individual sports. Such sort of complete and comprehensive domination of one's sport at the world level was unheard of. Rajeev had now walked the realm of legends.

The Committee International des Sports des Sourds (CISS), the international body that organizes the Deaflympics, is attached to and is recognized by the International Olympic Committee (IOC). In recognition of the extraordinary achievements of Rajeev Bagga at the Deaflympics from 1989 to 2001, CISS decided to bestow upon him the ultimate honour. He was officially declared the 'Deaflympian of the Century', an award also recognized by the IOC. No other athlete had got that citation in the deaf category. He was to win two more golds at the 2005 Deaflympics held in Australia where he was also recognized by the CISS-IOC combine as a 'legend athlete' and taken around in an open Jeep around the athletics stadium.

As Rajeev himself says, 'The string of honours bestowed upon me by CISS, the premier sports authority for world deaf persons, attached to the IOC, left me happy and satisfied. I had brought huge laurels for my country. Every time I saw the Indian flag being unfurled at the medals ceremony, I had goose-bumps and sometimes tears in my eyes. I had only wanted to play for India when I started out in 1985. I had never imagined that I would win so many gold medals for my country and that I would also be a national champion in both the singles and doubles in the 'hearing' category, and that I would not only be ranked number-one player in the country, but that I would dominate the sport all over. The official title of "Legend" bestowed upon me by the IOC was also very unique. I remember that instead of taking part in the march-past in the opening ceremony at the 2005 Deaflympics at Australia, I was taken around in an open Jeep waving to the cheering crowds. This was indeed a very special moment for me, something I will cherish forever.'

Between 1989 to 2005, this phenomenal player won fourteen gold and four silver medals at the five Deaflympics, and two more gold medals at the World Deaf Championships. He won the national singles and doubles titles, represented India at every top international event in the 'hearing' categories, ruled domestic badminton for four years, was ranked World Number One in the deaf category for sixteen years, and reached a high world ranking of 38 in the International Badminton Federation's (IBFs) rankings in the open/ 'hearing' category.

By any measurement, by any barometer, the world has not seen a sportsman like Rajeev Bagga. He has brought immense pride to his country and to his family. He has made light of his disability and has shown the world that all hurdles can be conquered if you put your mind to it. He has taken the world head on and has been truly victorious in every way.

And in return, what has he got back from the country he so proudly played for? Or indeed from Maharashtra, the state he represented with incredible distinction in domestic badminton? Nothing. Nothing at all. Not even gratitude for having done good work in the only sphere that he could.

In fact the then sports minister of Maharashtra could not even recall the name of this national and international champion from his state, despite twenty-seven years of Rajeev's dedication to the game, his sixteen successful medal-winning Deaflympics, and his gold medal-winning world championships. Rajeev is a legend all over the world, but is totally unknown in the musty ministerial corridors of the Mantralaya. Brigadier Bagga had applied on Rajeev's behalf for a flat from the 10 per cent quota reserved by the state government for outstanding citizens, including sportsmen, who have brought laurels to the state. Maharashtra's sports minister had to refer to his secretary to find out who this player was. The application, made in 2001, is still being kicked around like a football by the shameful powers that be. The Bagga family has all but given up.

In 1989, when the Indian team comprising Rajeev Bagga and Sandeep Dhillon came back from the World Games for the Deaf in New Zealand, they were called to Prime Minister Rajiv Gandhi's residence. He welcomed the delegation and told Sheila Dixit, then minister for parliamentary affairs to call Sports Minister Margaret Alva and ensure that both Rajeev and Sandeep received a cash award from the ministry. At that time an Olympic gold medal winner was supposed to be given a cash award of ₹7.5 lakh, and a silver medal winner, ₹5 lakh. The team stayed in Delhi for five days with fervent hopes that they would be handsomely rewarded. But there was no call from any one. No one bothered. They returned empty-handed to Bombay.

Later at the Sapna Awards, a prominent central minister who was the chief guest also promised some remuneration. Nothing happened. Mr Chidambram of the Congress Party and chairman of the Deaf Sports Association (DSA), promised that before the next Deaflympics in 1993, Rajeev would be richly awarded for the laurels he had brought to India. He said that the gold medals would be evaluated. Nothing happened.

Meanwhile, Rajeev missed the 1992 Barcelona Olympics for the 'hearing' by just one point. This was first time badminton was entered as a medal sport. The DSA president sent a note to the IOC requesting that Rajeev be included as a wild-card entry, as the 1989 Deaflympics champion. The Indian Olympic Association (IOA) forwarded this note to Fazil Ahmed, president of BAI for endorsement and, typical of him, he refused, saying that Rajeev should have come to him first. Thus, whatever little chance Rajeev had of playing in Barcelona was lost in the ego tussles and the red tapism of the BAI.

The four gold medals he subsequently won at the 1993 Deaflympics also brought no recognition from the Government of India. Nothing happened in 1997 or 2001 or even 2005. Rajeev Bagga, despite being a world champion in every way, a legend who would have been embraced by any other country for his mindboggling haul of sixteen gold medals, was not given even an iota of the respect and honour that he deserved. It was as if he just did not exist. After every Deaflympics he would dutifully make the rounds of the prime minister's residence and the sports minister's office, for the photo-ops they wanted. But he got nothing in return. Not a single rupee according to Brigadier Bagga.

The story of the Arjuna Award, the highest government award for Indian sportspersons, was even more stressful and insulting for Rajeev. The BAI did not initially recommend his name for the award in the open category, even after such outstanding performances worldwide. The DSA then took up the case and approached the Government of India with documents supporting Rajeev's claim to the prestigious award. The ministry, in turn, sent the papers to the BAI asking it to endorse the 'hearing' category national titles won by Rajeev.

The BAI, still under Fazil Ahmed, refused to endorse Rajeev's name. The ministry had no choice but to use its power to announce the Arjuna Award for Rajeev, even though by this time the BAI had written twice to them refusing official endorsement of the award for the deaf-mute genius. The press by this time had understood that something was wrong and totally supported Rajeev for the award.

However the one institution that always stood rock solid behind him was his employer, Hindustan Petroleum Corporation Ltd. (HPCL). 'We cannot thank HPCL enough. They not only gave him a job at age eighteen, but promoted him couple of times, and always supported financially and in whatever way we asked them to. The officials at HPCL were superb,' says Brigadier Bagga. Rajeev started earning the day he turned eighteen, and much before his older siblings, says his happy sister Sangeeta.

By 2002 Rajeev had moved on to England as his wife was a British citizen. But his heart still beat for India and he played the 2005 Deaflympics for the country, amongst other tournaments. But even after being termed an Olympic 'Legend' and still getting no recognition or monetary benefits, he decided to cut the umbilical cord from the country of his birth. He applied for British citizenship, was accepted with open arms, and henceforth represented his adopted country at the Deaflympics and also at senior masters events in the 'hearing' category. And, indeed, he went on to win many more medals for Britain.

'The last straw as far as I was concerned was the fact that I had to pay my own expenses while playing for India in the 2005 Deaflympics. I still won three gold medals but with no recognition or respect for my achievements coming forth—only broken promises—I decided on my return to Delhi that I would never play for India again. I went to my HPCL office in Mumbai and resigned after thanking them for all they did for me, and flew off to a new life in England with my wife,' says the ace badminton star.

But Rajeev, who is now settled in Coventry, England, with his wife and a son, is a happy contented man. As a certified coach he coaches the national deaf teams of Britain and Austria and also works also for the local municipality as social worker. He has won many laurels for his adopted country. Rajeev has twice won the All England Veterans singles title in the over-forty age group, as well as medals at the World Senior Badminton Championships as well as the National and European championships. He also represents his country in beach volleyball in the veteran age group. He is treated as a legend and was a torch bearer for the Olympics. The world deaf community adores him. And yes, his adopted country and his county, Coventry, have bestowed many awards and huge recognition on him.

Rajeev has enjoyed some of the terminologies that members of the media, locally and internationally, have bestowed upon him. 'Wrist of Fury, Silent Warrior, Silent Volcano, Shadow Warrior, The Racket That Speaks, Touch Winner, On Par-No Handicap, are the ones I have really liked over the years,' he says with a twinkle in his eyes.

He is not a bitter person today for having been shabbily treated both by the government of India and the state government of Maharashtra. 'For myself, though I never got any monetary help or incentives from authorities for any of my international achievements, I am happy that I won the respect of the Indian people, specially my badminton fans who still remember and adore me. This is far more important. I really wish that Indian sport be cleared of petty politics and the partisanship it indulges in. Though I am really happy now as a British citizen, I still feel for India, the country of my birth.'

As far as physical handicaps are concerned Rajeev says, 'I want to add that while functional disabilities exist, the biggest handicap that exists is in one's head—that is, in attitudes. Both able-bodied and differently abled people need to recognize this fact. We all need to look at the individual and not at the disability that an individual has.'

SATYA PRAKASH TEWARI
The Lion Hearted

It isn't a calamity to die with dreams unfulfilled,
but it is certainly a calamity not to dream.

~BENJAMIN MAYES~

As a teenager Satya Prakash Tewari had a dream. He wanted to emulate the great cricketer Sunil Gavaskar and, like his idol, play cricket for India and bring glory to the country in the international sports arena. He lived and breathed cricket, dreaming of the centuries he would score against all and sundry. And if he failed in becoming a Gavaskar, well, there was a fallback option, his second most cherished dream. He was enamoured by the men in uniform. Yes, if he somehow missed wearing Indian colours in cricket, he would certainly wear the Indian army uniform as an infantryman. This precocious teenager lived the perfect life, cocooned and enveloped in his dreams till 6 August 1981, when a horrific accident shattered his body and his soul. The mental trauma, the shattered body, the dark future or no future at all; and then the desire to commit suicide also surfaced.

Satya Prakash went through all the emotions, but somehow clung to life and went on to become a celebrated differently abled sportsperson, who brought outstanding honour to India.

This, then, is the story of Satya Prakash Tewari.

Satya Prakash Tewari was born on 6 April 1966 in Pratapgarh district of Uttar Pradesh, where he lived for about a year before he was packed off to Mumbai where his father had a job with the Bombay Electric Supply and Transport company, more popularly known as BEST. He was the youngest sibling and the only son among three children. The parents, like in all orthodox Indian families, doted on the only son. The family first lived near Victoria Terminus before shifting to Wadala, where he joined his first school, the Seetaram Prakash High School. Satya Prakash Tewari studied there till the ninth standard, before the family relocated to Ghatkopar in east Bombay, where Satya Prakash's father was granted a flat by BEST.

Childhood was idyllic, full of fun and frolic, games and that carefree attitude that was typical of a lower-middle class family. There were few clothes for Satya Prakash but enough to eat in the house. The parents wanted the children to be strong and steady in physique. But yes, studies were also a priority which the children were told not to forget. Satya Prakash, or Satya as he is known, was a merit student, he says, till the sixth standard. 'I used to be regularly in the top five till sixth standard, diligently doing my studies, doing my homework in time, etc. But somehow after the sixth standard, my focus shifted and along with other boys in the building I started putting more time on the ground close by, playing cricket, football or whatever sport we thought of on the given day.'

The result was that instead of his usual grades he started slipping and his rank reached among the bottom five instead of the top five. But Satya was not too perturbed as time spent on cricket was bearing fruit. It was, after, all much better than spending time on studying mathematics or geometry, both of which he found difficult to grasp. In the eighth standard he was selected to play in the Junior Inter School Tournament for the

Harris Shield, as an all-rounder for his school. The die-hard cricketer played for his school in 1978 and 1979.

At home, his mother became a natural ally. While father used to get upset if he did not find Satya with a book in hand, mother would come to the rescue of the Gavaskar-to-be. The natural athlete in him also saw him effortlessly winning the 400 and 800 metres races regularly in school sports. But for the well-built, lean and tall Satya, cricket was what he wanted to excel at. He was a natural all-rounder and idolized the then superstar, the opening batsman par excellence Sunil Gavaskar, who was in all aspects the sports icon of the country

'I used to hear commentary on the radio very often and loved to hear what experts said about Gavaskar. I wanted to be like him. I also liked Kapil Dev, but Gavaskar was my real favourite, my role model. When television had just been introduced, Test matches used to be shown on the old black-and-white screens. We did not have a TV, but someone had one in my colony and all of us boys would watch Gavaskar playing the likes of Holding, Holder, Roberts, Garner etc. of the West Indies. I would watch till he played and leave the room when he got out.'

The thought of becoming a doctor or an engineer, the two most sought after professions in those times and the dream of every parent for their son, never occurred to Satya. He just wanted to be a cricketer and had even joined the National Cadet Corps (NCC) so that he could become disciplined and physically strong—again the main motive was that NCC activities would help in his chosen sport.

And, of course, there was Amitabh Bachchan, the reigning demi-god of Bollywood. Satya used to adore the 'angry young man,' as the actor was labelled for his roles, and saw almost all of his movies, even trying to emulate Amitabh's mannerisms and style, as much as possible. Which young boy of that age did not dream, at least sometimes, of following in Bachchan's footsteps and becoming a movie star?

But his father put a stop, at least temporarily, to all the fantasizing that Satya indulged in. He was now in the tenth standard and studies had to take utmost priority. His father was clear about this and so the playing gear was locked away. Yes he could spend some time with his friends on the ground, but mostly he had to drown himself in dreary books. 'You have to pass the Senior Secondary Certificate [SSC] board exam, that's it. And you must get good marks. Cricket will not take you anywhere. So forget about it and concentrate on your books,' was the sermon given to the fifteen-year-old time and again. Though he would sneak out now and then, to hit or bowl a few balls daily when his father was not around, he knew there was no running away from the iron fist of his father. He had to study hard and pass the tenth standard exam. Satya consoled himself with the thought that after the exams he would again take up the bat and the ball, and try his best to become a professional cricketer.

In a sense, Satya was also impressed whenever he heard elders talk about the 1971 Indo-Pak war and the heroics of Indian soldiers. The stories of sacrifice, valour and bravery of the jawans in that war, that he heard his elders talking about, made a deep impression on his young mind. He knew that if not a professional cricketer, he wanted to become a soldier in the Indian army when he turned eighteen. 'The war was still fresh and by the time I was about ten years old, I was beginning to understand what the soldier stood for. I also had the deepest respect for the local policemen. Anyone in uniform was a hero to me. I did not know what my future was going to be, but I was sure that I would love to be either a cricketer or a man in uniform. I simply wanted to do something for my country, make India proud of me in some way,' says Satya.

He was well-known and popular in his school because of sports and his participation in the NCC. He loved to flaunt himself in the deep khaki uniform of the NCC. But of course everything, all his fantasies and high-flying thoughts were brought down with a crash, at least for the year when he was in the tenth as his biggest fear—the geometry and maths papers—stood like demons in front of him. He had to surmount this problem, as failure in this board examination would just not be tolerated by his father.

The Almighty was behind Satya, as he surprised everyone in the family by not only conquering the fear of angles in geometry, but actually scoring a respectable 56 per cent overall, which amounted to a high second class, something that made the entire family happy.

Satya wanted to graduate in commerce but, since maths was part of the curriculum, he decided to drop the idea. He was advised to take up science, without maths, in junior college. However, he was still not clear what he wanted to do in the future. Nevertheless, since college had to be joined, he joined the Guru Dutt Mittal College in Sion, in central Bombay, in early July 1981.

'Of course during the vacations after the tenth exams, sports had again taken priority in my life. Cricket was again a passion. And as soon as I joined college, I made a beeline to get myself enrolled for selections to the college team. Practice sessions were to start after the monsoons. I had no idea what I was to do in future, but knew only that playing cricket was to be an important part of my life, a life that had started changing once college started,' remembers Satya.

Destiny had other things in mind. Satya had crossed fifteen years of age and was just a month old in college when, on the fateful day of 6 August 1981, a tragedy was to occur which was to shatter his mind and body, wrench his dreams and fantasies away from him, and cripple him for life.

The day was dull, dreary and dark, with the monsoon venting its full fury. There was water everywhere. So much so that in some low-lying areas of the Central Railway line, rail tracks were submerged and some local trains had been cancelled. 'It must have been around 11 in the morning and I was trying to get home from college. I walked to Sion station to catch a train for Ghatkopar. There was no direct train and I had to change at Kurla. Since there were fewer local trains running that day, I had no option but to catch an outward-bound train for Kurla. It was a mail train going out of Bombay. I was in the last compartment. I saw so many other passengers getting down at Kurla station where up-country trains, like the one I was in, normally slowed because of water on the tracks, before gathering speed again. So I followed the other passengers and got down from the slowing train, too, even though I was wearing rubber slippers and had some books in my hand,' says Satya, remembering that fateful day which crushed all his aspirations and dreams.

In a hurry to get out of the train, Satya slipped and fell with his torso on the platform and both feet beneath the train footboard. At this point the train began picking up speed and dragged him a good thirty meters or so. Satya does not remember what happened next as he became unconscious. When he came to, he was surrounded by people, screaming and looking horrified by the accident. He was in excruciating pain. He did not know it at that time as he flitted in and out of consciousness, that both his knees had been crushed to pulp.

It is ironical, but he says now that he was lucky that he was in the last compartment. Otherwise he surely would have been killed. He was again very lucky as the local railways staff, showing great presence of mind, immediately rushed him to Sion Hospital. He could hear the conversation on the way in the ambulance and it suggested only that he was going to die very soon. He still remembers those words in Marathi—'Hi tar vachnar nahi, kiti blood gela, [He is not going to survive; see how much blood he has lost.]' The pain had numbed him by this time.

The one thought uppermost in Satya's mind, who was unaware of the extent of his injuries, was that his father would be angry as he would reach home late. Little did he know that he was never to walk again and that his life was now going to turn upside down. 'I don't know how the hospital authorities were able to contact my family but very soon I saw many employees from BEST in my room. My father had still not come as he was in some meeting and had not yet been informed. But I clearly remember one senior official from BEST saying that this group would donate all the blood needed and that money was not to be an issue as he himself was going to get some ₹50,000 due on retirement, which was in fact just a month away He told the medical team in the intensive care unit, "Please save this boy at any cost. His father is my boss, but more importantly he is a good boy, a good sportsman who has won many medals in school and is a good cricketer in the making," ' recalls Satya.

Time was running out and the medical team decided to operate straightaway. It was decided that both Satya's legs would have to be amputated, one from the hip socket, while a small stump could be saved in the other. The operation took almost six hours and when Satya regained consciousness he found himself in the emergency room with drips inserted into his arm. Two more operations took place under the supervision of Dr N.S. Lad, head of orthopaedics. Satya was still not aware that he had lost both legs as the heavy drugs and antibiotics ensured that he remained in a daze for many days. But he saw his parents, flitting in and out of the room, restless, listless and with a sense of despair and defeat writ large on their faces.

After a few days, still heavily drugged, Satya was moved into a normal ward and it was here his world of innocence, a world where he dreamt of either being the next Sunil Gavaskar or an infantry soldier fighting for the country, came crashing down. His dressing was being changed and with the effect of the drugs now receding, he realized he could not feel his legs.

'I could feel my arms and other parts of the body, but had no feeling where my legs would have been. I screamed and screamed, but in vain. No one could understand my anguish. In just one second or one moment of naivety or stupidity or childishness, whichever way one looked at it, when I had tried to jump down from a moving train, my life had been totally finished. I had no future, I would never walk again—how would I face the world again? People would sneer at me, call me names, call me a cripple, for the rest of my life. Such thoughts clouded my brain and I slipped into unconsciousness.'

When he woke up, his relatives surrounded him, all trying to be brave and cheerful, and offer him solace. His father and mother tried to smile through their tears. Some said 'don't worry, everything will be alright'. Some said 'you will be as good as new'. Some said they would always be there to help him, etc.

'It was all good to hear. But they simply could not understand what I was going through. After all they had not lost their legs, they were not the ones who would never walk again, never play cricket again. Would they ever be the heroic soldier I was going to be? Could they not see the darkness ahead in my life? Could they not feel my pain? All such thoughts raced through my mind.

Of course I was still too young to realize what was going through the mind of my parents—their only son, now crippled for life. But I could still see the anguish on my mother's face. She was deathly quiet and avoided looking into my eyes. Then I started crying and so did she. After some time all became quiet and deathly still. We had all cried enough and with eyes dry, now the decision had to be taken as to how I was to be taken home and how I was to live out my future. My physical wound was almost healed. But what about the wound to my psyche, my mind? Would I ever be a man enough to lead my own life?'

'And,' he continues, 'there was this one person with whom I had a close relationship of sorts who cruelly told me over and over again that my life was now finished. What can you do on your own, nothing at all—this person said. This hurt me very much, even though at that time this was the bitter truth. But the way this person put it, was something I remembered for a long time and I prayed to god to somehow give me strength to prove this person wrong.'

Satya spent about sixty days in all at the hospital, undergoing physiotherapy on many days. Dr Atul Shah and Dr Parkhi are two names that Satya remembers, of people who tried to give him hope. He says that this was a brilliant team of doctors and if not for them he would not have survived the trauma that he went through.

He had come home, having survived a horrendous accident. But what sort of life he was going to live? Did this life have any future at all? 'I knew there was nothing left for me. My future was a big fat zero. No cricket, no joining the army or doing anything at all. My biggest worry was, how was I going to live? How was I going to survive? I had no strength left in me. I could not even sit as there was no balance in my body, nor lift even a kilo of weight. I was so weak and it was in this condition that I was brought home to this very flat where I am talking to you. But I must confess here that the physiotherapist at Sion Hospital, Dr Neeta Shah helped me a lot, giving me hope. Initially I could not sit without any back support and two people were required to set me up against a wall or put some pillows for back support. I learnt how to sit from them but the learning process continued for a long time.'

Another problem were the severe bedsores on his back and, in fact, Satya was operated on for those as well. And the doctors said that though he was being sent home, the parents really had to take care of bedsores as they would become a chronic problem and could be very dangerous. He was alternatively made to lie down on his stomach or on his back. He couldn't lie sideways as he had no legs.

'I had another major problem to deal with. I could not go to the toilet on my own as I would often fall down even from a sitting position. My parents were the only support I had at home. I can't thank them enough for what they did for me and in fact my father is still doing for me. They had to again treat me and train me like a newborn baby. They helped me during toilet, helped me eat, helped me sleep. They were in attendance twenty-four hours a day, setting everything aside. Their lives now revolved totally around me and my needs. Father would go to office but not before he ensured that all my ablutions, etc., were done in the morning and I was wearing fresh clothes. My mother would then take over and help me through the day. I used to think about this a lot and was often embarrassed. They were old and instead of me helping them, they were now forced to look after all my physical needs. This is selfless love and caring can come only from parents. Nobody else can do this. I have no words to thank them enough. There should be awards instituted for caregivers who help people like me. But I doubt if the society as a whole really cares about us physically challenged people.'

In such situations time really moves slowly. It was difficult for the teenager to pass the minutes doing nothing, let alone hours just sitting or lying down, staring into nothingness. Satya spent a few months like this. Then on a follow-up visit to Sion Hospital, he was advised to go to the Artificial Limb Centre (ALC) at Haji Ali in south Mumbai. This is a central government institution, well-known for helping paraplegics and/or amputees, and its success rates are renowned. The medical fraternity at Sion Hospital, ever optimistic, told Satya that he would be walking again within no time after he visited the ALC. Some even dared to suggest that he could well be jogging on the Mumbai Racecourse which was adjacent to the ALC.

He met Dr A.K. Mukherjee, the head of the institute and is all praises for him. Says Satya, 'Dr Mukherjee gave me a reason to live again. His zest for life was compelling and he showed me and told me how life can still be meaningful and be lived to the fullest. He also convinced my father that the slight stump left in my right thigh had to be removed totally since I was a growing boy and that bone would grow in future leading to complications. This conversation took place in front of me and I told him that since I already had undergone four operations, one more would not make much difference. He looked stunned that a boy, not yet sixteen years of age, was speaking with such confidence. But I looked at life differently and told myself—what more did I have to lose? If I died in the course of the operation, no harm done. As it is I had already lost so much in life.'

Dr Mukherjee took great care of Satya and personally operated on his right leg. That year, there were some special programmes as the ALC was celebrating its silver jubilee. Satya was admitted and underwent much physiotherapy. And it is here that his outlook to life started changing in a way. In those days polio was a huge menace in the country and he would see many people, including small children, walking around with callipers, or on crutches; people of all ages and sizes, bearing the pain of life but struggling along gamely. He still remembers a small girl of about five years or so, lying in bed with both legs afflicted by polio, still smiling and chatting away like any child of her age would.

He also came across another patient, Gokarna Prasad Chaturvedi, at ALC. Chaturvedi, who hailed from Indore, had come to get operated on both feet which had twisted ankles, as a result of which he was not able to walk but hobbled along. He had an amazing and unique personality recalls Satya. The sheer optimism of this man astounded Satya.

'He was like Rajesh Khanna in the film *Anand*, full of life and fun. He was like a hurricane, never took no for an answer from anyone, became the darling of all hospital staff and was known by everyone within a month of his arrival. I was fortunate to meet him and learnt a lot from him. His confidence was incredible and though he was older, around thirty years of age, I started to stick around him as much as possible as he was a real livewire, a great company. He often broke rules, never slept at 9.30 p.m., the time set for lights-off, and insisted that the ALC get us a TV so we could watch programmes like *Chitrahaar* and the serial *Mahabharat*, as well as the feature film on Sunday evenings. He was a real leader, a real persuader.'

Satya admits that he was really embarrassed and even ashamed of his handicap. He did not know how to react to people or how to confront them for the smallest of things. And negative remarks, even from close relatives at times, saying that his life was over, or what would happen after his parents died, used to depress him a lot. He even thought of committing suicide, not thinking how his parents would take it, what they would feel at losing a young son. But Gokarna Prasad's presence helped him overcome all such negativity.

'I took courage from my surroundings at ALC, from the patients who had lost more than me, from those who were paraplegic or polio-afflicted from birth. At least I had walked and run and enjoyed cricket and other games till I was fifteen years old. I had those memories. Many people here did not have even those. As I sat on my cot, facing the Haji Ali Dargah and watched the world go by, I told myself that come what may I would try to infuse some meaning in my life. I watched flocks of birds flying out over the sea and often wondered where they went. They had to have a destination. Would they not get tired and drop into the infinite ocean? I marvelled at their energy, at their bravery and their mental strength. What was my destination going to be? What would I do once I was back home? The one thing I now knew was that I had to prove my detractors wrong. I was going not only going to live, but would try my best to live a meaningful life.'

Satya tried the limbs made for him, but since the legs were lost from the stump, it was not easy. He did try to walk with crutches and started going to the toilet on his own, but finally had to give up. The problem was that the famously uneven and bad roads of Mumbai did not allow him to walk. Once or twice he lost his balance and fell down and it took four people to get him up and get him going again. Finally, after some two years at the ALC, Satya and his parents decided that it was time to move on and face life as it came.

However, the medical team at Sion Hospital was still not

willing to give up on Satya Prakash. They referred him to the King George Infirmary at Worli where a higher level of physiotherapy awaited him. He would come here in an ambulance, work out for couple of hours and then be sent home. Sometimes they would make him stay overnight. Finally though, he and his family came to the conclusion that nothing more could be done. He would have to use a wheelchair for life and this was the bitter truth which had to be understood and accepted.

Says Satya, 'This phase of my life was over and I had to move on. The medical field and my doctors could do no more. I had to accept my handicap. I had learnt so much in life in the three years that I was confined to these various hospitals. The ups and downs of existence, the pain and anguish of patients, the helplessness of us mere mortals in so many different ways. And I saw that physical handicap can destroy relationships and lives. Seen through a microscope, life could be ugly. I saw spouses of both genders simply leaving each other if one met with an accident and lost limbs and it became apparent that marital desires could not be fulfilled. I saw a father being brought in an emergency situation, surrounded by relatives and close family. But once the handicap became apparent and bills zoomed, everyone left him one by one. Siblings left each other, and the son left the father and in some cases, vice versa. Only the mothers were left in the end to grieve. The mother- and- child relationship is perhaps the purest. In my case I was blessed with wonderful parents.'

Satya was just about nineteen years old and he was home thinking deeply about what he could do to earn a living. 'I had been brought up with deep, abiding traditions. Come what may I was not going to steal or beg. I might be crippled and wheelchair-bound all my life, but I would try to stand on my own feet—as the cliché goes. For my own satisfaction and for that of my atma, my spirit, it was essential that I lived my future with dignity.'

The father who was about to retire from his job with BEST applied to the company to set up a small shop at the BEST Shopping Centre, near the East Ghatkopar bus depot which was just few hundred metres from where the family lived. In any case, whatever savings he had from the job had all been spent on Satya's treatment. The application was backed and supported by the BEST trade union and its leader Mr Narayan Phenani. Accepted on compassionate grounds by the Chief Personal Officer Mr Dandekar, and General Manager Mr Kerkar, Satya was allotted the shop he wanted, in 1985, where he ran a STD/ISD booth which used to be very popular in those days. He also started stocking groceries and other items to convert the shop into a small multi-purpose store. At least now he had something to look forward to. He soon became an earning member of his family, a support to his father, who had retired by now but had also taken up a job in a private company as a security officer. Satya now had his dignity, he was earning and supporting his family, something that gave him immense satisfaction.

But again there was a twist in life. Typical of north Indian families who married off their children young, Satya's parents, too, started to think of arranging a match for him. He resisted because he knew that in his physical state it would not be correct. And also that he was still just nineteen years old. But the parents wanted him to share his life with someone, preferably a normal girl. They were worried about his future. In case they died early, who would look after Satya, was perhaps the worry uppermost in their mind. The social worker who looked after his case was also against the marriage, correctly saying that Satya was far too young at nineteen to get married.

But at the insistence of his father Mata Sharan, and he was

far too dependent on him, Satya agreed and wife Usha entered the Tiwari household. And thus, the married phase of his life began which gave him two wonderful children, a son Rohit who came first, followed by daughter Sudha. For the next few years Satya became deeply immersed in married life, shouldering all the responsibilities expected of him.

But tragedy and calamity, which had become close to Satya, struck again, leaving him helpless and very lonely all over again. Usha died within three short years of marriage due to a burst appendix which was not properly handled by the hospital where she was rushed. She left behind Rohit, who was then two years old, and Sudha who was also a toddler. Life again became a major struggle for Satya, who himself was just twenty-two years old. His parents, like the proverbial messiahs again came to his rescue, picking up the threads of life and adopting the grandchildren as their own.

'No one thinks of the sacrifice the caregivers give to handicapped people. Be it the wife or the parents. They live as much a dreadful life as we do. In my case my wife who was my support for three years, my parents who gave me hope and selfless love so many times and again after my wife died, were sheer paragons of virtue and love. I would not have survived and lived till today had it not been for them,' says Satya.

Life slowly again came back to normal after this sudden trauma. Satya started spending lots of time in the shop. Whatever feeling of embarrassment he felt at his handicap started diminishing fast as friends, old and new, started visiting him to help run the shop or just to share the local gossip. Time started passing with enough earnings now to take care of his family. For the next five years or so he worked hard to consolidate and expand his shop's revenues.

But there was this void in Satya's life. He had that burning desire to do something more. The remarks of that one person who had been close to him and who had said his life was finished and that he was not capable of doing anything worthwhile, haunted him now and then. Till his wife was alive he had not really bothered about it, but now he wanted to do something to prove this one person and, indeed, other sceptics wrong. He wanted to prove to the world that he was as good as any 'abled' person.

Satya was most lucky that he had a legendary differently abled sportsperson living in the same building as he did, Rajaram Ghag. Ghag, a paraplegic, had been the first Asian and the second man in the world to swim the English Channel in 1988 with his sort of handicap. He was a champion long-distance swimmer and one of the first such sportsmen to catch the nation's eye. Satya had seen Ghag make his way about around in a wheelchair, but had never had the courage to meet the man in person. Finally, around 1994, he went to Ghag's ground-floor flat and presented himself to the legend.

His life was to change again. 'I was on my way to becoming a raja in life, helped no doubt by this man also named Raja. This was a new beginning to my life. He told me to start playing some sort of sport to achieve some meaningful status. In those days there was hardly any arena where people like us could play any games. After my accident all I had played was some carom, sitting on my wheelchair. Swimming I had never done so that was not an option at that time. Rajaram then told me to start building my arms with some sort of weights and to try to enter some paraplegic sports meet where I could throw the discus, the shot-put and the javelin, or to try out the wheelchair race. I agreed with him and started in earnest. I now had a direction in life. And sports was again going to take centre-stage, something

I loved way back when I was a bubbling teenager.'

Satya had no coach to start with but he got hold of a shot-put ball and a discus and started throwing these at a ground nearby. Ghag saw this young man getting more and more interested in sports and suggested that he go with a few others to Chennai to take part in an all-India meet for paraplegics. Ghag said he would also come, but backed out at the last moment and sent one of his cousins Vijay Kadam instead. Satya, who after losing his legs had never travelled anywhere outside the city, was now in a dilemma—whether to go to Chennai or not. There was hesitation, and a hint of fear. But Ghag persuaded him to go. 'It will do you a lot of good,' he told Satya.

The squad from Mumbai landed in Chennai and were told at the venue that their entries had not been received and that instead of a three-day event, it was going to be a two-day event only. Kadam and Satya somehow persuaded the organizers to reconsider and were allowed to participate on the condition that all the three events—the discus, shot-put and javelin throws—be finished in one day itself. Satya did not win anything, just got a participation certificate.

However two things happened on this trip which were to ensure that India got an outstanding champion in the days to come. First, Satya got over his fear of himself and his handicap by travelling for the very first time outside his comfort zone, Bombay. Indian society in general and Indian Railways in particular, are notorious for being criminally negligent when it comes to providing facilities for our wheelchair-bound citizens. Just try to imagine how a wheelchair can be wheeled into a station where there are no ramps, then pushed onto a train compartment which has couple of high steps, but no ramp, leave alone enter the tiny toilets of our national trains. But Satya somehow managed and that gave him supreme confidence.

Secondly, participating in a sports meet after almost fifteen years brought out that competitive spirit in him, something which had remained dormant. Vijay Kadam was a wonderful companion on this trip and in the three more days they had in Chennai, he dragged Satya on a whirlwind tour which included all the beaches in and near Chennai, and also to its many temples including a trip outside Chennai to Tirupati Balaji. 'This was a memorable trip in every way. I enjoyed myself thoroughly thanks to Vijay Kadam, and most importantly for me, got bitten by the sports bug all over again. I wanted to do better and better in sports—that was now my dream, my mantra in life,' says Satya.

With the blessings of Lord Tirupati, Satya earnestly started training with a group of wheelchair-bound athletes and also began participating, first at city- and then at state-level, and then slowly at the All-India National Championships organized by the Disabled Sports Federation. Sports and its ambience became a passion that became all-consuming.

'Initially it was wheelchair races, but I did not have a proper wheelchair. I borrowed a chair Rajaram had got from England, which was light and more manoeuvrable. But my real interest was in the throws and I used to watch whatever athletics meets were shown on the sports channels. I learnt throwing action watching Bahadur Singh, the Asian Gold medallist and later coach of the national team. I bought a shot-put and a discus disc and on my own started training at a nearby ground. Some local boys helped me. The 1996 National Sports Championships for the Differently Abled were being held in Chennai and Rajaram told me to start heavy training. Since I was young and strong, he told me to participate in the wheelchair races and also the throws. "It will be tiring but you will know where you stand in the country," he told me a couple of months before the championships.'

Satya won gold in the 100 and 200 metre races and in the relay race, silver in shot-put and fourth place in the discus throw. The army contingent from the Services Rehabilitation Centre, Pune, was also there in full force and Satya saw them sweeping up most medals in athletics including the throws. He confronted a paraplegic soldier Nir Bahadur Gurung, and learnt the correct throwing style while wheelchair bound, from him. Gurung was later to have an outstanding international career wherein he won immense laurels for the country.

Elated by his success in Chennai, Satya soon got into a pattern of training almost three to four hours daily and started improving by leaps and bounds. He repeated his success in the 1997 and 1998 nationals and was soon the star, and expected to be selected for the 1999 Far East South Pacific (FESPIC) Games* to be held in Bangkok. Differently abled sportspersons from all over Asia trained hard to participate in this event which was held every four years and was recognized by the International Olympic Committee (IOC). The selections were to be held at Nagpur in September 1998 and determined to be selected for India, Satya raised his training to five hours a day. 'My hands would bleed at times and my muscles would cramp. The back also hurt as sitting in a wheelchair for hours also created problems for me. But I wanted to be really fit before reaching Nagpur to ensure selection.'

Satya had already faced the whims and discrimination of selectors—the bane of Indian sports—when he and Gurung were not selected for the 1996 Atlanta Paralympics in spite of coming first and second in the selection trials at the Sports Authority of

---

*From 2006 onwards these games were called the Asia Paralympics Championships.

India (SAI) facilities in Bangalore. Unknown players were selected, while Gurung and Satya were left twiddling their thumbs. This was his first taste of humiliation at the hands of Indian sport officialdom, and obviously more was to follow in the years to come.

Satya reached Nagpur only to fall sick with a viral infection and went in for a shot-put throw while running fever and fell short by 20 centimetres from qualifying in his classification. In differently abled sports, classifications are as per grade of disability. He came back to Mumbai dejected but talking to Rajaram Ghag, Satya realized that there was still a small ray of hope for the selections. The Disabled Athletes Sports Federation (DASF) decided to hold another trial at the army centre in Pune where those athletes who had missed out by 25 centimetres or less in the throw events would get one more chance. He had another month to train and after praying fervently to Lord Tirupati, he landed at Pune to throw 5 metres and 65 centimetres, some 40 centimetres more than the qualifying mark of 5.2 metres.

He had won a huge battle. He was now going to wear the Indian colours and represent the country with pride. But the euphoria soon fizzled out and he came crashing down with a thud from dizzying heights of joy when he learnt that he would have to fund his own expenses as the government of India would not pay a dime. So now a new war had to be fought. He had to find resources somehow and time was short—just fifteen days before he had to green-signal his name on the list of the selected 'Indian Squad'.

'I had no choice but to beg all around. My family physician Dr Lasaryia agreed to help and so did some friends. I had to raise ₹35,000. The doctor told me that whatever balance was left on the last day, he would gladly fill up. I went to many places and had ₹20,000 confirmed before going to the Pepsi soft drinks people. They were my clients as we sold only Pepsi amongst colas. Initially they agreed to a miserly ₹1,000. Then I met Mr Mudgule, their Mumbai region head at his Chembur office, and he was very disturbed and sympathetic seeing my handicap and the tide turned. Though it had not been a policy of the company to sponsor any sports other than cricket, he did promise me and in fact ensured that I got ₹10,000 from his sources. Then came a blessing with Clayton Murzello, sports editor of *Mid-Day* newspaper. Hearing of my plight he sent reporter Mufeed Rizvi to interview me and this was the very first time my name was published in a newspaper. I collected another ₹5,000 thanks to them, and finally my doctor, as promised, helped me with another ₹5,000 for my personal expenses on the trip. I was now all set for my first trip abroad and my first experience in an airplane.'

Rajaram Ghag was also in the Indian squad, selected for a swimming event. He had been abroad many times and therefore acted as a guide of sorts for the uninitiated Satya, who was overjoyed when he reached Bangkok. Everything was so different, so efficient and so clean. More over the local people and the Games organizers were extremely cordial, polite and helpful. He saw in contrast that the officials of the Indian contingent were negligent, least bothered about helping the athletes and were mostly busy sightseeing and shopping. This is a complaint that most differently abled Indian athletes still have about the officials who accompany them to international meets.

'No one told me where to get registration done, how to get the chest number and how to reach the venue. All I knew was that my discus throw event was starting at 10 a.m. As a result I left almost at 7 a.m. for my event, without breakfast, and on my own. Luckily a local volunteer saw my plight and guided me and I reached at almost the very last moment. I was the first of twelve throwers in the list in our classification and almost immediately, without any thought or moment to get my breath, I was thrust forward for my attempt. Because of my nervousness and the fact that I was not mentally prepared to throw immediately, my first throw was a foul, and the second below my expectations. The third was the best and I still managed only a fourth place in the discus throw event.

'I had missed the bronze medal by just 22 centimetres. Our manager said "Don't worry you did well. The fourth place is good enough as this is your first time." But I could not sleep that night. I was upset. I wanted to go home with a medal. But I consoled myself that my main event, the shot-put was next day and that I should concentrate on that. And next morning I was ready and knew exactly where to go and what time to reach there. Again there were twelve throwers, this time from China, Australia, Korea, New Zealand, Thailand, Malaysia, Pakistan, etc., all champions of their own countries. But I threw with full concentration and focus and won the bronze medal with a 6.92 metres effort. I cannot tell you what a relief it was. Finally I had achieved something on my own. I forgot my handicap and all bitterness towards life vanished.

'And when the Indian flag was hoisted at the medal ceremony, I had tears flowing down my cheeks. This was the one moment I had been waiting for, wanting to achieve something for my country, make India proud of me. I had given a fitting answer to my detractors, to all those who had doubted me, especially to that one person who had said that I was good for nothing after losing my legs. I won many international medals after this in many other sports, but this first bronze was the one I remember the most.'

Satya won another bronze two days later with a huge effort in the javelin throw and was really overjoyed. He could not become the next Sunil Gavaskar or an infantry soldier in that olive green uniform, but he had brought immense pride to the country in his own way. The irony was that the differently abled Indian contingent brought home more medals from the FESPIC games than did the nation's abled contingent which participated in the 1998 Asian Games in Bangkok, held just about a month earlier in December at the same venues.

This irony was not lost on Prime Minister Vajpayee who hosted a lunch for the disabled medal winners and announced a ₹12 lakh cash award for the Disabled Athletes Sports Federation (DASF), as well as individual awards for the medal winners. He confessed, however, that he had not been aware, before the contingent came to meet him, that such games even existed. Satya received ₹10,000 from a happy prime minister.

The DASF also publicly announced that it would give cash awards to the medal winners, but not one rupee was sent to them. This was a story that happened often. But Satya, high on octane now, just wanted to play sports as much as he could. The DASF was now substituted by the Paralympic Committee of India (PCI) and, by 2006, the government started funding the trips of such athletes. He won three gold medals at an international meet in the Belgium in May 2002 in shot-put, javelin and the discus throw and was selected for Busan FESPIC games of 2002. In a fashion typical of Indian sportsdom, they took him there but forgot to send his entry for any of the three events that he normally participated in. The result was that he simply spent his time cheering on his teammates in Busan.

Destiny was to look after him better than the officials that clutter Indian sportsdom, and badminton would prove to be a sport in which he would excel in future. He used to play a bit of wheelchair badminton, but once he learnt from the grapevine that a world badminton event was going to be held, he started practising hard for it and appeared for a selection where he was successful.

'I won a silver medal at World Cup Badminton at Bangalore in December 2002 in men's doubles and this ignited a passion in me all over again. In July 2004 I won a bronze in doubles [wheelchair] and a silver in doubles [sitting] at the FESPIC Badminton championships. Another bronze came at the third FESPIC Games 2006 (renamed from that year on as the Asia Paralympic Games) at Kuala Lumpur, Malaysia, in the wheelchair badminton men's doubles. In December 2008 I won another bronze in a doubles wheelchair event at the Asian Paralympic Badminton championships and then in November 2009 I got a gold in the men's doubles wheelchair and a bronze in the singles at the IWAS World Wheelchair Games organized by the PCI. I was selected for the 2010 Guangzhou Asia Paralympic games, but on landing there we found out that there was no doubles event where I stood a good chance of winning another medal for India. Our Association had goofed up yet again and I came back empty-handed.'

Satya Prakash Tewari, in a glittering sports career, went on to win sixteen international medals for India, and over seventy-five medals at the national level. He has become a legend of sorts and has shown that handicaps are more in the mind. He has no regrets that despite bringing so much honour to the country and to his state of Maharashtra, he has hardly got anything in return from the government or the many people in power who have left behind a trail of broken promises. These include promises to buy him a light-weight world-class wheelchair which would have helped him perform better.

The only person who helped Satya in 2004 and was true

to his word was Harish Baijal, the police commissioner (traffic) that year, who read a newspaper report in *Mumbai Mirror* and then acted on his promise of getting him a top-grade wheelchair.

It is good that Satya is strong of body and mind. And that in spite of not having the best equipment available, he still managed to pursue excellence with focused devotion. But some sense of disappointment and hurt evidently exists as he questions why Indian society and the government does not bother much about the achievements of the para-athletes and the paraplegics who have brought much more honour to the country in their chosen disciplines than have abled athletes.

'Whenever we go abroad for international meets, the coaches of other countries are trained to deal physically and psychologically with disabled athletes. We have no coach in any discipline trained to understand our needs. All of us are left to our own devices. There are general coaches, but no experts in the handicap categories that we carry with us. That is one main issue. And I also want to know why we are not remembered or honoured as much by the state or the central government? Everyone knows Abhinav Bindra as our Olympic gold medallist but no one knows that Murlikant Petkar won a paralympic gold in 1972 and Devendra Jhajaria won gold in 2002. As far as Asian Games go, the abled athletes have not got even half the number of medals we have won over the decades. Yet there is hardly any recognition.'

Today Satya is not so much bothered about his handicap, but wishes that society would wake up and understand the needs of wheelchair-bound people, so that in future such people can participate in social engagement on equal terms and as much as abled citizens. 'We have a lot to give to the society even though life is very difficult for the handicapped,' he says, but adds that society must be inclusive. He is also critical of many non-governmental organizations (NGOs) which take government grants to help the disabled, but hardly any help percolates down to the needy.

This life story of a mentally abled but physically disabled legend cannot be complete without a typical ending. Satya Prakash Tewari overcame a horrendous accident, overcame physical and mental trauma, was visited by tragedy many times, yet displayed enormous courage and perseverance to win sixteen international sports medals for India in the most competitive arenas. He could not become the next Sunil Gavaskar or a decorated soldier, but he fulfilled his new dream, that of seeing the tricolour fly proudly at sports podiums worldwide thanks to his abilities, hard work and never-say-die spirit. However, while he could achieve enormous success in the sports field by his grit and determination, he came out as a failure in areas where he and others of his ilk are conveniently overlooked by an ungrateful nation.

Satya Prakash Tewari tried three times to get the coveted Arjuna Award, but was unsuccessful. He applied for a state government apartment given to top sportsmen in Maharashtra, but does not know where his files are, despite having applied many times. The cash compensation or rewards from the sports ministry at the Centre for winning medals at the Asian and world levels promised many times in front of the media and dignitaries, have also not found their way to him. Not a single rupee.

Yet the sporting spirit in him is still alive. 'I will continue to be a sportsman and will try winning more laurels for my state, my country. That is my duty. What the country and state do for me is up to them. Officials and politicians can turn a blind eye towards my victories, but they cannot understand or take away satisfaction I derive from my achievements. No one can take that away from me.'

NIR BAHADUR GURUNG
The Quintessential Street Fighter

Tho' much is taken, much abides; and tho'
We are not now that strength which in old days
Moved earth and heaven,
That which we are, we are;
One equal temper of heroic hearts,
Made weak by time and fate, but strong in will
To strive, to seek, to find, and not to yield,
tho' many obstacles come, not to yield, not to yield.

~ALFRED TENNYSON~

Belonging to an army family—his father fought bravely in the Second World War and most male members of the family were soldiers in the proud Gurkha Regiment of the Indian Army and many saw conflict from close quarters—Nir Bahadur Gurung too had a vision of winning many awards and decorations for bravery. A proud but illiterate Gurkha, a native of Nepal, he overcame abject poverty to somehow come to Darjeeling and join the Gurkha Regiment with dreams in his eyes. He made it into the army but then fate played a hand.

His spine was crushed in a most freakish accident when he was barely past his teens, when tonnes of ammunition fell on him with such force that his rifle, too, broke. Yet, barring a brief period when he thought of committing suicide, he decided to tackle life head on. And in the bargain, brought India some of the highest honours which can be achieved at the Asian and world levels in paraplegic sports. At the national level his records are too many to count. Nir Bahadur is a true soldier who never gives up. 'Muh chupane se kya milta hai saabji [What does on get by hiding one's face sir?],' he asks with candour in his singsong voice. Most interestingly his first medal at the national level came when he was twenty-nine years of age and his first international medal was won at the mature age of forty-one! He is a real fighter in true Gurkha style, one who never gives up or thinks of defeat.

This is his story. A story of unparalleled bravery.

Nir Bahadur Gurung was born in Shillong on 11 March 1958. He had many siblings and was the third oldest. His father was a soldier with the British Indian Army and saw serious action in the Eastern sector in Burma and Malaysia. Nir Bahadur was brought up with stories of bravery and courage and always dreamt of emulating his father. When the British left after 1947, his father's commission was transferred to the Gurkha Regiment of the Indian Army and, on retirement, the senior Gurung was allotted a piece of land in a village outside of Shillong. However, following the Chinese aggression in 1962, the army decided to take over the land given not only to the Gurung family but also to many others, and establish a Regimental Headquarters there. The Gurung family was paid good compensation and asked to move itself out in 1962 from that area. Nir's family stayed in the Shillong area for another four years or so before trekking to Nepal with the help of the army. This move to Nepal, when Nir was about seven or eight years old, did not prove fruitful in any manner, however.

The family settled down in a very backward, downtrodden village of Nepal near the foothills of Mount Everest. The place did not have any facilities as such and there was no school in and around the area for miles. Malaria was one scourge everyone was worried about and, indeed, with no medical facilities for miles around, there were many deaths in this and the surrounding villages. Nir's family too suffered one tragedy after another as most of the children died an early death leaving Nir with one sister and one brother alive.

Given this background, Nir, of course, did not know what formal sports were, but still, along with his siblings and children of the neighbourhood, found various ways to pass the time. As a typical naughty child he was more interested in running around and playing games than in anything else.

Nir's father, who drew a pension, decided that he would build a school and ensure that some semblance of education was provided to the kids in the area. 'I studied in this school till fifth standard. The school was only till this standard and therefore whatever education I had was over. My father died in 1974 and then we had major problems as we were a big family at that time. From the pension father got, which was transferred to my mother's name, we were able to buy a small plot at a higher altitude and then the whole family worked on the cultivation of this land.'

Nir and his family had no other source of income and whatever they could grow was consumed by the family. Sometimes when climate ensured that crops failed, then the family could not eat and at that time the boys worked as guides or Sherpas for foreign tourists. It was a hard life, but made Nir and his brothers strong in body and mind. 'We were a happy lot. We had nothing much, at times not even two square meals, but my parents told us never to beg, always to work hard. There is always some work to be done, my father used to tell me. The land was hard to till and quite unforgiving, but then it was all we had. And yes, the pride of belonging to a Gurkha soldier's family. A family well known for its bravery in times of war.'

In 1976, Nir was the beneficiary from a Nepal Government scheme, though he could not really derive much benefit from it. The government had begun gifting parcels of lands in uninhabitable areas, free of cost to boys over eighteen years of age, in the hope that soon the area would become populated and new villages would come up. Nir's land was in a dense jungle area which was difficult to till and full of mosquitoes. Though he tried his best, nothing could grow there and the fear of malaria ensured that apart from cutting and selling wood, nothing else could be done. Poverty remained as it was, even though Nir now owned a fair amount of land.

One day in December 1977 his father's younger brother, a soldier in the Indian Army, came up and convinced Nir to join up. Both of them went to Darjeeling where the uncle informed the recruitment officer that Nir was his younger brother and this facilitated Nir's entry into the Indian Army as a sepoy in the Gurkha Regiment. In those years, unlike today, units within the regiment also had their own caste system and caste-based recruitment was carried out. Nir Bahadur thus joined the Gurung unit of the famous regiment. The Gurkha Regiment also had Rai, Limb, Brahmin and Kshatriya units.

His training finished in July 1978 and Nir shifted to Panagarh in West Bengal where the regiment was transferred. From Panagarh the unit was sent to Gurdaspur where it was deployed on the border with Pakistan. Nir Bahadur however was soon sent to Shillong for an extensive driver's course in 1980, as his unit had earmarked him and found him strong and fit to drive the enormous Shaktiman trucks of the army.

He came back after some six months of the intensive course, now totally trained to drive army trucks. Life in the Gurkha Regiment really suited Nir. He is all praise for the culture and hospitality that he has seen in the forces. 'People used to say that there is discrimination in the army and that soldiers do not get enough to eat, etc. But I found this all wrong. I was really very happy in the Indian Army and there was no distinction between Nepalese and other units. We were all treated the same and with respect. Life went on for me at Gurdaspur, and despite frequent border skirmishes, we led a peaceful life.'

Fate however had sinister designs in store for Nir Bahadur. The date was 13 January 1983. Nir clearly remembers it as the day his world came tumbling down. His unit had been asked to take trucks filled with live ammunition for field firing practice to Hoshiarpur, some 40 kilometres away. Nir was not driving the truck but was sitting inside along with other soldiers, guarding the ammunition. The truck passed through an area called Chakkivan, which was actually a shortcut to the destination though the truck had to go up and come down a hill. The road was not good and, from the top of the hill, with the rock face on the driver's side, the truck slid on the dangerous icy surface, as the driver lost control and the brakes also failed.

'With the driver screaming that the brakes had failed I told him to get the truck on the rock wall as the opposite side had a deadly fall. I shouted to get the truck to somehow hit the wall so that it would slow down, the driver tried but with the truck gaining speed he lost his cool and whatever little control that he had. The truck did hit the rock wall but then suddenly turned turtle and slid along the slope for almost 30 metres before coming to a stop, luckily for us, on the wall side of the road. If we had fallen down the cliff and the ammunition had exploded, not only us but seventeen more soldiers who were in the truck would have died, plus the explosion would have critically damaged areas and villages around us.'

Four soldiers were killed instantly as the heavy ammunition boxes, some weighing up to 300 kilos, fell on top of them, crushing their skulls. Nir Bahadur did not die, but later wished he had. His skull was fractured and was bleeding, two ammunition boxes fell on his spine, shattering it, and he also had fractures in his arms. The impact was so severe that his rifle was broken and bent in two places. Nir Bahadur Gurung was in the prime of his youth and not yet twenty-five years of age.

He lost consciousness and woke up at the Pathankot Command Hospital, where they kept injecting him with painkillers and sleep-inducing drugs so that he did not feel the pain and also remained oblivious of the damage done to him in that accident. The Army medical team just did not allow him to regain full consciousness any time in the forty-five days that he was in the hospital. So severe were his injuries.

'When I was finally allowed to be fully conscious, I saw that my whole body was plastered and there were tubes running all over my body. I was told that I had eight major fractures. I could not move and was in excruciating pain all the time. I could not move at all, so severe and tight was the plaster put on my various fractures. I was not told that my spine had been totally damaged and since I could not feel much of my body as all of it was covered by the plaster, I did not realize that I would never walk again in my life. In this static condition I was transferred to a bigger hospital in Delhi.'

In Delhi the plaster was peeled off and Nir was again in deep pain. He started bleeding from the eyes, nose and had major trouble urinating as he passed blood there too. And here, on the second day, he realized that he had no sensation in his legs, but was told it would return slowly as he had been in plaster for a long time. As it was, his legs had lost most of the muscles being inactive and in plaster for long time. But one problem that really upset his equilibrium were the two huge bedsores he had developed. And these were very painful. The senior doctor, of the rank of Major General, met Nir on his rounds and asked him if he was comfortable.

'No sir,' he said and showed him the bedsores. 'I am not feeling any sensation in my legs also. I do not know what is wrong but please do something about my legs and the bedsores.' The doctor said that he could not be treated in this hospital and ordered that he be sent immediately to the Paraplegic Rehabilitation Centre in Pune. That night Nir was told by his nurse that his spine was totally damaged and that he had very little chance of recovery. But whatever little chance he had, the Pune centre was his best bet.

'I did not know the impact of these words as I am not a literate person. But when I asked in detail I came to finally understand that I would never walk again. My life was shattered and whatever dreams I had were not going to be fulfilled. Ever. I would remain wheelchair-bound, unable to lead a normal life. I had told my mother just few months back to look for a nice Nepali girl for my marriage. That was not to happen at all. I realized that I was doomed to lead a very lonely life and that society would look upon me as a cripple. I wanted to be a soldier all my life. But what good is a soldier with no legs? I was certified as a paraplegic.'

Within a week, for some reason the Army Medical Corps (AMC) had decided that Nir Bahadur be sent instead to Lucknow, home to one of the spinal injury centres of the armed forces, the other two being Pune and Chandigarh. The doctor in-charge there, Colonel B.P. Singh, was aghast that the patient had been kept in Delhi and Pathankot for almost three months. With a severe spinal cord injury Nir should have been sent to any one of the spinal centres named above on a most urgent basis. At first they refused to admit the hapless Gurkha Regiment soldier, but finally relented. Colonel Singh operated and removed a big amount of tissue to relieve Nir of the bedsores. He also saw to it that both fractured arms were aligned and then re-plastered for some time so that later he was able to get an almost full range of movement and abilities in his arms.

Nir spent almost two years at the Army Hospital in Lucknow, but each night he had nightmares. He imagined what life would be like, what his future would be. How was he going to earn a living? Marriage was out of the question as, with no sensation beneath the waist, he could not enjoy marital bliss, nor would the girl who would marry him. And if the army abandoned him, where would he go? The thought of a completely dark future unnerved and scared him. Finally, one dark day he decided that it was not worth living anymore. He started thinking of ways to commit suicide but realized that in the hospital this was not going to be simple. As it was he was bedridden and not allowed to go anywhere outside the barracks.

When finally the day came when he was going to be discharged, he told Colonel Singh that he wanted death. 'What nonsense are you talking? I cannot do any such thing. We want you to go home now, as we have done whatever we could do,' said the doctor.

'Sir I will not go home. I have no future, no life left. Please inject me with poison and kill me. Otherwise I will try to find ways to hang myself.'

Stunned, Colonel Singh got a counsellor on board and, gradually Nir Bahadur was convinced that he could still do something worthwhile in his life. They also got the army to extend his services, but Nir was to choose whether to be shifted to Pune or Chandigarh for further treatment, as the medical team in Lucknow had done all that it could. His mother had been able to come to Lucknow once and had broken down on seeing his condition. She also wanted him to come back to Nepal, but Nir would have none of it.

So in May 1985, some thirty months after the horrendous accident, Nir Bahadur Gurung shifted to the Pune Paraplegic Rehabilitation Centre of the Indian Army and started building a new life for himself, a life that would give him honour, respect, dignity and satisfaction. He did not know it yet, but he would eventually go on to become a para sportsman par excellence. A true legend.

He was under the care of Colonel Joshi and saw that most of the inmates in this wonderful facility were either paraplegics or quadriplegics with little or no sensation or movement in all four limbs. But all were Indian Army soldiers. Injured in wars, battles, skirmishes and horrendous accidents, like the one faced by Nir Bahadur. These men were warriors, proud of the army's traditions and its discipline, always ready to lay down their lives for the nation. In Pune, too, faced with a harsh life as physically disabled people, these inmates still had a sense of belonging and discipline, qualities that can be imbibed only by those who spend a lifetime in the services.

'I got some confidence and that feeling of comradeship when I saw all these wheelchair-bound soldiers and within a few weeks had made lifelong friends amongst these brothers who had same mobility problems as myself. I saw that apart from trying to learn various vocational skills, they spent lots of time playing different sports. The army provided coaches for all sorts of games. And since I was not literate, a new vocation was not cut out for me, but I thought why not use my strength and take part in wheelchair races. Yes I was young and strong and a Gurkha above all and Gurkhas never accept defeat. So I used the huge compound racing from one corner to the other. I did weight training also to get more power in my arms and shoulders and soon was ready to take part in any sports meet if the Centre agreed. I had also learnt that sports participation was a major part of rehabilitation of us paraplegics and the army supported it wholeheartedly.'

Almost two years of training went by and Nir was improving day by day in wheelchair mobility, which required raw power, As for sports, he tried many but started to play table tennis which he liked immensely. In November 1986, he came to know that the army would send a contingent to the National Sports Championships for Paraplegics, to be held in Bombay in January 1987. Nir Bahadur doubled his training and was fighting fit when he hit the track. On his debut he won the gold medal in the 100 metres race.

From then on there was no looking back for this legend in the making. He came back a hero to Pune and the coaches there started giving him coaching tips in shot-put, discus and javelin throw as well. Nir Bahadur had that brute strength which they wanted to harness for next year's edition of the National Paraplegic Championships. In February 1988, the meet was held in Chennai and Nir Bahadur stunned everyone by winning gold in 100 metres wheelchair and 4x100 metres wheelchair relay races. He did not disappoint his coaches and won silver in the javelin and the shot-put throws too.

'I could see my life now in front of me. I now knew what I

wanted to do. Sports was to be my main focus and I wanted to win as many medals I could at the national level for the army and my adopted state of Maharashtra. Sports gave me that thrill and I loved to compete and travel. Sports also gave me respect and adulation, which I thrived on. Hard work was no problem for me. After all, what was I to do with so much time at hand?'

Nir Bahadur broke all sorts of records at the national level. From 1987 till 2010 he won fifty-nine medals in track-and-field events, including thirty-three gold and twenty-five silver medals. The events include wheelchair races, and the three throws, namely, javelin, discus and shot-put. In the wheelchair table tennis championships at the national level, Nir Bahadur won another fourteen medals from 1988 till 2011, of which twelve were gold medals, revealing his ruthless domination of this sport at the national level.

This also shows his incredible fitness which he maintained from age of twenty-nine when he played in his first National Games in Mumbai to the ripe old of fifty-three, when he won his last medal in 2011. Suffice it to say that, in all probability, India has not seen a better paraplegic national-level athlete in history than Nir Bahadur Gurung, and that it will be very difficult for his stupendous feats to be surpassed in the near future.

However, winning at the national level was not going to cap his goals and ambitions. Even though he had started out late in life, Nir Bahadur Gurung wanted to win international medals for India at the Asian and world levels. A bigger stage was waiting to see his exploits.

In 1994, Nir learnt about the Far East South Pacific (FESPIC) Games held every four years. 'I came to know about this from former paraplegic sportsmen and decided that I also must enter these games. I started training doubly hard, and continued a harsh training schedule for almost six months. I was selected for the 1995 games held in Beijing, China, but alas, came back empty handed.'

He however understood what more was required of him and swore to himself that in the next FESPIC games in 1999, to be held at Bangkok, he would win a medal in his classification. He underwent heavier weight training for his arms and shoulders and decided to concentrate only on the three throws and withdraw from the wheelchair races, as, however hard he tried, he could not find a sponsor to buy him the lightweight chair used by all foreign athletes. Each day was spent in at least a 100 shot-put throws, and 200 discus and javelin throws. He would throw, race to bring the projectile back, and start all over again. It was sheer hard work, but had to be done.

'I used to train so much on my own that at times my right palm would bleed and my muscles would cramp up. But I continued every day and I could see an improvement in all my throws. I again won the selection events for the 1999 Games and arrived in Bangkok confident of doing well.'

Nir came fifth in javelin and missed the discus throw bronze by one place—he came fourth. The shot-put line-up was the last and he knew it was now or never. There were twenty-two competitors, all geared up to do their best for their countries. His very first throw put him in contention for a place in the top four. He qualified for the finals on the strength of that one throw and then went 16 centimetres better to slot himself in third place, which eventually won him the bronze medal. Delighted and in tears at the sight of the Indian flag being unfurled at the medals ceremony, Nir Bahadur also vowed that in next FESPIC games at Busan in South Korea, he would win at least two medals.

All the medallists were invited to have lunch with then prime minister, Atal Behari Vajpayee, who was moved and delighted to be amongst the country's disabled medal winners and announced that his government would donate ₹12 lakh to the Disabled Athletes Sports Federation (DASF) and, at the insistence of Nir Bahadur, he was moved enough to also announce cash awards of ₹15,000, ₹10,000 and ₹5,000 thousand for each gold, silver and bronze medal winner respectively. He also promised that if he remained in power by the next FESPIC games, the awards would be much more. 'You are the pride of India,' the prime minister told the contingent.

Nir Bahadur continued his winning ways at national- and state-level meets, and was almost forty-four years old by the time the 2002 Games approached. But his fitness, most amazingly, kept getting better and better. He could shame people half his age in sheer strength, stamina and reflexes required for top paraplegic athletes. The bulging biceps and strong shoulders were going to bring India glory, hardly seen before in para-games in Asia.

The Busan FESPIC games approached and Nir Bahadur was at the peak of his form, frequently throwing well over qualifying distances. Measuring his own throws he realized that he would be throwing better than what he had done at Bangkok. But so would be the others, and he knew that each and every opponent was to be respected. Winning that bronze in Bangkok had done wonders for him, he was no longer nervous, and in fact was hungry for success.

'I was ready to shed blood for the country. In practice and training back home I was looking strong. The first event was javelin and my throw of 15.12 metres was challenged by only one athlete. But after six throws I still maintained the second position and won a silver. In discus, too, my throws were big, with my best effort after the sixth throw being 19.30 metres, good enough for a silver. And on the final day my favourite shot-put was on. The Chinese and Koreans were very strong, leading all the way. I entered the finals of last eight athletes at the fifth position and had three more throws to go. In my anxiety I cut the line in the first throw and was faulted with a red flag going up. When my turn came again I threw only 6.30 metres. This was disappointing as I was still in the fifth position The best throw was 6.74 and second best at that time by the Korean player was 6.54 metres.

'My turn came again. It was now or never. I thought of my family and our goddess in Nepal whom we worshipped. I prayed for strength and asked the goddess to give me that one chance so that I could bring glory for my country which was nurturing me and which had sent me all the way here to Busan. And in true Gurkha style with the war cry on my lips I grunted and threw the iron ball with all my strength. I touched 6.66 metres. No other opponent could cross this distance. I had won my third silver medal, a feat unsurpassed till now. No one had won three silver medals before me at the FESPIC games. I had in my own humble way created history and brought pride to India. I had repaid my debt to India and to the Indian Army which had looked after me so well all these years.'

Atal Behari Vajpayee was again the prime minister. The country had gone into elections after fighting a savage war with Pakistan in the Drass-Kargil sector. The disabled sports contingent was invited to meet him at his residence for high tea. Nir Bahadur Gurung was in his element, the star of the show, joking with the prime minister and gently reminding him of his promise four years ago that he would ensure that para-athletes got more cash awards from his government.

The prime minister, true to his word, announced much

enhanced cash awards of ₹5 lakh, ₹3 lakh and ₹2 lakh respectively, for the gold, silver and bronze medals. Nir Bahadur, was happy that he would clear ₹9 lakh, but was still was courageous enough to tell Vajpayeeji that he was discriminating against them when able-bodied athletes had been showered with officially announced cash incentives of ₹15 lakh ₹10 and ₹5 lakh each for the same medals. 'Don't worry son, if I am still the prime minister the next time you come I will give you exactly the same awards as the able-bodied sportspersons. You have my word on it. This is a good start so I urge you all to accept what the government is giving now,' said the prime minister. Then Vajpayeeji smiled and asked Nir Bahadur, 'Gurkhaji you have won so many silver medals. Why not exchange them for couple of gold medals next time?'

'Sir, I am getting old, but I will try to live up to what you have said and do my best,' replied the soldier. The prime minister was amused, but chided Nir Bahadur by saying, 'You are a Gurkha and an Indian soldier. What is age to you people? You are taught to climb mountains bare handed—what is a mere gold medal? I am sure you will get me one before I leave this chair.'

This statement stayed in the mind of Nir Bahadur for a long time and, in true Gurkha style, he vowed again to move mountains and get that elusive gold medal for India. But two things happened before the next Asia Paralympic Games which were held at Kuala Lumpur, Malaysia in 2006. First, he decided that he would henceforth concentrate only on the discus throw and specialize in it. And second, he went for selections for the 2004 Athens Paralympic Games and threw far enough to qualify for his first 'Olympics'.

'But I also started to suffer a bit from spondylitis with constant pain in my neck, and this coincided with the time as I was training for the Athens Games,' remembers Nir. He did well enough to reach the top eight from amongst thirty throwers, but after reaching the finals, his best throw could get him to the sixth position only. Nir was disheartened, specially because all eyes were on him and the Indian contingent was sure he was good enough for at least a bronze. But once the leader threw some three metres further than his nearest competitor, the rest lost heart, Nir amongst them. The contingent however was overjoyed when one of them, Devendra Jhajharia, threw a world-record distance in the one-armed javelin throw and claimed the gold.

Till 2004, all para athletes selected to represent India by associations recognized by the government of India, had to pay their own expenses including airfare to the venues. The reasons for this are best known to the authorities. While able-bodied sportspersons selected to play for India, had all expenses taken care of by the sports ministry, the disabled athletes were on their own. Nir Bahadur got a pension from the army and almost all of it went into his travelling and other expenses. Sometimes the army took care of the airfares. If not for the benevolence of the army, Nir Bahadur and so many others would never have won these untold glories for the country. But logic prevailed and in June 2004, the government finally recognized the need to fund the disabled contingents for multi-sports events held under the banner of the IOC, and world championships held under the banner of the world federation of the particular sport.

Then a major tragedy occurred in middle of 2005 but typically of a Gurkha soldier, Nir Bahadur overlooked medical advice and continued as nothing had happened, even though by not adhering to the doctor's suggestion of taking rest, he endangered his life.

He had stood first in the wheelchair races of the Pune International Marathon in 1990, 1991, 1992, 1997, 2000 and taken second place in 1989 and 2002. These were races of limited distances, since wheelchair-bound athletes ran either four or seven kilometre races in such marathons worldwide.

For the 2006 race, Nir Bahadur, ever the fearless as his name suggests, decided that he was strong and fit enough at age forty-seven, to do a full marathon, that is, the full 42 kilometres, as a wheelchair athlete. The organizer of the event, one Mr Sawant, was not prepared to allow this. Nevertheless, not one to give up easily, Nir started training in earnest, wheeling 35 to 40 kilometres every second day, to get in shape for the big day. At the same time he tried everything possible to get clearance from the organizers to participate in a full marathon, to the extent he challenged them that if allowed to participate in the full marathon, he would not only finish the full distance, but he would surely defeat many able-bodied runners, beating them to the finish line.

Indian Athletics chief Suresh Kalmadi was also approached and though he wrote a letter to Sawant in support of Nir Bahadur, permission was still denied. They told him that they could not spare a motorbike-borne 'pilot' vehicle and an ambulance to accompany Nir Bahadur. By this time he was easily wheeling himself to a distance of almost 45 kilometres in practice, a spectacle never again seen in Pune, as he burnt the tires of his wheelchair on the roads of the city, applauded by many.

He was not allowed to participate in the full marathon, which was depressing and had a psychological impact on him. Added to that was the heavy physical training which he had done for so many years. All this took a serious toll on him. He started getting pains in his chest and was taken for treatment, where a block in one of the arteries necessitated an angioplasty and a stent being put in to allow proper blood flow. Then he was told to take complete rest for at least six months and not take part in any hectic physical activities. He was upset and hurt at not being allowed to compete. He did not want any sympathy or extra help in any way, just the courtesy of being allowed to live his dream to the fullest. But the heart problem left him stunned.

'This was a shock for me. I thought I was really fit and healthy but this angioplasty business showed me that at the end of the day we are all mortals. Yet to my mind this "total rest" business was simply not on. I had so many things to do still. And though I respected what the doctor said, I thought to myself that if I continued some training at most I may die. But then I had already cheated death before and had even wanted to commit suicide, but was talked out of it. I told myself that god did not want me to die so soon. God wanted me to live and win more medals for India. And even if I died who was there to grieve for me? I would like death to come when I was in some sports meet or doing training.' So against all caution and medical advice, Nir Bahadur Gurung was spotted back on track, training and doing what he wanted, within a month of the angioplasty.

The 2006 Asia Paralympic Games approached and were to be held in November at Malaysia. Nir, now participating in only the discus throw, decided that nothing less than a gold would do. After all, Prime Minister Vajpayee had wanted a gold medal and Nir had promised him one. Training was focused and nothing was left to chance. 'I would have two sessions of three hours each, every day. I gave up everything else for some six months and put in my best in training. I was really throwing big distances in this intensive training period. Lots of time was spent gaining strength. I could not have been fitter than this. I was really satisfied with myself. I knew that I was good for the gold. One thing I must confess here Sir, I am very stubborn. Once I decide to do something I will go all out and do my best, come what may. So though I had by now developed a heart problem, it was not going to come in my way at all.'

The first three throws of the Indian soldier crossed 21 metres and his best was 21.36 metres, good enough to give him the lead, which he maintained without much problem. No one threatened or challenged him. He was in a zone of his own. Nir had created a new Games record and won the most cherished medal of all—the gold. This time not only was the triclour unfurled, but the national anthem was also played while all participants, spectators and the media stood at attention.

'I can't describe that feeling, sir. Even today I get goose bumps just thinking about it. There is something about the anthem and the national flag. And for a soldier nothing is more sacred. I had tears rolling down my eyes when the flag went up. I had brought India the best gift I could.'

And in doing so he had also redeemed the promise made to Prime Minister Vajpayee. Nir Bahadur was almost forty-eight years old when he snatched that gold medal, making light of his age. He proved to all and sundry that age is just a number, something to acknowledge and then tuck away at the back of the mind.

The Indian squad came back to India and the medal winners were taken to Delhi by the PCI with the hope that, like before, the prime minster would be delighted to meet them. But the government had changed and Vajpayee was no longer in office. The medallists were not allowed to meet the new prime minister. The sports minister also did not have time to meet these extraordinary champions. Their dreams of being respected and acknowledged for a job well done, their expectations of getting a cash award as promised, all turned to dust.

For Nir Bahadur, who was sure that his feat would be recognized and applauded and that he would get a ₹15 lakh cash prize—the same as announced for able-bodied atheletes—this came as a double whammy. First, as the previous prime minister had hinted the awards would be brought into line with that given to the able-bodied recipients; this did not happen. He got zilch, not even a single rupee. Second, the thought that senior cabinet ministers could not find even ten minutes from their schedules to congratulate him and other disabled athletes, hurt and bewildered him.

Later on they learnt that since the PCI was not recognized as an official body by the government of India at that time, the ministry decided that the para athletes could not be rewarded or acknowledged. It was only after Sunil Dutt became the union sports minister and took interest in the plight of the disabled athletes, that his huge backing to the PCI ensured that they were recognized as a National Sports Federation.

After the 2006 Asia Paralympic Games, Nir cut down on athletic events and started concentrating only on table tennis where he won medals at the national level till 2011. He also indulged in some weightlifting, where he, true to his sporting genius and enormous strength, got so good that he was selected in the national team for the Asia Paralympic Games, the last one for him. But says Nir, that some sort of cheating by local organizers in Guangzhou kept him out of medal tally, otherwise he felt that he was good enough for a bronze in the discus throw, his favourite event and also in his weight-lifting classification where he stood fourth.

'I was not allowed to participate in my classification by the local officials. They put me in a higher classification. Our Indian officials also did not protest. I was good for a medal but local officials were afraid of me since I was a gold medallist in the 2006 games. I was also cheated out of a bronze medal in weight-lifting too, where an Australian opponent lifted faultily as his arm was not in the correct position. I was fourth in this event and should have been given bronze, but against all rules the Australian team produced a medical certificate which was upheld by the judges, when they should have rejected the certificate produced at the last moment, and after the event.'

A crestfallen Nir Bahadur returned to India empty handed. But his spirits soon rose as he won the singles gold medal at the Paralympic National Table Tennis championships in Ghaziabad in 2011. Earlier, in 2010, he had participated in his last National Para Games in Haryana and threw his way to a silver in the discus and the shot-put events.

Today, at time of writing this, Nir Bahadur is at the ripe age of fifty-five and says that he may not take part in athletic events at all but still wants to participate in table tennis, both at the national and international levels.

'Eye-sight is a bit of a problem now days Sirji,' he says with a candour and transparency that comes easily to honest and humble champions. 'But I will continue in sports till I physically can. There is glory in sports and after all what else can an illiterate Gurkha like me do? This is the only thing I am good at.'

He has achieved huge success any which way one looks at his career. But he has somehow lost out on the rewards and appreciation that should have come his way, even in small quantities. He was not given the Arjuna Award which should have been given to him way back in 2002, when he won three silver medals at the FESPIC Games. The sports ministry was silent, atrociously so, when Nir Bahadur won the elusive gold medal at the 2006 Asian Paralympic Games. No one from the government met him or his fellow medal winners, giving the flimsy excuse that the Paralympic Association was not recognized by the government. And most shockingly, the government of Maharashtra did not deem it fit to reward this senior athlete with the Shiv Chattrapati Award for excellence in sports, even after he won seven international medals of the highest calibre and an astonishing seventy-three medals at the national level.

'They tell me in Maharashtra that I am not a native or domiciled in the state. I applied three times but was denied this reward. I have stopped applying now as I feel insulted. And as far as the Arjuna Award is concerned, I do not understand the reasons at all. It is all just petty politics. I am told that had I known someone important I would have got both awards. But why should that be a criterion? Have I not done enough to justify these awards? Let me ask you, sir, if I am good enough to fight on the front as a soldier, be ready and willing to shed my blood for the country, then why am I not good enough to get an award from the country? And, sir, a couple of more questions are always on my mind and I cannot find any answers. If the government of India pays the expenses of us paraplegic athletes to participate in the FESPIC or Paralympic or Commonwealth Games, then that automatically means that we are recognized as a national team. Why then deny me the Arjuna Award as this should have come to me automatically?

'And, sir, as far as the Chattrapati Award is concerned, when we soldiers fight on the front, do we fight only for Punjab or Haryana or Bengal or Tamil Nadu? Don't we lay down our lives for the entire country? And since I am staying in Maharashtra since 1985, am I not domiciled here? Have I won the medals for any other state at the national level? And do my international gold and silver medals not belong as much to Maharashtra as to India? I have no answers to all these questions always buzzing in my head.'

Well neither do we have answers to all such questions which torment Nir Bahadur Gurung, the quintessential street fighter, the street-smart Gurkha soldier. He has done the best he could do for the country. Hopefully someday the powers to be in the state and country, will also wake up and do their best to appreciate and applaud this simple Gurkha, who brought unforgettable laurels for us.

MURLIKANT PETKAR
Hero Extraordinaire

Out of the night that covers me
Black as the pit from pole to pole
I thank whatever Gods may be
For my unconquerable soul
In the fell clutch of circumstance
I have not winced nor cried out loud
Under the bludgeoning of chance
My head is bloody, but unbowed
Beyond this place of wrath and tears
Looms but the horror of the shade
And yet the menace of the years
Finds, and shall find me, unafraid
It matters not how strait the gate
How charged with punishments, the scroll
I am the master of my fate
I am the captain of my soul

~WILLIAM EARNEST HENLEY~

In the annals of Indian sports one would be hard put to find a sportsperson, able-bodied or differently abled, who has led the magical life of Murlikant Petkar. Had we not met him, gone over his documents, confirmed what he went through and how he survived, we would have found his story unbelievable too. Even the dream merchants of Bollywood would not have dreamt that somebody like Murlikant Petkar could ever exist.

This then is the true tale of a boy who ran away from home at age twelve to escape a mob out to lynch him, landed up in the Boys Battalion of the Indian Army, was taught the skills of a soldier in his teenage years, became a national-level boxing champion for the army, reached Kashmir at the age of eighteen only to be hit by seven bullets early in the 1965 war against Pakistan (one bullet is still lodged in his spine). Thereafter a paraplegic, he went into sports and then won India's first Olympic gold medal in 1972 in Germany, and the first gold medal at the Commonwealth Games in 1970. It may be difficult to digest and believe but there it is.

Murlikant Petkar is a real Indian hero. He has won huge laurels for India and, as the first Indian to excel at various paraplegic games, has led the way for other wheelchair-bound and differently abled brothers to win international medals and honours for the country. He has done us proud, as a soldier and as a sportsperson of outstanding calibre. The country, though, has yet to do him proud. Not only is he yet to receive the Arjuna Award—the highest honour any sportsperson can receive—but the government is also in the process of stealing away his land by de-recognizing his ownership and reserving it as a playground.

Murlikant Petkar's extraordinary journey commenced in 1947 or 1948, he is not sure which of the two years he was born in. For purposes of this mini biography, however, we will use 1947 since his army records and those at the Tata Engineering and Locomotive Company (TELCO), where he worked later for the most part of his life, cite 1 November 1947 as his date of birth.

He was born in Islampur village in Maharashtra's Sangli

district, in a family headed by a father who was a certified freedom fighter and had a small tailoring shop. He also received a small freedom fighter's pension which was simply not enough for the endless needs of his six children. Murlikant's housewife mother thus brought up her children amidst great financial hardship. Murli, as he was fondly called, was interested in sports from childhood and used to spend all his time playing hockey, football, or rural sports like gilli-danda, kabaddi, kho kho etc. Endless hours spent in pursuit of these sports made him lean and tough with strong bones and good stamina.

The Sangli/Satara belt of Marathwada in Maharashtra is famous as a centre for wrestling and some of the best-known wrestlers, or pehelwans, as they are called, have come from this part of the country. The local akhadas or wrestling arenas owned by one pehelwan or the other, were really famous and drew youngsters who watched in awe as the burly wrestlers went about their training and mock fights. And there was always an air of festivity if there was an official dangal, exhibition bout in Islampur or the surrounding villages.

It was only natural for young Murli to gravitate towards the akhada at Islampur which was run by Ganpat Rao Khedkar, one of the most famous wrestlers in Maharashtra. These akhadas also gave lessons to young strong boys and soon Murli was getting talim or lessons in how to be a good wrestler. With hardly any food at home, the hours spent at the Khedkar akhada became a sort of boon for the young ten-year old. He was asked to make the cold thandai—crushed almonds and other dry fruits mixed in cold milk—a favourite health drink of wrestlers. This thandai, and ghee were the staple supplements of the pehelwans and more often than not, young Murli got a couple of glasses as his share for all the hard work he put in. Growing into a tall sprightly lad for his age, he soon became the favourite amongst the senior wrestlers. They sought him out for a warm-up with mock bouts, before they got embroiled in the serious business of their vocation as professional wrestlers.

'Early childhood was a good time for me,' recalls Murlikant, sitting in his flat in Khadki, a suburb of Pune. His thoughts are sometimes hazy and he gets emotional as he tells us his story, harking back through the years that have made up his life. 'We were poor and did not have enough food at home to feed eight mouths. My father tried his best, was respected in the community as an honest man, but could earn only as much as the work allowed him. My days were largely spent in all sorts of sports and I was really good at all of them. I had a good strong body and once I joined the akhada of Ganpat Khedkar, I really came into my own. For the first time I also got real and fulsome nutrition in glasses of thandai. I recall spending hardly any time in Islmapur High School where I was enrolled, as I really wanted to become a professional wrestler, a well-known pehelwan like Khedkar. But my life took such an amazing turn that I had to run away from my family and my village at the tender age of just twelve.

'A neighbouring village called Kanderi had organized a dangal and our wrestlers supported by our villagers, went there for the bouts. As per customs prevailing before the bouts, a pooja was held and coconuts broken by the headman of Kanderi.' The headman also happened to be married to Ganpat Khedkar's sister, which made him a son-in-law of the Khedkar family—generally a sensitive and delicate relationship in the traditional Indian set-up.

Murli recalls that for the exhibition match the headman announced that his son Shivaji Patil, who was around Murli's age, would fight any youngster for a purse of ₹5, a princely sum in those days. Normally for matches or bouts between children, the winner's prize used to be coconuts and batashas, a dry white sweet made of raw sugar. Ganpat Khedkar nodded to Murli and he stood up to take the challenge, even though he was shorter than Shivaji Patil. He had learnt the tricks and art of wrestling well from a master like Khedkar. And as Murlikant himself says, 'I was always very competitive and whenever I took part in sports I simply had to win. If I lost I used to sulk for hours and would not feel better until I won the next time.' Losing was something he never cherished.

For about five minutes the two adolescents kept circling each other till Shivaji clapped his thighs hard, soon followed by Murli, indicating that a serious bout was about to begin. By now the crowd was getting restless and soon enough someone laid down a white cloth on which the ₹5 was duly placed. Thereafter the crowd began throwing in more coins making the stake higher, in this winner-take-all bout. Now Murli did not know how much money had been thrown in, but guessed well enough that it was increasing by the minute and had to be much more than the ₹5 that had started it all.

The crowd asked the headman whether it should be this a normal or an exhibition bout, or whether it should be stopped. Like a true sportsman the headman declared that the bout would have three rounds. The judges also announced much to the approval of the crowd that, as with adult wrestlers, this would be a 'chit-pat' bout. In other words, the first to fall with his head hitting the ground would lose as per the unwritten rules that governed rural wrestling.

Murli looked at Khedkar who nodded and gave his blessing. In two lightning moves he had picked up Shivaji and lifted him aloft, holding him up high by the waist and the shoulder. This was a classic position from where one could throw the opponent down and Murli did just that, much to the delight of the appreciating crowd which knew a thing or two about wrestling.

The crowd went delirious with delight and remained euphoric until someone in the crowd shouted that Khedkar had deliberately trained Murli to defeat Shivaji, so that Khedkar's brother-in-law the headman would be made to look small in public. A simple bout between two youngsters suddenly turned into a planned public insult designed to make the headman lose face. The events that followed were to scar Murli for life. The crowd, deciding that this victory was an insult to their headman and their village, started braying for Murli's blood.

Ganpat Khedkar saw drastic action was needed and that he and Murli had to escape before the situation became really ugly. So he grabbed most of the winner's cash and, surrounded by his supporters, dashed out of the village towards the state highway, chased by the Kanderi villagers. On the way he thrust a fistful of notes and coins into Murli's pocket; later this turned out to be the really princely sum of about ₹12. Murli was lifted and put on the first truck they encountered and the driver promised a sum of ₹5 to take Murli to the final destination. The truck sped away and deposited Murli in Pune city some seven hours later around midnight, hungry and bewildered.

'I spent the night, awake and frightened, at the spot where the truck had left me. I missed my family, specially my father and since he had not come for the wrestling bout. I wondered if he was aware of my predicament. I could not think of going back as I thought the Kanderi villagers would kill me. Luckily, one of my father's sisters lived in Pune and I knew the area where her house was. In the morning I reached her house after searching the area for some time and met her and my uncle. I told them the story and he agreed not to inform my parents for the time being, as we thought that Kanderi villagers must be looking for me and Ganpat Khedkar. I did not know what had become of Khedkar. I stayed in this house for a week or so before my uncle took me to the local recruitment centre of the Indian Army.'

Murli was taken to the army recruitment centre at around 10 a.m. and, seeing his health and physique, was immediately accepted, made to sign some papers and made a part of the Boys Battalion of the army. By 4 p.m. the same day he was put on a train to Bengaluru, then known as Bangalore. Murli's uncle told him not to worry and that at an opportune time he would tell his parents about his joining the army. The boy was still just twelve years old, not even a teenager. The year was 1960.

Murli liked what he saw of the army. There was discipline no doubt, and there were studies, too, but what interested him most were the exercises and the fact that he could play as much hockey, football or any other sport he liked. And yes, there was enough food all the time. Within a year or so he became really good at hockey and was selected to play for his Command* against other teams in Karnataka. He scored many goals, was fearless and nearly made it to the Karnataka team to play in the all-India championships of the Boys Battalion. He was dropped twice at the last stage simply because he was a Maratha boy and the Karnataka team wanted only local boys from the state. Upset at this treatment he vowed never to play hockey again and started taking an interest in martial arts, boxing and hand-

---

*The Indian Army, at present, is divided into the following Commands: Eastern Command, Western Command, Northern Command, Southern Command, South Western Command, Central Command and Army Training Command. Murli would have represented the Southern Command.

to-hand combat training.

His favourite sport was boxing and Havildar Kutty, the trainer, soon realized that he had a really ferocious and fearless fighter on his hands. 'I liked boxing because here either your teeth got broken or you broke your opponent's teeth. No bhaigiri or brotherhood here as in hockey. I was on my own. If I won I would be selected for the state and then nationals, if I lost—well there was another chance after a few months. And I had strong shoulders and arms because of wrestling and hockey. I was fit and strong and looked forward to the bouts in the ring,' recalls Murlikant with glee.

He was so good at it that very soon he was in the Command team and was selected to represent his Command against the Bombay Engineering Group (BEG) at the Inter-Unit Championships in Pune. He won all his fights. He did not visit his aunt's place, and even though he was now fourteen years old, he did not know whether his parents were aware of his whereabouts.

Going back to Bengaluru he took part in the Southern Command Championships, came out a winner, and was selected for his first National Championships in the Army Boys Battalion. He won here, too, and was selected to represent the army at the Junior National Championships to be held in Jabalpur in1963. It was there that he met one of his relatives, and, for the first time heard that his parents were well, but in distress because they did not know whether he was dead or alive. Apparently his aunt and uncle in Pune had forgotten, or chosen not to inform his parents in Sangli about his whereabouts. Murli had also not bothered so far, as he was still afraid that if he went home the villagers of Kanderi would get to know and kill him.

He repeated the feat of winning the Southern Command title, the National Championships in the Boys Battalion and then the Open Junior Nationals the next year in 1964 too. As a reward for his great two years as army boxer, he was selected to represent the Indian Army at the International Services Sports Meet to be held in Tokyo, Japan. In between, when he was not putting in hours in the boxing ring, he was undergoing exhaustive training in hand-to-hand combat, rifle shooting and other skills required of an Indian Army soldier.

So towards the end of the year 1964, Murlikant Petkar, now seventeen years old, who had hardly travelled in his own home state of Maharashtra, was set to jet out to Japan. 'I had never seen a plane up close, only high in the sky. I had never thought of flying—not even in my dreams. And here I was, afraid to get inside a plane, wondering what would happen if it crashed, because one of my teammates had told me that these machines also crashed and everyone died. Dying while boxing was okay with me, but a plane crash was something else. I tried to turn back and run away, but seniors of the squad caught hold of me, pushed me in, strapped me and ordered me to be quiet. The take-off was a nightmare and when it took off, the plane was shaking and I went white. I could not breathe. But once the air-hostess came and started giving food and drinks, I guess I became alright.'

The competition in Tokyo was spread over four days and in the first three days Murli, who had by then been nicknamed 'chotu tiger' or the young tiger by his team, had knocked out six fighters. 'I was fast and quick and for me a knock-out was the only option. I had lot of anger in me. While fighting I would think of my being forced to run away from home, not being allowed to play hockey for the state and that anger would spill out in my boxing and I would take it out on the opponent.'

The semi-finals saw him at his ferocious best as he knocked out a boxer from Turkey and then the finals loomed, which had to be played the same evening. Murli was confident and looked forward to wining this international title, but an equally big hitting boy from Uganda hit his chin so hard in the second round that Murli was knocked out for two days. 'I just not know what happened. This boxer was very good, he did not allow me to get under his guard and hit me often. I never saw his right hook coming and he knocked me off my feet. I was out for two days. But in the end it was all fun. I was happy to have won a silver medal for the Indian Army.'

He learned a lot on this trip, including how to eat with a fork and knife. 'I had never seen a knife and fork and did not know how to use these to eat food. Since all teams were staying in a type of youth hostel, we had a common dining area. And all the others were cutting bread with the knife and I tried but broke seven plates while trying to learn this art. I used too much force in everything I did, I suppose. It was very embarrassing for me but there was a nice matron there and though she did not know any Hindi and obviously I did not know any Japanese, she patiently explained to me and showed me how to eat with these instruments. My officers were upset, but she did not allow them to shout at me and was very sweet.'

Murli returned with the squad and was transferred soon to 1 EME Centre* in Secunderabad, where he began training for the 1965 nationals to be held at Bengaluru. There he again won. He had tremendous confidence in himself and his abilities as a boxer. The training was hard and critical and his eighteen-year-old body was really filling out. He had not visited his village or met his parents since he had fled Kanderi village. But he had no regrets

*EME refers to the Corps of Electrical and Mechanical Engineers of the Indian Army.

as he was happy in the army, training now to be an armourer.

The General Officer Commanding (GOC) Southern Command was a sportsman himself and was very happy with the national titles Murli had won for his Command. As a reward he asked Murli if he wanted to go on a trip sponsored by the army. 'I had not taken any leave from the day I had joined. So he asked me if I wanted to visit any place in India and immediately I said, 'Sir, please send me to visit Kashmir.' This one decision was to change Murli's life yet again totally and in a most dramatic fashion.

Along with ten other boys selected from the Southern Boys Battalion, Murli landed in Kashmir and was attached on temporary transfer to the 108 Gurkha Regiment and put to train as an armourer at the 109 Light Aid Detachment workshop within the unit. The first seven days were heavenly as this strapping lad from Islampur in Sangli saw the memorable sights of what is truly 'paradise on earth'. The Gurkha jawans took him to Gulmarg, to Pahalgam and, of course, gave him guided tour of Srinagar. He was after all a star boxer of the army—a celebrity of sorts. Murli soaked in the sights of the snow-capped mountains, the cascading rivulets and the green pastures in October 1965. Winter had yet to set in and the climate was lovely.

On his tenth day with the Regiment, during siesta time between 3 and 4 p.m., everyone heard the long wail of a siren. He and many others mistook it for the whistling call to come to the Mess, some hundred metres away from the living quarters, for evening tea. Murli did not drink tea and therefore he and a few others stayed put in the barracks. The wail in fact was a war siren announcing an unprovoked attack by the Pakistani Air Force (PAF). The Gurkha Regiment, so close to the border, was a priority target for the PAF, which bombed and strafed the entire area. There was blood and gore everywhere. Murli ran out with the others and was aghast when he saw broken limbs, spilled intestines and shattered bodies strewn all over. His friends from EME Secunderabad, his new friends from the 108 Gurkha's, maimed and scarred for life. Many died while standing in line for the evening tea. The remaining Gurkhas in that small unit of the LAD workshop swore revenge and as the senior officers came running in, Murli and other soldiers were ordered to recover the bodies, collect the rifles and help the injured.

'Our leader was Havildar Gurung Thapa and he took command instantly. We immediately took the injured to the nearby army hospital and then reported back for duty, still shaking with disbelief. Thapa gave us orders to immediately load our rifles and get into the trucks which had already assembled. We had been ordered to go to the front in Sialkot sector and take up a defensive position just in the centre of a hilly area, while the enemy infiltrators were already established on top. There was a road below us on which Indian army trucks were busy taking troops to the line of control (LOC). We reached, dug in and started firing. The first night was brutal and by the morning we were exhausted and running out of ammunition. The enemy was getting more and more reinforcements. In fresh firing from the top I got hit by many bullets, nine I was told later. One bounced off my skull fracturing it, and one skid past my right cheekbone damaging my eye. One hit my spine and lodged there, while one went through the shoulder. Both thighs were hit and both calves as well. The impact of the bullets was such that I was thrown from our position to the road below, and there an army jeep passing by could not stop in time and went over my legs. I was screaming in pain and all I saw and remembered last was that there were some Red Cross workers who were helping the injured. I lost consciousness thereafter.'

Later he came to know that his condition was so bad that he had been shifted from one hospital to another and landed in Delhi after some seventeen months. He had lost his memory and did not even remember his own name. The nurses in Delhi nurtured him. He was totally bedridden.

One day there was an inspection of his ward by the Commandant of the hospital, a doctor who was a General. Murlikant was lying at the edge of his bed, not certain of what was happening when, in the melee of junior officers making way for the General, he got knocked off the bed and hit his head hard on the floor. Unbelievably, and in true Bollywood style, he suddenly regained his memory and remembered that he had been riddled by bullets fired by Pakistani soldiers. He was lifted to the bed. His mind went back to that fight on the hill and Murlikant concluded that after his injury he had been captured and that this hospital was in Pakistan.

When the General reached his bed to enquire after him, Murlikant shouted a war cry, got his fingers around the officer's neck and pressed his windpipe. 'I had been trained to fight and kill Pakistani soldiers. I thought I was still in Pakistan and this hospital I thought was Pakistani. I screamed and told the other doctors and soldiers to stay away from the General or I would kill him. The General tried to assure me that he was an Indian doctor but I refused to believe him as there was no identity card on him or on his bodyguards and the medical staff surrounding him. And he was not wearing the field combat uniform. In my mind the Indian army uniform was the camouflage uniform. The guards with him even pulled out their hand-guns, but I had a solid grip on the General's windpipe.'

There was much shouting and cursing, but Murli was not giving an inch and the stalemate continued till a senior nurse appeared and brought her ID from the nurse's station which finally confirmed to Murli that he was indeed in Indian territory and that the medical staff belonged to the Indian Army.

The harassed General got his breath back and saw the humour in this whole episode and forgave Murli for being so blunt and aggressive. 'In fact he praised me for following the ideals of Indian soldiering and said every soldier should be like me and never forgive the enemy. He later on invited me to his office for a cup of coffee,' remembers Murli fondly.

Murli also realized, after he regained his memory, that he could not use his legs and was informed that he was 95 per cent paraplegic. He also had no control on his urination or on his bowel movements. He was wheelchair-bound for life. He had been in the hospital Delhi for about a year and was just past his nineteenth birthday. He had undergone seven major surgeries on his skull, eye, knees and back and one bullet was still lodged in his spine, which the doctors refused to remove for the danger it would pose to the spinal cord.

Not knowing what the future had in store for him, he one day requested the General to send him back to Maharashtra and if possible shift him to INS Ashwini—the navy's premier hospital* in Mumbai. He had not been back to Islampur for almost six years, from the day when he was forced to run away to save his life and a transfer to Mumbai or Bombay as it was known, meant that he would be close to his family and village.

This was move was again to bring about a huge change in his life. He was set to immortalise himself in the field of paraplegic sport, but after some astonishingly dramatic moments which

---

*The Indian Navy's medical establishments all carry the prefix INS or Indian Navy Ship, hence INS Ashwini.

would thrill any celluloid hero.

At INS Ashwini, he fell into a daily schedule which saw him swimming and playing other sports like shot-put, archery, table tennis, javelin etc., under the watchful eye of a senior army doctor called Jawale. Swimming was basically a therapy to strengthen his back and shoulders. Murli was slowly getting his strength back and was also dreaming of a reunion with his family. But when the reunion did occur, he was in for a rude shock.

'I think it was somewhere towards middle of 1967 that I could finally meet my parents, who came along with my elder brother. They were aghast seeing my condition. My father and brother were shell-shocked and would not talk to me at first. My mother did not react this way. I told them that I was now thinking of leaving the army as it had no place for a handicapped soldier. And that I would join a school back home, educate myself and try to be an earning member of the family. But my brother would have none of it. He said that no one could look after me as I had no control over my bowels and urination. He said that since I was now a langda, a person who had no use of his legs, I would be a burden on the family, which was not earning enough as it was. My father kept quiet during this outburst. My mother kept on crying and I was also very emotional. I had never been hurt so much in my life as I was when I heard what my brother said. My father's silence on the issue wounded me more than any Pakistani bullet could. I felt sorry for my mother. But suddenly I resolved that all of them must leave.

'I had some past salary from the army, about ₹10,000 with me and I gave ₹5,000 to my mother and bid all of them farewell. Till today I cannot forget that helpless look in my mother's eyes. She pleaded with them that she would look after me, but my brother and father remained stone-hearted and unmoved. I was still a teenager, but that one moment on that fateful day I realised that a mother-child relationship is the purest. It has no malice, only acceptance, no looking for rewards, only caring and unblemished love.'

The family went away, but left a depressed paraplegic behind. It was at this stage in his young, brave but burdened life that Murlikant decided that he did not want to live and that he must find ways of committing suicide. Being bedridden, hanging from the fan or something high and strong enough to carry his weight was out of question. He contemplated shooting himself, but procuring a gun or a rifle would be difficult and without accomplices it was not possible. Knifing himself would be messy and in any case would take hours and if found out in time, he could be saved. After all he resided in a hospital. He decided after a lot of thinking that the easiest and best way was swallowing a handful of sleeping pills.

Using a fair amount of cunning, therefore he began telling the nurse looking after him that he wanted a pill as he was finding difficult to sleep. Unwittingly, because she wanted to help this young man out of his misery, the ward nurse became an accomplice. Murlikant soon collected some thirty pills, which he judged were enough for the task on hand. He set up his date with destiny and bought a packet of the best agarbattis or scented incense sticks and some flowers. With all ingredients ready, Murlikant was now all set.

'I had no desire to live anymore. My own blood had disowned me. Barring my mother no one cared for me. I had decided on the day I would end my life, but I had to do a couple of things before I left this cruel world of the living and joined my ancestors above. I had some money left with me and that fateful day I threw a lunch party in my room for all my new friends at the hospital.

In the evening I called for a taxi and went to see the famous Taj Hotel and had my dinner there. It was a sight, with many well-dressed patrons wondering loudly how I was allowed in. But no one could stop me as I had enough money in my hands. After the dinner I went to a clothing shop and bought a pyjama and a shirt. I wanted to go out in style. Then I bought three half bottles of whisky, rum and vodka and returned to INS Ashwini. I was satiated and fully ready to meet my creator.'

Just before he sat down to drink and take the sleeping pills, the hospital sweeper came running to Murlikant and requested him to lend him ₹10. A popular but illegal form of gambling that used to take place in those years was called 'matka' and one Ratan Khatri used to run this infamous but hugely lucrative and popular form of street gambling. The sweeper wanted to gamble on a number that had come in his dream. 'I wanted to help him and make him happy, so instead of ₹10, I gave him a hundred-rupee note. He went away happy with joy but soon came running again. He said I should also put some money on his number. I agreed, since where I was going money was not needed. I gave him another hundred-rupee note, but told him to put my money on one number more than him. That is the last digit was to be one number more.'

Murlikant started his departure ritual around midnight by lighting the agarbattis and sprinkling the flowers all around where he sat, and also offered prayers to God Hanuman, whom he had revered all his life. All done, one swallow of liquor with one sleeping pill was followed by the next. Chanting the *Hanuman Chalisa*, in some thirty swallows he gulped all the pills and was soon asleep with both the liquor and the effect of the pills hitting him hard. Not being a hardcore alcoholic, Murlikant did not realize the effect that almost one-and-a-half bottles of mixed hard alcohol was going to have on him. Getting up with a splitting headache and a gurgling stomach at about 4 a.m. the next morning Murlikant vomited till his stomach was empty. The fact that he had emptied the contents of his stomach meant that the effect of the sleeping pills was almost nullified. He was still in a daze though and went back to sleep with a very heavy head, only to be woken at around 9 a.m. up by a screaming and highly excited sweeper.

'I opened the door and there he was, along with two people whom I had not seen before. The strangers were from the matka syndicate and they whispered to me that I had won ₹40,000, a huge sum in those years. I think it was around September or October of 1967. I was stunned and did not know how to react. I soon felt for the first time since I got riddled by bullets, a sensation and need to urinate. The money and this sensation which showed me that I could have some control over my urine, made me ecstatic. The commotion outside my room soon brought hordes of my friends and medical staff, with everyone congratulating me on my good fortune. I had done my best to commit suicide last evening and here I was, suddenly having gained a small iota of control over my body and also richer by a fortune, which I did not know what to do with.'

Murlikant decided then and there that he would not keep this money with him. More importantly he decided that God Hanuman had willingly allowed him to live and that his life must have some meaning hereafter. The Khatri Matka people gave him an address to collect the money and went away.

He met Dr Jawale the next morning and requested that he be given two escorts and an army truck to bring the 'winnings' back to INS Ashwini. The cash was brought to his room and Murlikant, still undecided what to do with it, first of all threw a party for all at the hospital, including his sports teacher Jawahar, who had been appointed by a sports trust run by the famous cricketer and philanthrophist Vijay Merchant to help rehabilitate injured and paraplegic soldiers at INS Ashwini through sporting activities in cooperation with the armed forces.

After a long time spent pondering over the question, Murlikant finally decided what was to be done with that huge amount of cash still with him. 'When I was going to collect cash the day before, I saw some blind people trying to cross the road near Victoria Terminus (VT) station and it struck me that with all my handicap and disability I was still better off than those who were blind. This impairment is the worst of all physical handicaps. Society was and still is mostly immune to the needs of the handicapped population. We all need help, but the blind need the most. I decide that I would give away all my money to the National Association of the Blind and again requested Dr Jawale that I be escorted by two soldiers in our truck to give away this money. He was very happy and readily agreed and in fact even came along with me.'

Having given away whatever money he had, Murli now decided to start his life with a new slate and do well in sports, bring laurels to the army and to Maharashtra. Under guidance of coach Jawahar and help from the Vijay Merchant Trust, the young soldier—who had in any case been very good in sports as a child—was soon thriving in almost all the disciplines he put his hand in. Obviously given his handicap, boxing, wrestling and hockey were out of question. Swimming at the Navy pool in Colaba was one thing he really liked as it helped him get stronger. But with nothing else to do the whole day, Murlikant was soon trying his hands on everything from archery to shot-put, javelin, table-tennis, wheelchair racing, etc.

By December of 1967, the Trust and the army put up his name for the State Championships for Paraplegics where he did everybody proud by winning gold medals in archery, table tennis, shot-put, discus and javelin throwing, and weight-lifting. Sponsored by Vijay Merchant and the Parsee Gymkhana of Mumbai, Murlikant repeated this feat in 1968 and in 1969 at the National Paraplegic Games and won four gold medals for the state, repeating this feat again and again till 1973.

By early 1969 coach Jawahar had got hold of the various qualification distances and timings of international meets and Commonwealth Games paraplegic events and realized that with some more training and pushing Murli could be among the medal-winners at international meets as well. He was young, strong and willing to put in the required hard work. Soon the training became more focused and harsher, but Murli was in his element.

'The first international championship I was selected for was the 1969 Stoke Mendeville International Paraplegic Meet in England and our Indian squad was again sponsored by Vijay Merchant and the army. We were well received at the airport and again at the venue by the expatriate Indian community, which was cheering for us in large numbers. I had really trained hard for this event and was in good form. I had been entered in 50 metres freestyle swimming and shot-put. In my swimming race I won India its very first international gold medal in paraplegic games. I felt really happy and proud at what I had achieved. Our Indian flag went up first as the national anthem was played and I got emotional, and like a soldier I saluted the flag while sitting in my wheelchair. The Israeli and German flags followed at second and third place. I was given my medal by Queen Elizabeth who asked me many questions about my injury and I replied through our official interpreter.'

The same year Murlikant went to Mexico for another paraplegic championship and again won a gold medal in swimming. He was now very confident in his swimming event and became one of the hot favourites for the 1970 Commonwealth Games to be held in Edinburgh in Scotland. He had qualified for 50 metres freestyle swimming, javelin throw and shot-put throw.

'We were informed about three months before the event that an Indian squad would be participating and accordingly we stepped up the training schedule under our new national coach R.P. Singh. I was putting two hours in the pool daily and also three to four hours on the track for the throw events. Dr Jawale saw to it that I got a good diet and all the facilities that I wanted. No one had won a Commonwealth Games gold for India before and he told me that I had it in me to go for glory and get that gold for the country. I promised him I would get that gold.'

A well-trained and really focused Murlikant redeemed his pledge to Dr Jawale and broke the existing Commonwealth Games record, winning the gold in 50 metres freestyle. He then went one better by winning a silver medal in the javelin throw and a bronze in the shot-put. He was presented the gold medal by the then British prime minister, Ted Heath.

In 1971 Murlikant was a sure shot for the Stoke Mendeville International Paraplegic Meet and did not disappoint as he powered his way to one more gold medal in swimming and the silver in the Javelin throw. By this time Murlikant had started hitting the national media headlines and on return was awarded the Best Army Swimmer medal by the then Chief of Army Staff, General Sam Manekshaw. Another great honour was when he was invited by Prime Minister Indira Gandhi for a tea reception at her residence in New Delhi where she rewarded Murlikant with a purse of ₹2,000. An ecstatic Vijay Merchant, the man behind all this success announced that the next year in 1972, India would send its first contingent to the Paralympic Games*, which were to be held immediately after the Munich Olympics. And that twenty-five-year old Murlikant Petkar was to lead this contingent of paraplegic sportsmen of the country.

The stage was thus set for the biggest test for Murlikant. Destiny was beckoning him and he knew that if he won a medal at the Paralympic Games, he would be immortalized in the annals of Indian sport.

He trained with full focus and beat the qualifying time every day in the pool. He also decided that he would focus only on this event. But this time, he wanted to not just win a medal. He wanted to create a sensation. Murlikant did a combination of weight training and fast-paced swimming daily, spending up to four hours in the pool and the gym. The distances that he swam were a combination of 25 to 50 to 100 metres, pulling himself as fast as he could.

There used to be a Colonel Nicholson who motivated Murli every day. 'Colonel Nicholson would come every day to the pool with a bottle of Chivas Regal, the best Scottish whisky available in those times. My coach would read out the world record which was, if I remember correctly, 32 seconds for the 50 metres freestyle race. I had already broken the Commonwealth Games record. Nicholson had this army baton in his hand and he would jog all the way when I swam. If I equalled the record I would get two pegs of that whisky and he would applaud me. If I did not equal or failed to come close, he would thrash the water with the baton and scream, "Not good Petkar. You better pull up your

---

*These games had been started by the International Olympic Committee for paraplegic athletes.

socks boy, you are not only going to represent India, but also the finest army in the world—and don't you forget that." But he was a real gentleman and was the sports in-charge of the army battalion at Colaba in those years. He saw to it that I got extra glucose, meat or whatever food I wanted. But liquor, only if I equalled or broke the record. Otherwise I was not allowed to eat outside or even travel outside the training arenas lest I meet with an accident or something.'

However, following a barbaric attack by Palestinian freedom fighters on Israeli athletes in the Munich Games village, the Paralympic Games were pushed back. Many athletes had been brutally massacred. The world was aghast and host Germany were really bitter at what had happened in their homeland. The Interpol and other investigative agencies descended on Munich and it was decided by the hosts to not only shift the Paralympics to Heidelberg but that the event would start some fifteen days later than the dates released earlier.

This tragedy and the subsequent push back of dates, threw all preparations to the wind. Murlikant thought he would not peak at the right time. 'I was put off a bit, but the national coach decided that we should all take a break for a week so that the body would be well rested, and then start training again following the same parameters as before. This did the trick and I was in a really keen mood and great shape by the time we landed in Germany.'

There were some 120 swimmers in the field and five heats before the finals in the 50 metres freestyle. Murlikant had a slight problem to overcome every time he swam in a race. Because of the injury on his skull, the area where the bullet had grazed him was still soft. So he had to be really careful at the finish. If he did not control himself he would hit the edge of the pool and do himself a serious injury. To avoid this therefore he used to station one of his helpers at exactly 5 metres from the finish, and that too on his left side which he favoured to come out for a breath while swimming.

Here at Heidelberg, the manager of the Indian squad had to really emphasize upon the hosts the peculiar problem Murlikant faced. Impressed by the fact that such a brave soldier was in their midst, the German organizers were extremely cooperative and saw to it that a local volunteer was stationed at the required distance for Murlikant, wearing a red cap which could be easily seen.

Murlikant thus raced to first position in all the five heats before making the semi-finals on the third day, where he was again the first swimmer to reach the finish line. 'It was really exhausting, but exciting at the same time. There was a gap of two hours between each heat and the assembled crowd, many of whom were Indian Punjabis, used to applaud me every time. The Indians in fact would meet me soon after a race and offer me all sorts of inducements to win. It felt nice to be followed and feted by so many of our countrymen. In fact right through my career I have always received love and appreciation from the ordinary Indian in every part of the world.'

The finals saw the eight best swimmers in the paraplegic world assemble to fight it out for the medals. It was taken for granted that the Indian ace would win and Murlikant did just that, making India proud by shattering the world record on his way to the gold. History was made as he became the first Indian to win an individual Olympic gold medal. No one had so far won one either at the Olympics for the able-bodied, or the Paralympic Games. The crowd went wild and he was feted all the way as he was wheeled to the podium.

'This was my moment. I had worked really hard and this was my reward. Who would have thought that an almost illiterate boy from Islampur village in Sangli district of Maharashtra, who had run away from home, who had survived so many bullet injuries in the 1965 war, and who had lost his memory completely for many months, would one day be an Olympic gold medallist, that too with a new record. The tiranga went up and fluttered proudly as the national anthem was played. I could not stop my tears as I saluted the national flag. I do not know if I had been able to kill an enemy soldier, but at least I had brought an Olympic gold medal for my country.'

He landed in India a real hero, owner of that elusive gold medal which had been and still is a dream for all athletes who represent the country on the Olympic stage. The Governor of Maharashtra and Sam Manekshaw, a Field Marshal by then, sent their representatives to receive Murli at the airport. But the one man whom Murli thanked profusely at the airport was none other than Vijay Merchant, who had made all this possible. An army convoy took him to INS Ashwini, where a standing ovation by almost 3,000 soldiers of the armed forces at the Colaba Naval area awaited him. A photograph was taken with his medal, and this picture adorns the hospital till today. The hero was then flown to Army Headquarters in Delhi where the Field Marshal personally met him and congratulated him and received the Olympic gold medal on behalf of the army.

For a man who had cheated death twice, once at the hands of Pakistani soldiers at beginning of the 1965 war in Sialkot sector, and next when his suicide mission went wrong, this was now a life worth living.

A few months later Murlikant decided to leave the army as an active soldier-cum-sportsman. Iconic industrialist J.R.D. Tata, along with his senior official Mr Moolgaonkar, visited INS Ashwini to meet some soldiers who were recuperating after serious injuries in the 1971 war against Pakistan. Tata also requested a meeting with Murlikant Petkar, a champion he had read a lot about. The chairman of Tata Sons was overwhelmed when he heard Murlikant's entire story and asked the hero how the Tatas could help him. He said, 'Sir, I don't want any cash award from you nor any piece of land. If you really want to help me, give me a job. I know the army has been very helpful to me considering my physical condition. But this is no place for a paraplegic like me. I would be grateful if I were offered a job but with one condition, sir. You must also allot me living quarters within 200 metres or so from the job area so I am not dependent on anyone and can wheel myself to my functional area.'

Tata also set a condition when he offered Murlikant a sports supervisor's position at TELCO in Pune. He made Murlikant promise that he would continue taking part in national and international meets, sponsored by the Tata corporate house. Murlikant gladly accepted and parted ways with the army in October 1972 and shifted to Pune. He had overcome humongous odds to achieve great heights—very few manage to do either in one lifetime. Murlikant was only twenty-five.

He decided he still had to cross another personal frontier, before really settling down to a new life away from the army. He had not been to Sangli ever since that wrestling bout, nor met his parents since that episode in 1967 when he was let down by his father and older brother. In Pune, some of his relatives met him and asked him if he wanted to get married. He was wary but agreed to see a few girls provided they were apprised of his physical condition before the meeting took place. He was earning ₹3,000 a month at TELCO, had a monthly lifelong pension from the army, was an individual-event Olympic gold medallist, and a real-life hero to boot. Many girls were charmed enough to meet him and finally one was chosen who bore him a son and four daughters, including a pair of twins. The marriage was attended by his parents and siblings and amidst emotions and festivity the bitter past was forgotten. Constant physiotherapy and exercises had helped him get more sensation in lower limbs, regain more control over urine and bowel movements, and he could stand up on his legs, but with some struggle. The army, though unhappy that it would no longer have him on the rolls, agreed to make him a lifelong patient at the Paraplegic Rehabilitation Centre in Pune, where he still goes for ten days of physiotherapy treatment every month, even after so many years.

The bullet is still in his spine and his head still hurts. But the soldier in him or that desire to win in every sports competition—that fathomless fighting spirit—never died. From 1973 to 1984 he continued to dominate the state- and national-level paraplegic sports scene, winning at almost any sport or event he set his mind on. He was rewarded with the Shiv Chattrapati Award by Maharashtra in 1975 and was recommended for the Arjuna Award in 1973, 1974 and again in 1975. But for reasons unfathomable, he did not get this award. He won the Commonwealth Games gold in 1970, the Olympic gold in 1972 and in one last fling at the international level at the ripe old age of thirty-five, he stunned everybody in paraplegic sports circles around the world when he swam his way to yet another world record timing in the 1982 Far East South Pacific (FESPIC) Games in Hong Kong.

As far as Indian sports went, no one had ever dominated his event with such force as Murlikant Petkar. Perhaps we can only name deaf-mute badminton star Rajeev Bagga, who won sixteen gold medals in five World Deaf Games, as coming close to Murlikant in terms of achievements. These two are by far the best ever sportsmen produced by India at any level. No one has won the gold medal at the Asian Paralympic Games, the Commonwealth Games and the Olympics from India, except Murli. We in India struggle, and indeed have gone through many top-level games without winning a medal—and here is one person who won gold at all the three Games. When the Rajeev Gandhi Khel Ratna Award was introduced in 1991-92, he had already retired from international sport, but he still tried to be named the ratna or jewel of Indian sports, which he really is, but was overlooked as usual.

In 1974 he was allotted some land by the government of Maharashtra in Sangli for which he says he paid the market price, but which has lately been taken away from him and reserved for a sports ground robbing him legally of that one and only reward he has had for all he has done for Maharashtra state and for India. Yes, he gets a sports pension from the state, but the government of India has refused to give him a sports pension stating that under their rules no paraplegic can get a pension.

What a life this soft-spoken legend has led. Running away from a crazy mob which wanted to lynch him when he was just twelve years old, landing in the Boys Battalion of the Indian Army, being whisked away to Bengaluru where he learnt boxing, selected to go to Tokyo where he knocked out six opponents before he himself got hit so hard in the final bout that he was unconscious for two days; then being rewarded for his medal-winning performance with a temporary duty to Kashmir, where his arrival unfortunately coincided with the start of the 1965 war with Pakistan. He was hit by nine bullets (one is still lodged in his spine), run over by an army jeep as he fell, and thereafter lost his memory for almost eighteen months. He recovered it in true cinema style and then had guns put on his head as he almost choked a General to death—because he thought he had been captured by Pakistan, was a prisoner of war, and therefore killing at least one Pakistani army man was his birthright as an Indian soldier.

Then, at INS Ashwini in Bombay he was so deeply hurt by his family that he tried to commit suicide but was saved miraculously. That same morning he won a princely sum in local gambling, which he promptly donated to the National Association of the Blind, even though this huge amount of money could have helped him a lot in material terms.

He started life anew at the young age of twenty, focusing solely on paraplegic sports and went on to shatter the world 50 metres freestyle swimming record three times while winning gold medals at the 1970 Commonwealth Games at Edinburgh, the 1972 Olympics for paraplegics (the Paralympics) in Heidelberg, and at the Paralympic Asian Games in 1982 in Hong Kong. All unbelievable, all true. If there is a real life hero in India, any which way one looks, it has to be Murlikant Petkar. Does he have any regrets in his 'charmed' life?

'Destiny has been both cruel and kind to me. I have enjoyed my life, and today I am satisfied. It was my destiny to be crippled and be a paraplegic, but then who would have thought that I would do so well in the world of paraplegic sports. It was my destiny to be hit by nine bullets, but then god let me live for some purpose. I have received the love of all our people all my life. No regrets as such, except a couple of questions which come to my mind and torment me at times. I simply do not understand why I was denied the Arjuna Award or even the Khel Ratna, or why my land is being taken away from me here in Sangli. Have I not done enough to deserve these awards? What more could I have done to get these honours?' What more indeed could have

Murlikant Petkar done? A soldier, grievously injured defending his nation, who yet went on to win the biggest honours for India on the global sports field.

It is the collective conscience of this country that has to answer the questions that torment this genius, and to correct the embarrassment which is actually our national shame.

TARANATH SHENOY
A Genius in Every Way

Success is not final, failure is not fatal
It is the courage to continue that counts

~WINSTON CHURCHILL~

Taranath Shenoy was born deaf-mute and with vision in only one eye, impairments that could have spelt lifelong helplessness and doom for anyone. Taranath could have gone that way, but for his determined mother and extended family which decided that he must lead as normal a life as possible from the start. He went to normal schools, played normal sports with his siblings and numerous cousins. He was taught from start that failure at attempting anything was not wrong; not attempting at all was wrong. Failure in life was to be accepted. Not trying at all was not to be accepted.

He started swimming when he was four years and was soon winning races, but a chance long-distance swim changed his entire life. The decision to become a long-distance swimmer catapulted him to the national headlines and ensured that he walked the realms of legends. He became the fastest differently-abled swimmer in the world to cross the English Channel—considered by experts as the Mount Everest of swimming. He got bitten by a shark which he could not hear and which came in behind him from his blind side. The shark bite did not stop him but a couple of hours later, painful cramps stopped his first attempt in 1983, some 17 kilometres into the swim. Determined as ever and not one to give up, Taranath came back strongly to cross the English Channel the very next year in 1984, thereby becoming only the second Indian, since Mihir Sen's record attempt in 1958, to do so. In 1985 he became truly a legend when he swam the channel both ways in one attempt, finishing the marathon in roughly 21 hours, just 6 nautical miles short of his target, the coast of England, thanks to a dense fog that had settled on on the Channel.

Making the impossible look possible is one thing that Taranath excels in and he has made light of his serious impairments. His life is highly motivational for those who care to learn from him.

'We handicapped, or "differently abled athletes" as you say, are treated with so much respect abroad. In India it is a torture from the time you land at the airport. There is much sympathy and society looks after all your needs abroad, here life is a struggle most of the times.' But Taranath also feels that one should not cry over things. Just get along with what you have and strive to be a good human being. 'Never look back in life,' he says. Most part of this story is told to us by his elder sister Vidya Koppikar, a medical professional who has followed Taranath's life very closely.

Taranath Shenoy was born on 10 June 1959 at Pai Hospital in Matunga, Bombay, to a middle-class joint family that was self-contained and fairly prosperous. His father had been active in the freedom movement and, after Independence, ran a restaurant which was the mainstay of the family. Taranath had, amongst his many siblings, an older sister Lata, also born deaf-mute. The parents came to know after almost a year of his birth that both the children were deaf-mute. The entire extended clan was shocked and distressed, but soon after his parents, specially his mother, took charge.

Taranath's was an orthodox Hindu family. His mother belonged to a family of priests and pandits—Taranath's maternal grandfather hailed from the Bhat family and was head priest at the Karkal temple in their village—and this could have proven problematic for Taranath because of his impairments. In the 1960s, families hid rather than advertise loudly that there was someone handicapped in the family. It was considered a bad omen. His mother put her foot firmly down on any suggestion that Taranath had to be kept away from society, and added that, 'No tantriks or black magicians or sadhus who want to cure Taranath will be tolerated or encouraged. I do not want any dhongi people around him. We will make him strong and make him stand on his own feet. He must learn to handle the problems that will undoubtedly come his way.' She ensured that Taranath and his sister, Lata were treated as 'normally' as everyone else. They were not to be favoured, nor shown undue sympathy. Both had to solve their own problems.

As Taranath explains in his life sketch, 'Well I understand, when all doors close, the Almighty opens a window. In my case the window—my parents—were far bigger than the door. By my good luck I had very understanding parents who not only taught their deaf-mute son how to negotiate life and be strong, but also to look at the world with appreciation and love.'

Taranath was also born with bilateral congenital zonular cataract in both eyes, which meant that he was almost 70 per cent blind. Despite many operations at a very early stage of his life the doctors were unable to save his right eye. With progressive zonular cataract in his left eye, Taranath had just 60 per cent vision.

Then in 2009, thanks to medical progress, another operation to his left eye restored vision to almost 80 per cent, according to his sister Vidya Koppikar.

The large extended family had almost 100 people eating daily from the kitchen. The restaurant in the lower-Parel area, surrounded by cloth mills in central Mumbai, was always full says Vidya, and the family was prosperous enough to send all the children to study in a good school, eat well and also donate handsomely to charity. Taranath and his siblings, however, also had to work in the restaurant if waiters did not turn up. 'It was fun, you know, sometimes cleaning up utensils and waiting on tables, but that taught us to respect everyone. But mostly it was games for me as all kids in that family compulsorily had to be out playing something or the other. I was not teased by any local boys as I hardly interacted with them,' explains Taranath. Lots and lots of children in the joint family obviously meant a childhood full of fun for Taranath.

Initially, Taranath and sister Lata were enrolled in a school for deaf-mutes at Peddar Road, run by an English lady called Margaret Moore. Within two years however, his mother shifted them to a school for normal children called the Sunanda High School at Tardeo, where both siblings proved to be diligent students who did well in studies. Taranath was a topper in school because his levels of mental concentration were very high. 'This is common for all swimmers and top athletes as they have that ability to extract the maximum out of a limited time. They are not distracted easily from their focused thinking—and this trait is there in Taranath too,' says Vidya.

However a teacher called Sandhya Apte was directed by the UNICEF and the school to come and give tuitions at home to the two deaf-mute children. Taranath studied in this school till his tenth standard and has happy memories of his student life. 'I had good friends in the school as I was always good at sports like running, swimming etc. No one troubled me, well not much anyway. At least no one looked down upon me because of my handicap. I fondly remember my school days,' explains Taranath. He also says that it was when he started getting better at swimming that he was subjected to lot of verbal and non-physical abuse that upset him very much and left him vulnerable at times. We will come to that a little later.

Taranath's tryst with swimming actually started by accident. His older brother Sharad used to suffer from asthma and the family doctor advised the children's mother that Sharad take up some regulated physical exercise, if possible swimming, which would strengthen the chest region. Once the decision was taken that Sharad, who later went on to become an ace swimmer in his own right and a surgeon to boot, would regularly go swimming, all the children in the joint family also started trooping in to the Mahatma Gandhi Swimming Pool at Dadar. 'Some ten to twelve of us would take the 62 number bus and go to the pool where we had appointed a coach, Mr Khedekar, to teach all of us. Taranath initially had some reservations but he was thrown into the pool when he was just about four years old and against all expectations took to the water like the proverbial fish,' recalls Vidya.

He won his first race at seven years of age at a meet which was akin to an inter-school event run by the District Sports Officer. The small cup he won as a trophy still adorns a shelf in his sitting room. Then winning became a regular feature, and what is significant is that Taranath won his early races and indeed later even long-distance races, against able-bodied opponents. He remained at a slight disadvantage in that he could not hear the whistle signalling the start of the race. No amount of pleading was of any avail that some method like waving a red handkerchief be used so that he could see it and dive into the pool. He then got one of the competitors to pat him on the rear just as the whistle went so that he could dive in, but that always meant he was a second or so slower at the start. 'It was a simple thing to do and that would have helped me, but no official was interested in helping me. Some even suggested that a deaf-mute like me had no reason to be there at the races, since anyway my life was anyway doomed. Why was I ruining the chances of other boys? I did not need any sympathy—all I needed and requested was a level playing field, but that was always denied to me.'

With coach Khedekar doing a great job, Taranath won many inter-school and open sprint races till the twelfth standard. But other coaches and participants, including the chief coach at the pool, which was owned and maintained by the Bombay Municipality, were extremely envious of this young swimmer whose potential, everybody knew, was huge. They would verbally abuse him, which of course bounced off him. Then things got nasty as they began puncturing his bicycle tyres, eating or throwing away food from his tiffin while he was swimming, etc. The chief coach would deliberately try to ensure that Taranath did not get any tips, or make him swim with much bigger boys who could intimidate this young boy.

By the time he was nineteen years old, Taranath had made a name for himself in shorter races on an all-India basis. Around this time, 1978 or 1979, local swimmer Avinash Sarang had drawn media attention towards long-distance swimming. Taranath knew him and after much discussion, fed up with the unfair tactics used against him in shorter races, he decided to shift to long-distance swimming. This was soon to become his forte. Again, the senior coaches at the Mahatma Gandhi pool proved to be obstructionists, not allowing him to swim the long hours he needed to build his stamina and confidence. Much later, when he became a name, all these problems faded away.

Deputy Municipal Commissioner Khairnar had tried to intervene in those initial days at the request of the family, but could not do much. Khairnar had himself been a target of the underworld mafia and had escaped a bullet injury. 'I have been severely injured but am continuing my work. My advice to you (Taranath) is to ignore all barbs, abuses and insults—just concentrate on what you are doing and you will be famous one day. We can gag a few of these guys, but not everyone. And coaches are Municipal employees or contracted, so we cannot do much there,' he told the family.

The siblings, especially Vidya, did not give up and, after lots of running around, they finally found a benefactor in Julio Ribeiro, then the police commissioner of Bombay. The police swimming pool at Worli, though not as big as the Dadar pool, was put at Taranath's disposal free of cost. He was also given two bodyguards to ensure no outsider distracted him. It was here that Taranath really dug in deep and started preparations for long-distance swimming races that were to come up from 1979.

'I am really grateful to the commissioner. In a way he helped shape my life. I used to swim five hours in the morning and five in the evening, swimming between thirty-six to forty hours weekly. I would leave the pool only when my body started to go numb. It was hard work but I really enjoyed that. I wanted to succeed in any case and make a name for myself,' says the ace swimmer.

Taranath also wanted to continue studies after his Senior Secondary Certificate (SSC) examination which he passed in April 1979, and study commerce, but the family, specially sister Vidya, advised against this and told him to continue swimming and make a name for himself as that would make it easier for him to land a job. He therefore had lots of time at hand and was able to concentrate and focus on his passion.

'I had real passion for swimming, though at first when my mother insisted I learn the sport, I had resisted. But once I started winning at the state and national levels my interest really grew. I used to stand first at both normal and the handicapped meets, and this continued till I was about eighteen years old. But my interest in short sprints started waning and I wanted to switch to long-distance marathon swims, and I was glad that I shifted focus. It was in long-distance marathons that my true ability and capability came to the fore. I found sea swimming easier because of the buoyancy of sea water, but having one eye and that too not fully operational was a problem as I could not see far enough and had to guess the height of the waves. Big fishes were another major problem. From one side I just could not see any big fish approaching and hearing was, of course, out of question.'

In 1979, to gain confidence in sea-swimming, he swam from Dharamtar to the Gateway of India in Mumbai, and then from the Indian Navy's ship INS *Hamla* to the Gateway of India. In that same year, he went to Gujarat for his first long-distance swim at the notional level—from Chorwad to Veraval, a distance of some 18 nautical miles. Here, he met with a major hurdle and his career would have never blossomed had it not been for some quick thinking and obstinacy on his part. He explains in his own words what happened.

'When I landed at Chorwad the organizers could see that I was very fit and the probable winner of this race. They did not know that I was deaf-mute and when I could not talk back, they at first wanted to disqualify me on basis of my handicap. This was nothing but cheap local politics. But since I insisted on taking part they thought of another trick and got the doctor—who was present to certify the fitness of all participants—to declare that I had a cardiac problem and therefore should not be allowed to swim. My coach Vinod Guruji was shocked, but both of us were not going to give up in any case. My boat was put aside from the race but the main judges on the shore had not noticed this, as they were almost a mile away.

'I jumped into the sea and my coach followed and we signalled the boat to follow us. With fast and powerful strokes I soon started overtaking other swimmers. Vinod Guruji soon caught hold of a nearby observer's boat and they helped him climb in thinking he was one of the failed participants.

'To everyone's surprise I swam the distance in record time and was the first to complete, defeating all able-bodied competitors. The organizers soon learnt that I had swum as a disqualified candidate and I was denied the first prize. But they were highly embarrassed as I was surrounded by all the participants who applauded me and they had to record my entry in Marathon Swims, as having completed the distance though I was disqualified.'

As soon as he returned, Vidya took him to Dr Date, a renowned cardiac specialist and tests showed that Taranath actually had a strong heart and did not suffer from any problems at all. Taranath had embarked on a new journey by cocking a snook at all his detractors. The fact that he had actually come first in that marathon and that too in record time, was not lost on the senior coach and his ilk and they had no choice, however begrudgingly, to welcome him back to the Dadar Pool, where he soon took on training for his next goal without any further problems and harassment.

Taking his successes and swimming feats into consideration,

he was offered a job by the Central Railways sports department as a Superintendent, which he happily accepted in 1980. With the worry of 'getting a job' over at quite an early age, Taranath, was now set to give fins to his dreams.

His first international distance or marathon swimming target in 1981was the body of water between India and Sri Lanka called the Palk Straits, a treacherous sea spanning over 24 nautical miles. Practising at the Dadar pool for almost ten hours a day, Taranath prepared for his first international outing meticulously. Financial help came from sister Vidya who was a practising doctor by this time. She had been present at the Chorwad to Veraval race, and also came for the Palk Strait attempt to give moral support. With coach Vinod Guruji on the 'pilot' boat, Taranath set off to conquer this first of the 'twelve seas', his career target, and did do so in style.

Overjoyed at completing this feat, Taranath immediately set his sight on the 'Mount Everest' of marathon swimming—the English Channel. He wanted to swim from Dover in England to Calais in France the very next year, and wanted to be the fastest handicapped swimmer to do so. Mihir Sen was the first Indian citizen to have achieved this feat way back in September 1958 and had become a legend in Indian sport circles. Before him, the very same year, Brojen Das of British-Indian descent had also crossed the Channel in August 1958 in record time. Taranath wanted to be the second Indian and the first deaf-mute and sight-impaired person in the world to swim the Channel in 1982.

This was not so easy. Locally, no one in Bombay came forward to help him in any way. That was before the age of the internet, and communication was very slow. He wanted the address of the Channel Swimming Federation, but no one shared it with him. Finally, it was the great Mihir Sen who came to his rescue and provided all the addresses Taranath needed. Financial help was also required, since the expenses would touch almost two lakh rupees, way beyond the reach of this middle-class family. Taranath wrote to the President of India, but even though the President's office forwarded his application to the sports minister, nothing came of it.

Family and friends rallied around and collected half the amount. Virendra Hegde, a trustee of a temple in Karnataka, offered a big helping hand. Mr Dhabolkar of Air India, and his secretary Mrs Gajalkar, also came to Taranath's rescue, announcing that two return tickets would be provided whenever Taranath was ready for his adventures. This was a tremendous gesture and the family remains extremely grateful to the national carrier for its unstinted support to Taranath in his career. Commissioner Ribeiro also tried his best and pitched in. Former police official and sports psychologist Mr Bam was of great help as well.

Vidya is very critical of one former cricketer now deceased, who was famous for his philanthrophy. According to her, this pillar of society scoffed at the idea of providing support in any manner. He in fact told Vidya that being hearing and sight impaired, Taranath's very idea of swimming the Channel was ridiculous. 'Let him first learn Braille, and become competent in life—then we shall see what can be done,' is what he told her.

Taranath in the mean time went about practicing and putting on fat on the body with a special diet, as this was necessary to combat the really cold waters of the Channel, where the temperature sometimes dropped to almost 6 degrees Celsius or 7 degrees Celsius, even in summer.

Vidya also wrote for assistance to Prince Charles of Britain, and, surprisingly, that letter not only reached Buckingham Palace, but was actually answered by his father, the Duke of Edinburgh and husband of Queen Elizabeth. 'I am delighted to know that Taranath Shenoy, deaf-mute and with lack of sight in one eye, is taking the step to swim across the English Channel. A brave attempt indeed. I wish him all success and will be delighted to help him in any way that may want. I have instructed my office to arrange an escort for him from the airport and provide help for hotel accommodation etc, and he may call up my office,' is an excerpt of what he wrote.

This thrilled the family immensely. Vidya recalls, 'We were so surprised that we got a reply from the Palace in London. Here in India no one bothered to write to us. The President of the country did have the decency to let us know that the sports minister would look into the matter, but the sports minister did not get in touch with us. Neither did the state government officials here in Mumbai. Look at the decency of these people in England. Anyway, we had to skip getting back to the Duke as we did not know how much the hotel would cost and we were on a tight budget. Taranath landed in London and then went over to Dover on the south coast where he and Vinod Guruji stayed at the YMCA hostel for the duration of his training.'

The local coach there put him through the steps and training was harsh, almost ten hours daily, five in morning and five in evening. He had to get acclimatized and get used to the weather. Vinod Guruji could not stay for the entire duration of sixty days, but local coach Mr Leay Dixon, knowing Taranath's condition, agreed to help him as much as possible.

Taranath used to get homesick and lonely and sometimes Vidya would call long-distance and Dixon did not know how to answer her. She told him to just give the receiver to Taranath and he would 'feel' the vibrations from the receiver through Vidya's voice and that would satisfy him. That was his way to connect with the family back home and stay motivated.

The day loomed when his local coach announced that there was a green signal for his attempt the next day. So with shark repellent applied and prayers said, Taranath jumped into the cold sea on 10 August 1982 for his attempt to swim across the English Channel. He was doing well at almost the half-way mark at about 17 kilometres, piercing the waves with his pilot boat nearby carrying the coach and one marksman on board to shoot sharks if they came too close, when suddenly he was overcome by painful cramps in both legs and a wave of nausea hit him. There was no going forward and he was forced to abandon this attempt. The diagnosis revealed that he had a slight blood pressure problem, mainly because he had not been able to put on as much weight as was needed. The 1982 attempt was wiped out and Taranath returned home burning with a desire never to make this mistake again.

'It was a failure no doubt about it, but I did not want to dwell on it. I was angry at myself and was upset. But at the same time I told myself tomorrow was another day. I may have lost the battle—but the war was still to be fought. I was a sportsman after all and had to take this in my stride,' says Taranath, remembering his frame of mind and his determination after that unsuccessful attempt.

He returned home and, almost immediately, with renewed vigour and extra focus, started the training routine all over again. But he had a couple of medical problems that plagued him. First he had to be operated for blood clots and then his patella (knee cap) got dislodged. That had to be looked into. Then it was back to swimming national long-distance competitions again, to gain more experience. He also talked to sports nutritionists and other experts and put on weight like never before, to attempt a second

Channel crossing, but this time decided to swim from the French side. That is, from Calais to Dover, just for the heck of it.

He landed in Europe around the middle of June 1983, giving himself all the time to put on more weight if needed and prepare as well as he could to swim the full length of the Channel this time. The second attempt was no less adventurous. 'A small shark came from nowhere and bit my left leg. I could not hear it nor see it till it was too late. But luckily it happened just 5 kilometres or so from the end, and I swam on undeterred and finished my swim. I had decided to create history by becoming the fastest handicapped swimmer and my timing of ten hours and fifty-four minutes was a record at that time. It made me so happy that I had achieved what I had set out for.'

The myriad brickbats and the many hardships would have led lesser mortals to have called it a day. The worst was when coaches told him that he was no good as he could not understand what they were saying. A deaf-mute had no place in a pool. They treated him as if he was a lesser human being, someone beneath contempt and not to be bothered about. As the *Times of India* once wrote about him, 'Taranath was born as history's favourite dartboard.'

He was born with two unrelated handicaps, of the eye and the ears, a very rare disorder, and yet had conquered his demons himself. He carved out his own destiny. The failure in his first attempt in 1982 did not deter him, but made him come back stronger and with a vengeance—to complete an unfinished task. He understood that failure is not fatal. Courage lies in coming back to do what you want to do and, like Lord Krishna says in the *Bhagavad Gita*, 'Focus on doing what you want to do. Success will follow on its own.'

Taranath was not satisfied by just this one crossing of the

Channel. He came back again in 1984 to successfully swim the dreaded Channel again. But this time he decided to complete the return swim, too, for a new sensational record. He finished the first leg, swimming from England to France in ten hours and fifty-five minutes (which is officially recorded as his timing), and turned to swim back to England. Just 6 nautical miles short of his target, after some twenty-one continuous hours in the water, he was forced to give up because of the dense fog which enveloped the Channel. He was unfortunate and bitter but could do nothing about this. However he made one more successful attempt the very next year, without any problems.

He had already created history by becoming the fastest and the only swimmer in the handicapped category to achieve this feat of crossing the Channel thrice. The fastest he swam was the 1985 attempt, which he finished in ten hours and forty-two minutes. Luckily he was not bitten by any shark, but Portugese men-of-war or jelly fish, stung him many times in the last two attempts. 'But with the water being so cold I did not feel the sharp sting at first—it was only after few hours that I would feel the pain. But more than these creatures, the sting of human beings hurt me more. One ace swimmer told the press that being deaf-mute was no handicap and that the press was giving me undue publicity. My sister Vidya wrote back to the same newspaper, challenging this person to swim with both ears and one eye totally covered and then decide whether it had been easy for me. To date I do not understand why people were so jealous—after all I had done no wrong to anybody,' says Taranath.

He was awarded the Van Audenaerde Tankard, a special trophy for disabled swimmers. Taranath has a unique place in the list of swimmers for this special award as he is the only swimmer to get this award thrice, not only for his three Channel crossings, but also for his various feats all over the world. He was honoured by the government of India and awarded the Arjuna Award for outstanding contribution to sports in 1985. The Maharashtra government had already bestowed the Shiv Chattrapati Award on him in 1984.

Not satisfied with swimming the Channel thrice, Taranath then set his sights on other long-distance swimming marathons and went on to put his stamp of class with great determination on the following major seas, some of which he had already swum before: the Palk Straits (Indian Ocean) between India and Sri Lanka; the Suez Canal (Red Sea); and the Nile River between Helwan to TV Building and back to Cairo Meridien Hotel, Egypt—a distance of 24 kilometres; the Catalina Channel (West Pacific Ocean) between Santa Catalina and Royal Palms in the US; the Manhattan Island (North Atlantic Ocean) between Battery Park and Hudson River, US; the Straits of Gibraltar (Atlantic Ocean) between Spain and Africa; the Strait of Dardanelles (Marmara Sea) Turkey, between Europe and Asia; from Torregaveta, to Baia, to Bacoli (Liguarian Sea) in Italy; World Championship Long-distance Sea Swimming in the US (North Atlantic Ocean); World Championship Long-distance Sea Swimming in Western Australia (Indian Ocean); Cook Strait between South Island and North Island in New Zealand; and, of course, the English Channel. The only sea that he has not been able to swim is the Panama Channel in South America as that has been closed to swimmers because of heavy shipping traffic.

Taranath was made an honorary member of the Triple Crown of Open Water Swimming Association for having completed the English Channel, the Catalina Channel and the Manhattan Island Marathon Swim—a 47 kilometre-long circumnavigation around New York City. He is the only Indian to achieved this most rare honour reserved only for the best marathon swimmers. He was inducted into the International Marathon Swimming Hall of Fame in 1987 as an Honouree.

In 1990 Taranath was honoured by the government of India again and this time he was bestowed the Padma Shri award. He became so famous and well loved that in the 1990's local schools had a chapter on him till the sixth standard—all students came to know about his incredible courage, his determination and his never-say-die spirit. His life-story is one to inspire the younger generation of swimmers and, indeed, all of us.

Taranath has won many state and national titles in sprints, and wins till today in veteran age-group swimming competitions, but will always be known as the ultimate conqueror of the English Channel. The ultimate marathoner. He did not win any medals at the Deaflympics as there was no long-distance swimming event, and could not emulate, therefore, his close friend Rajeev Bagga, the deaf-mute badminton star who won sixteen gold medals at the Deaflympics and World Deaf Games in a span of sixteen years.

'I am happy with what I have achieved in my life. If I have any regrets, it is only that I could have done that return crossing of the Channel in 1984 and set a record in the world as an Indian citizen. But sometimes I do regret how we handicapped are treated in India. Abroad everyone takes so much care of us, helps us in every way. Here in India things can be different.' Another unique trait of this legend comes to the fore as far as his job in Central Railways is concerned. When Taranath joined the railways and saw the corruption he was confused and aghast. But his upbringing and sense of honesty instilled in him by his parents clearly showed him the way. Cash was brought to him to pass some bills and invoices, and since he refused outright, he was simply transferred as he was seen as an obstacle in what was a daily and 'normal' occurrence in the office.

He is still an active swimmer in the veteran circuit and spends a good number of hours coaching deaf-mute and even able-bodied kids. Does he have any message for his fellow Indians? 'We do not need sympathy,' says Taranath. 'What we require is a level playing field so that we can also learn to contribute to the society and to the country. My sister who is deaf-mute, has won the President's medal as the best employee in her profession five times. If she can do it, all of us can. But society and the government must get us jobs and vocations where we can contribute. The authorities must also explore how all of us can be helped to lead normal lives. Local transport, for example, is horrible in India. How do you expect the wheelchair-bound, or polio victims, or the blind to take buses, trains or walk on non-existent footpaths? How can they cross roads and do daily chores, which the able-bodied take for granted? These are questions that beg answers.'

Taranath Shenoy is a shining example of what can be achieved if one sets one's eyes on a goal, however difficult the journey. If we can each emulate even half of what he has done, we will become a better people.

MANSOOR ALI KHAN PATAUDI

A New Dimension to Courage

'The impossible is not quite the impossible, if you set your mind to it.'

~NIK WALLENDA~

Amongst all the subjects chosen by us in this book, Mansoor Ali Khan Pataudi, or Tiger Pataudi as he was universally known and revered, is perhaps the most unique. His being sight impaired, after losing his right eye at the age of twenty-two in a horrific car accident in England, may not have had too much of an impact on his daily life as his left eye was perfect, but the fact that he chose to play international cricket and excelled in it, despite having uniocular vision, and not binocular vision like the rest of us, marks him as one of the cricketing geniuses of all times.

Playing on uncovered wickets, with no helmets and without the help of all the paraphernalia we see covering today's batsmen, Tiger faced and conquered the likes of Wesley Hall, Charlie Griffiths and Andy Roberts—all fearsome fast bowlers of their time. An astonishing feat really if one considers that the ball came up to him like a missile discharged at almost 160 kilometres per hour and beyond. Yet he scornfully scored centuries, played fearlessly, and like a tiger prowled and marshalled the cover area as a highly athletic fielder. Any which way one looks at his record,

Tiger Pataudi, born with a great cricketing mind and acumen, was one of the most accomplished sportsmen India has ever seen.

With both authors of this book having played sports at the international and national levels, we salute this legend for what he achieved and what he stood for. We simply had to write about this extraordinary sportsman who showed the world how to conquer fear, and in this chapter we try to portray how he managed what he did.

Unfortunately Tiger is no more with us. We present the story of how he was able to play despite his handicap, and also try to portray some aspects of his personality through the words of his charming wife Sharmila Tagore, his close friends and fellow Test cricketers Yajurvendra Singh and Bapu Nadkarni.

A salute to Tiger Pataudi's genius.

Mansoor Ali Khan Pataudi was born with the proverbial golden spoon. Tiger was a nickname given by his parents, and Tiger described this in his autobiography, *Tiger's Tale*, saying, 'I have always been known as Tiger, though I do not know why, except as an infant it seems I had the tigerish propensity to crawl energetically about the floor on all fours.'

His father Iftikhar Ali Khan held the title of Nawab of Pataudi, a small state of some 25,000 inhabitants in what was Punjab during the Raj. Today Pataudi is in Haryana—after Punjab was bifurcated after Independence. Tiger succeeded his father and got the title of Nawab when he was just about eleven years old. Iftikhar Ali Khan had the unique distinction of playing Test cricket both for England (against Australia in December 1932), and for India later on and, in fact, captained the Indian team during its tour of England in 1946. He died while playing polo at the young age of forty-one. Tiger's mother

Devendra Jhajaria receives the Arjuna Award from President Pratibha Patil

Taranath Shenoy receives the Padma Shri from Prime Minister Atal Behari Vajpayee

Salman Khan and the Basha family (Farman, Antonita and their son)

(left to right) Rajaram Ghag, Nir Bahadur Gurung, Murlikant Petkar (standing) and Satya Prakash Tewari

Murlikant Petkar

Taranath Shenoy

Farman Basha at the 2010 Commonwealth Games

Rajaram Ghag

Mansoor Ali Khan Pataudi

Rajeev Bagga with his family

Satya Prakash Tewari

Malathi Holla

Nir Bahadur Gurung

Satya Prakash Tewari

Sajida Sultan was the Begum of Bhopal. For Tiger, there was no dearth of anything from the start, as both Pataudi and Bhopal were wealthy estates.

Iftikhar Ali Khan and Mansoor Ali Khan provided a rare instance of both father and son captaining the Indian national Test cricket team. In India, in any case, this is the only instance. Tiger was very fond of sports from childhood and in fact later also excelled in hockey, polo and squash. Sent to school in England, Tiger excelled at cricket from a very young age, both as a right-handed batsman and a right-arm medium pace bowler. He was a batting prodigy as a schoolboy, relying on his keen eyes to punish the bowling. Tiger captained his school team in 1959 and demolished the old record set by Douglas Jardine in 1919, by scoring a record 1,068 runs in the season. Wikipedia also mentions that he won the English Public Schools' Racquets Championships with partner Christopher Snell.

Tiger made his first-class debut for Sussex in August 1957 at the tender age of sixteen and also played for Oxford while he was there. Tiger was all set to set afire the cricket fields, not only of England during county matches, but also internationally as his sensational batting had already garnered lots of interest all over the cricket world. But destiny had other designs. Disaster struck on 1 July 1961 when he lost an eye and severely damaged his right shoulder in a horrific car accident.

Let us see what Tiger himself writes about this accident in his autobiography, excerpts of which were published in Mumbai's *Mid-Day* newspaper on 23 September 2011. 'With four other team mates of my Oxford team, we were coming back from Brighton to Hove after having dinner, for the next day's play against Sussex. We were in a Morris 100 belonging to our wicket keeper Robin Waters and it was such a lovely evening that my friends asked me if I would walk back the last lap home, but I was feeling far too lazy. I clambered on the front seat with Robin who was driving. I had just settled in when a big car came right on to the middle of the road, and on to us from nowhere and hit us straight on. I just had seconds to turn my right shoulder to take the impact, and when I hit the windscreen I must have broken my shoulder as I found it impossible to throw a ball for nearly two years afterwards. I also hurt my hand, but was not at that time aware of any other injury.'

While being taken in an ambulance to a nearby hospital, Tiger looked over at Robin who did not seem to have serious injuries apart from few cuts on his forehead. He told Robin about his shoulder and said he might not be able to play the match next day. Tiger had no idea that he had also injured his eye as he felt no pain.

When he woke up in the hospital at Brighton he was surprised to be told that he required an immediate operation on his right eye as it had a splinter from the wind-screen embedded in it. The surgeon, Mr David St. Clair Roberts performed the emergency operation and, according to Tiger, did a good job. 'Afterwards,' notes Tiger in *Tiger's Tale*, 'I learnt that I had lost the lens in that eye as it had dissolved due to the injury, and that there was also a coat across the iris. The pupil of the eye had been stitched up, leaving me practically with no vision. The eye was also out of alignment but a further operation was not possible at that time.'

Distinguished eye specialist Sir Benjamin Rycroft whom he met shortly afterwards, told Tiger to continue playing his passion—cricket—with one eye, as getting used to a contact lens would take a long time. He did try the contact lens and got almost 80 per cent vision in the injured eye but, as he wrote, 'the only trouble was that I was seeing two of everything.'

He faced the tragedy with courage, and the loss of almost 95 per cent vision in his right eye did not deter him from following his passion for cricket. Never did he feel at any time that the sport would not be a part of his life. He refused to believe that this was the end for him.

Tiger missed the season for his university but was back at the nets within a month of the operation, trying to sort out his batting and spending hours at it. 'For long hours George Cod, the Sussex coach bowled to me at the nets, while I worked out what I could still do and what I could not. At first I simply could not pick out the length of the bowling at all. Then I reached a sort of compromise, but I suppose it took almost five years before I could claim to be completely on terms with my handicap,' wrote the former Indian captain.

So how difficult was it really for Tiger Pataudi to actually go out and play the calibre of cricket that he did? Most of us cannot play any game with one eye, let alone a game like cricket, where the fast-hurled ball can cause serious damage. Famous eye surgeon, Dr Ranjit H. Maniar, who has been practicing medicine for thirty-three years and is head of the Department of Opthalmology at the Shushrusha Hospital in Dadar, Mumbai, is also a very keen follower of sports in the country, and opines that Tiger was simply superhuman in the garb of a cricketer.

Says Dr Maniar, 'Basically when you are playing cricket or any sport, you require binocular vision, where both eyes see the ball coming at you as one image. Whether it is coming in slow or fast does not matter, binocular vision gives you depth perception and this enables you to judge the ball correctly, mainly in terms of speed and direction. As far as Pataudi was concerned, it is said that he changed his batting stance a bit, taking a bit of an off-side facing stance where he turned around more towards the leg side—a side-on stance, with the left eye looking at the bowler. With that one-eyed single vision, with that depth perception, he was able to bat so efficiently. Now I do not know how he practiced or how he came to this conclusion, but whatever method he applied, he did so very intelligently and with great success as far as his game was concerned.'

He continues, 'Uniocular depth perception is obviously not as good as binocular depth perception. It is incredible that Tiger adapted to this at a fairly late age in life for a sportsperson, and then so soon after the accident. Normally it is easier for a child to do this, that is lose binocular vision and adapt to uniocular vision. In Tiger's case not only was he able to adapt at a late age and continue playing the sport he loved, but was actually able to continue excelling in it. And that is astonishing, unbelievable really. His eye-hand co-ordination was excellent, his batsmanship of the highest order, and his fielding in the covers had to be seen to be believed. He used to pounce on the ball so fast, literally like a tiger. Most athletic really. This was his greatness.'

Tiger Pataudi however wrote in his autobiography that he had not changed his stance as much as many believed. 'I don't think that I adapted a very open-chested stance. Actually I always favoured a position more square-on, that most textbooks recommend. I soon found out however that I could not hook any more as I could not follow the ball around, and I had to curb my natural inclination to drive half-volleys, because I was frequently beaten by the Yorker.' But as Dr Maniar illustrates above, Tiger did accept that life had become a bit tricky for him after the accident. He mentions in his book, 'As any boxer who has had one eye closed due to blows from an opponent will tell you, it causes loss of perspective of judgement and distances.' He accepts the fact that he had major problems in realizing the depth and distances of the incoming ball with his eye impairment.

According to Dr Maniar, playing on the uncovered wickets of those times, especially the wickets in England without a helmet, called for a superhuman effort from players with both eyes functioning, let alone Tiger, who had the use of just his left eye. 'His level of disability would be around 45 to 55 per cent of any normal player. Despite this he was able to perform so well. I wished I could have seen him play with binocular vision like any other player. What a sight that would have been. Even with one eye he was magical as a player, and so very successful as a captain.'

The doctor also feels that had both eyes been functional, Tiger would have played for a much longer time and retired much later. And he would have made long-lasting records. 'Laurence Rowe of West Indies had his career cut short because of an eye injury and corneal ulcers, otherwise the way he was going, he could have been the best ever from his country—perhaps better than even Brian Lara. These things happen unfortunately and we should be grateful that a couple of generations could witness the fantastic game of the Nawab.'

Dr Maniar also explains how covering the affected eye with his cap helped Tiger. 'Covering one eye meant getting the depth perception only with one eye. You know one eye was very good, while the other was very sub-normal. Plus there was a small amount of deviation of that eye—which we call a squint. Because of this problem, focussing and merging of those two images would be problematic. It was easier for him to shut that eye with a slanted cap and then focus with the leading eye—that is the left eye. But what a person he was. Awesome. You try walking around with one eye closed whole day long and see the problems you face. And here was Tiger Pataudi, slaughtering the bowling all over the world. As a sports lover I say hats off to him. And as an eye-specialist all I can say that he had a most superb eye-hand-body co-ordination, something most extraordinary. His adjustment to the disability was so good. No amount of practice on the nets could make him what he was. More than everything it was sheer will power, steely determination to succeed and fearlessness in facing most demonic pace bowlers that made Tiger what he was.'

There is no denying that Tiger had no fear when he went on the field to play cricket or any other sport. And as wife Sharmila says there was a different side to Tiger that showed his dead pan humour and reserve. She explains how Tiger approached cricket, and indeed life as such, with the eye impairment. 'You know Tiger was a very self-contained person by nature and also by inclination. So he hardly ever talked about things that bothered him. Small things like a headache may bother me and I would tell the world that I had one, but for him even if he had a fever, he would not talk about it, just lie down and wait for it to go. No doctors also till things really went out of hand. If we discussed his eye problem, he would ignore the whole conversation. If we persisted and asked him whether his average would have been better had he not had that unfortunate accident, he would get angry, annoyed.

'He did not want to go there, into what could have been. To him it was hypothetical. He would not like to revisit the past even with old friends when he relaxed after a drink or two. Except may be touching on the subject minutely in his autobiography, the subject was not discussed by him. Tiger was just not made that way. You know, he would not talk even about his father's death, not even to me. Forget the rest of the family or close friends. So the question of talking about his injury and what could have been, to strangers or outsiders, never arose.'

According to Sharmila, Tiger never looked for any sympathy

or credit and he never wanted to be known for that handicap. He wanted to be judged as he was. In a rare moment of candour, Tiger once joked with Sharmila, saying that he could have an average of 75, but had only around 35 due to having played with one eye as he had 'half the eyesight'. Sharmila, a superstar in her own right and one of the best-known actresses of Hindi and Bengali cinema, simply cannot understand how her husband could have played cricket at that level with the problem.

'I find it difficult to imagine that he could have with played such efficiency. I am now getting a cataract in my right eye and I find it so difficult even to walk down the stairs as judging distances is so problematic. Peripheral vision is also important in sports, not just tunnel vision. His right eye had only about 4 per cent vision left, and he could only make out light and darkness—nothing else; extremely hazy vision from that eye. Contacts were suggested so that he would not go cock-eyed, as his better eye would start compensating for the bad eye. He did try a contact lens but did not have the patience to deal with it and discarded it almost immediately as he was seeing two balls all the time.'

But Tiger was an exceptional athlete with a fantastic hand-eye co-ordination, says Sharmila. He started playing very soon after his surgery basically because he had been in such excellent form before the accident and wanted to capitalize on it. Tiger was a naturally gifted sportsman and the only game he had problems playing was racquets—an indoor game, similar to squash, played in universities in the United Kingdom (UK) and the United States of America (USA). It was a very fast game and he found it difficult to handle. Prior to his injury however Tiger was very good at this sport and played in the Winchester team which topped the league they played in, with his partner Christopher Snell. A proud Sharmila says that if you go to Winchester, you will find Tiger's name everywhere—mainly as captain of various sports teams. He was a real all-rounder.

Coming back to cricket, Sharmila says, 'Tiger was so good at his batting, his running, his fielding—and he was catching so well. Of course he moved out of slips as he could not do close in fielding as the ball came in far too fast. He moved to covers, but still how could he take those catches and stop those balls hit so hard. I always used to wonder. Tiger was also very analytical and applied his thinking to his batting. He developed his own technique of understanding and pre-determining how the bowler would bowl by the action of his arm. You know while we are talking about this, I now wish he had written some article or chapter in his book on how he adjusted to his injury and how he managed to excel despite the problem. All he would say is just one or two sentences about the injury and its aftermath and then keep quiet.'

Tiger was always educating himself about the bowlers he would face. He read about them as much as he could, of course those days there was no internet and hardly any television. His computer-like memory would always retain the action of any bowler he faced and remember it for years. But he would get foxed by any new bowler, someone he had not seen before, someone whose action he was not familiar with. Once his eye settled in however, he would master the bowler as early as he could. The initial period against a new bowler was difficult.

Let us see how Sharmila Tagore further describes her late and great husband. In her own words, 'I think he had tremendous guts, tremendous courage. You know we all get so low, so down when little things happen to us, little losses. And we feel so deprived. But in his case I feel that he was used to losses. He lost his father at eleven, suddenly he had huge responsibilities given to him, his mother's dependence on him—so he learnt to keep things within himself, and not to break down under pressure. He had this great fighting spirit which enabled him to bounce back to sanity.

'It requires courage to accept your problems and then fight back from a position that is way down and then come into international recognition. I agree with you that Tiger had great leadership qualities, and a good combination of brain and talent, apart from his natural athleticism and fast reflexes.

'Another thing that I noticed about him was that he could internalize and never blamed anybody else for anything. We talk when we want sympathy, or we want endorsement of something. We sometimes talk to get a response from others, you know how people say don't worry, things will get better—that sort of thing. He did not need all that. He was so self-contained. He had inner strength.'

Did Tiger ever show fear against fast bowlers like Charlie Griffiths, Wes Hall and Andy Roberts? And did he have a different style of practising at the nets?

'No, not at all, he had no fear and even if he had, he kept it to himself, never showed it at any time. He never ever brought this subject up with me, and we never discussed this sort of topic. Just imagine he faced all these bowlers without a helmet or other safety measures. As I said before he had fantastic reflexes, exceptionally good, and that took care of reacting to the speed. You know he used to wear his cap slanted to cover the right eye. That helped him. He was intelligent enough to adapt to current situations. So there was no fear, he just focused and concentrated on his game which he had real passion for. And of course when he got hit by that delivery from Andy, it was towards the end of his Test career and he had become old, reflexes were slower.

'He really was exceptional. He enjoyed the challenges of

cricket, he enjoyed facing and conquering these bowlers. In fact I would say that at a young age, Tiger relished the fact that he would face the best bowlers in the world. It was so sad that his huge talent was cut down in his prime by that silly accident, when he was just a five-minute walk from his hotel at Hove. Just bad luck or his destiny you can say.'

Sharmila also says that Tiger never brought up the subject of his impairment as far as his daily life was concerned. How he would deal with daily chores, driving or even hunting which he was so fond of?

'Well, very rarely would this subject crop up and that too if he broached it himself. He told me only once, before we got married, that he found it annoying and difficult to light a cigar or a cigarette as he almost missed the tip. Or while pouring water into a glass he spilled the liquid on the table because he would misjudge the distance or direction.'

Tiger himself wrote about this in his book, saying, 'When trying to light a cigarette I found I was missing the end of it by quarter of an inch. I was also liable to pour water from a jug right on the table, instead of into a tumbler as I intended. But gradually I got the hang of such actions and behaved normally. However night driving was a major problem as the headlights bothered me.'

Interestingly according to Sharmila, former English player and commentator Geoffery Boycott, never believed that Tiger played with one eye only. 'He had this conversation with my son Saif once, and told him that Tiger may have suffered a slight impairment or a small loss of vision and insisted that no one could play fast bowling as Tiger did, especially in conditions in England, without full vision or almost full vision. So Saif got upset and said, "What do you think, my dad is faking it! Something that has been so well chronicled in the media all over the world and you do not believe it." I really wish Tiger had kept a diary, or written about this problem. You know you are the first person asking this in detail to me.'

'The other thing that comes to my mind is his passion for hunting. How did he manage to shoot? Mind you he and all his cousins were brought up in that atmosphere where going to hunt was so very normal. He was a great shot but how he managed even after he lost the right eye is unique. Hunting was a challenge later on and he used to be happy if he succeeded. It was good for his self-esteem, his self-confidence. He had to excel in whatever he did as far as sports went. That is why he hardly ever played golf, he was far too impatient. Shooting in a way reinforced his own ability to himself.

'Tiger was not overtly philanthropic and did not want any publicity for whatever he did to help people. He was however always available to counsel and help anyone who approached him to deal with problems of losing eyesight.

'Tiger never liked talking about himself. But let me tell you we run an eye hospital in Pataudi under our Trust. A small but very active hospital and he always took a personal interest in it. He quietly started it and we are happily continuing it. We do some outpatients, some cataract operations and few major eye operations on a weekly basis. He always made time to talk to anyone who sought his advice. For example actress Nirupa Roy's son hurt himself gravely while playing with his friends. The sharp end of a pencil went into his eye. He spent hours with the child and the family. Another time some kids were blowing away mango flies and one got hit in the eye and Tiger was there looking after the kid personally. He had that soft side to him, a very humane side.'

Sharmila remembers a funny thing about Tiger. 'If he did not want to remember you or talk to you, even though you may have met him and chatted long enough, a day or so before, he would look right through you. I used to find that funny—I mean I asked him how could you not remember—but he would not answer. If the person persisted saying that they had met Tiger sometime back, he would say, "Maybe you were standing on my right side where I could not see you," immediately putting that person on the back foot, and would walk away. He also liked well lit rooms as compared to me as I liked dimmer light. He also slept always on a particular side.

'The other thing of course was that he was very competitive in whatever sports he played. I remember an incident when Saif was nine and at prep school there was a father–son match, and when these nine year olds were bowling, Tiger was gleefully hitting them for fours and sixes. His shots broke couple of car windshields of cars and people got upset. But Tiger had his fun. I mean he had to play to his best ability. So when we went in for tea, no one spoke to him—but he was least perturbed.'

Sharmila concluded, saying that another aspect of Tiger's personality was that he was very soft spoken that one had to really concentrate when he spoke. And he was a stickler for rules and discipline. 'When, as a captain, he asked people to be fully ready at nine a.m. the next day, everyone responded. He commanded respect by his own demeanour and led by example. He never raised his voice, even at home, but people knew how to respond to him. He could communicate in a few words. Even with us at home we knew how far we could go with him and when to withdraw. There was this "lakshman rekha" with him which he did not encourage people to cross. He was a very private person. And always with that deadpan expression—even while cracking a joke. His feelings or thoughts never flashed across his face. He was unflappable, never appeared troubled while at crease. Sledging was there even in his time—perhaps not as much as it is today. But these things evoked no response from him. Tiger was a tough man and he played cricket aggressively, but fairly. He was a good human being and a great leader.'

Tiger's great quality came to the fore with his relationships as a brand ambassador of the Delhi-based Venu Eye institute. According to Tanuja Joshi, managing director, Tiger had signed on to donate his eye to the institute and had expressed this desire to Sharmila and she ensured this was promptly done after his untimely death. In an article published by the *DNA* newspaper on 23 September 2011, Tanuja Joshi said, 'Every month since 1991 we have been having our eye clinics hosted by the Nawab of Pataudi at his hometown. He has directly helped some 1.5 lakh people regain eyesight. Every month we treat some 400 to 500 patients and he ensures he is around as much as possible. We roped him as brand ambassador in 2001. He never missed our annual programmes. He was great, extremely helpful and humane.'

Another person who has great words for Tiger is former India wicketkeeper Saba Karim who played more than thirty One-Day Internationals (ODIs), and a solitary Test. He got badly injured during the Asia Cup match against Bangladesh at Bangabandhu stadium in Dhaka on 31May 2000, while keeping wickets. The ball came off the batsman's pad and hit him smack in the right eye. There was permanent scarring on the macula and he lost 85 per cent vision. Saba underwent surgery but had permanent impairment of vision in the right eye. He explains how he got in touch with Tiger and the advice that the legendry cricketer gave him. 'My injury was quite similar to Tiger Pataudi's. My doctors at Shankar Netralaya in Chennai suggested that I interact with him and so I met him at his residence in Delhi. He was sympathetic to me and told me about the struggles he had faced and coped with. Till I met him I was fighting my injury and hoping I would regain normal vision. And it was Tiger who told me to accept my fate and move on. He said vision would not improve, and that I would have to rectify techniques to play at the level I was used to. He told me how to adjust and play with impaired vision. He also helped me make those adjustments that in many ways made life worth living. I used to be depressed and he got me out of that state. Depth found a new meaning for me. From improving my all-round skills in the game, it now meant "trying to judge the trajectory of the ball". Then there was this other thing, "double vision", which left me at my wit's end. Two balls were coming up at me all the time. It was Tiger who gave me the right cue.'

Saba says further that his conversations and interactions with Tiger were in many ways a wake-up call for him. 'Once while leaving his house, I was so concerned about my injury that I asked him how long it took him to recover. A chill ran down my spine when he answered, "Saba, I never did recover." He told me to accept what had happened and move on.'

Saba came back to play that one solitary Test after his operation and with his impaired vision. Tiger's help gave him enough courage to don the gloves. But with rapidly deteriorating vision it became dangerous to keep wickets for pace bowlers and Saba finally called it quits, but says that he cherishes the time he spent with the great man. More aspects about his personality and his cricket are brought out by two cricketers who knew him from close quarters, Bapu Nadkarni and Yajurvendra Singh. We present their views in a question- and -answer format.

Yajurvendra, who played for India between 1977 and 1979 and co-holds two world Test fielding records of five catches in an innings and seven in a match, was a very close family friend. There was a natural affinity between Tiger and the much younger Yajurvendra—popularly known as Sunny, as both belonged to erstwhile princely families and both had tremendous passion for the sport.

'Sunny, first of all when and how did you meet Tiger and what was your impression of him?'

'I had known Tiger for many years since he was friendly with my parents and my grandfather. The first time I actually saw him was when India won a Test match against Australia in 1964. You remember that lovely heroic win at the Brabourne stadium? My parents introduced me and I could sense that aura around him. Subsequently I met him at a few family occasions, but he was far too senior to me for me to actually have conversations with him.

'My first real encounter with him was when I had started playing good cricket and he invited me to play for his team at the Pataudi Memorial Tournament in Bhopal, which he used to organize annually. It was a prestigious tournament and his invite meant an invitation from the captain of India. When I went there, I think it was 1974, I could see the likes of great players like Gavaskar, Chandrashekhar, Solkar etcetera, many from the team that had such a great tour of West Indies in 1971.

'He said hello to me at breakfast and I was thrilled and then we went to field after winning the toss. He suddenly turned around and asked me in which position I fielded. I said "anywhere," basically meaning wherever you want sir, as I did not know what else to say. "Good," he said, "you must be a bloody good fielder. So you take the forward short leg—that will be perfect for you." That was a typical one-liner from Tiger. He was a man of few words. I had done close in-fielding before, but never at that position. He was captain of the Indian Test team, so I had no choice but to accept. I actually enjoyed it and took three catches that day.

'He complimented me and said I was great in that position and that is how I was always drafted in that position during my Test career—where I took a record number of catches.'

'So it was actually Tiger Pataudi who led you to become a specialist fielder in that position?'

'Yes. He in fact strongly suggested that I make that my pet fielding position. Anyway, getting back to that match, next came batting and he asked me where I normally batted and now knowing that I better be precise with him, I told him that I batted in the middle order. "Good," he said, "you will open today. And you better not get out early as Jaisimha and I both need some time before we come out to bat." He used to put that sort of pressure. But that is how I started also going in as an opening batsman.'

'Sunny, you were close to him. Did you two ever discuss his eye impairment in cricketing terms?'

'I did ask him couple of times and I was astonished at what he used to tell me. Initially when he started playing after his accident, he was seeing two balls and he started to play the ball which was close to him, on the inner side. Nobody in India at that time could understand what he was suffering. He was still doing well in county matches and so everyone thought there was no problem at all, that was the general assumption. There was a trial match to pick a team against England and on the basis of his past record in county cricket in England and seeing that he looked fit in the trial match, he was selected to play against the visiting Marylebone Cricket Club (MCC) team.

'In the second Test he scored over 50 runs and was selected for the remaining Tests. He had tremendous guts to be able to play so soon after that accident. I mean just imagine two balls coming at you at more than 100 miles an hour on uncovered wickets, hardly any protection against those fast bowlers from England, Australia and the Windies. Tiger then started playing with that cap covering his right eye and that blocked the ball further to him. Still, to this day I can say I have never seen anyone with his courage.'

'Do you know of anyone else who overcame such injury in the game?'

'Well years later I met Colin Milburn, the English player, during my 1979 tour of England with the Indian team. Colin was coach by that time of their Universities team. We talked about Tiger. Colin also had an eye injury similar to Tiger and he really marvelled at the way he had not only coped with the loss of eyesight but actually come roaring back as a top-class cricketer. "Because of Tiger I thought I could also come back and play but never could. I tell you what Tiger has achieved is unbelievable," Colin told me.

'Then you have the legendary Ranjitsinhji, who lost an eye due to a shooting incident could never come back to the game though he did try his best. Saba Karim, who kept wickets for India also lost an eye while playing and tried his best but could not come back. Tiger was an extraordinary person.'

'How do you think he was able to have that perfect timing in his strokes while playing with help of only one eye?'

'Well I think with time he adjusted to his style of playing. You know, interestingly, he told me once, "Sunny, I don't find much problem with pace, but at times I am foxed by the dipping of the ball, specially off flighty off-spinners." And this was a fact. The fast ball came at you and Tiger learnt to negotiate it well, but the trajectory of the spin flummoxed him. But you know he started encountering it by playing aggressively. He came down the track to hit spinners off the bounce. He was not in the mould of

Merchant, Hazare or Gavaskar, and never played in that format. If runs had to be scored he would do that. You know he used to play lofted drives. He always had that very positive attitude. He liked nothing better than hitting boundaries.'

'What about fielding?'

'Well that was another thing. He was one of the best fielders in covers. Actually you know it was Tiger who started those sliding stops which we see so much today. Tiger was the first one to do that and no one copied it as no one used to be as fit as him. And the funniest thing was that he was so flexible he could catch behind his back. Amazing really. You know his whole theory in cricket as far as fielding was concerned was that this is a game of 30 yards. He said that you have to take off like a cheetah in the first three or four steps. If the ball has passed you, nothing can be done—whether it is a run, or whether it is stopping the ball. If the ball has already passed you the chase is almost futile. So the fast reaction in first three-four steps was of utmost importance.

'I remember one catch he took at CCI. He was fielding at mid-on and the ball went high on deep mid-off. He sprinted some 30 yards and smack—he had the ball in his hands. Without any doubt, he was an excellent fielder. His throw was excellent. He was very agile and very quick. His throw was fast despite his bad shoulder. He was naturally fit and that helped in his fielding. I recall Chandu Borde telling me about the first fitness camp of Indian cricket held at the National Defence Academy (NDA) in Khadakvasla near Pune. The day after arrival the boys were asked to go for a five-kilometre run. By the time rest of the squad arrived huffing and puffing, Tiger was already back, had changed, was reading the newspaper and having breakfast.'

'Was he naturally fit?'

'Yes, yes. He used to train a bit but look at his physique. He was so lean and muscular. And he was very good at other games also, especially hockey and squash. Imagine, with one eye. He was very flexible and fast on his feet. He had animal-like reflexes. In hockey he used to play with the Bhopal team regularly. Aslam Sher Khan, the former international hockey star, was one of his protégés.'

'A hypothetical question now. Given what he achieved with one eye functioning, how would you rate him as a cricketer in the history of Indian cricket?'

'I think if he had both the eyes Tiger would have been by far the best cricketer India could ever produce. I am definite about this. I mean with one eye he had an average of almost 35 and that too on uncovered wickets against some of the fiercest pace bowling in the history of the game. He was the backbone of the Indian team during his time. If Tiger scored, then we would have a decent total. If he did not, then team was in trouble. Everybody depended on him to make runs. He has achieved something with the handicap he had that is so difficult to believe. He scored a double hundred, few other hundreds—can you imagine the concentration required to be on the crease for so many hours and not get out. Incredible.'

'And he was also a very brave person....'

'Indubitably. You know in the 1975 series against West Indies, the team led by Clive Lloyd, they had the likes of Andy Roberts throwing thunderbolts. Tiger did not play the first two Tests, which we lost, and then he was roped in especially for the third as captain. He had told the selectors that he could not see the ball clearly, but they told him not to worry, just to lead the team. He went in to bat and a ball by Roberts hit him on the chin and cut him badly. He got some respect-worthy runs after that. I met him later after the series was drawn 2-2 and he told me that he just could not sight the ball. I asked him then why was he playing. He answered "What else to do? I am captain again and it is expected of me that I do my best." Imagine putting all his reputation at stake against one of the best pace ball attacks in history and going in just because it was a duty given to him. That is bravery of high order in my book. He retired after that series.'

'How would you rate him as a captain?'

'An excellent captain in every way. He led from the front. He was the first guy who told us how important the Yorker was. His field placements were precise and effective. I played in those corporate matches and at times we would be struggling and he would come in, change the field here and there, get us a win and leave. Bowling changes were always well thought out and he was very disciplined and ensured everyone followed him.

'His cricketing acumen was fantastic—he knew the game very intimately. He brought in Gundappa Vishwanath, brought in Bishen Singh Bedi, he knew how to scout talent. He was the first to understand the value of spin in the Indian attack and value of close-in fielding. He asked for turning wickets in India to defeat foreign teams. Today Dhoni says the same things. His understanding of cricket was astute. He was way ahead of the times in thinking as far as the game was concerned.

'Then he fought for better emoluments for Test cricketers. He was a Nawab so obviously people knew he did not want any raise for himself. He fought hard for his players. He had some standing. He was a Nawab and that meant stature. That sort of stature I think came only with Ganguly later on. He led India to its first victory overseas. As a captain, too, he was perhaps the best we have had.

'A last question, Sunny. Apart from his cricketing genius and his sense of humour, what else do you remember him for?'

'Well, he did not like flying at all. So when in India, we would travel all over by train and at every station his people would wait for him with ice for his whisky, which he loved. At Bhopal station of course it used to be chaos once the train brought in the Nawab. He liked his shooting and yes, he loved listening to ghazals. Begum Akhtar was his favourite and he knew the entire family extremely well. He loved home-cooked food and whatever time he came home he would get into his lungi-kurta and eat home-cooked food. And eat with his fingers—no knife and fork for him. He was not much of a party person. He read voraciously; never slept without reading a couple of hours. He simply loved reading.

'You know at one of these matches in Bhopal he introduced me as his 'nephew' to the press and walked away. Immediately there was chaos as the press wanted to know how a Hindu prince like me could be related to a Muslim Nawab. I had to say this was family connection. He used to be always coming out with such one-liners. At one film party with Rinku (Sharmila Tagore) he was introduced to big-time producer Shankar BC. Now Rinku had told him before the party to keep himself in check and not make any jokes. But once introduced he could not help but say "Nice meeting you Shankar, but where is AD?" He just could not get over the BC suffix.'

Tiger's reserved nature ensured that he was not very close to most of the players he played with. Sunny was close because he had same sort of royal background and Tiger also knew his parents and grandfather.

At the other end of spectrum, Tiger became close to spin wizard Bapu Nadkarni, almost a decade older than the Nawab. Bapu came from a humble background and had a very open, congenial and endearing personality. Born Ramchandra Gangaram

Nadkarni in 1933, he was universally known as Bapu and made his Test debut in 1955/1956 and last played for India in the New Zealand tour of 1967. His last six years of international career coincided with Tiger's Test career which had started in 1961. Says Bapu, as he answers questions put to him, that Tiger was not deliberately aloof by nature. He simply had no choice. Bapu also refers to Tiger as Pat (short for Pataudi).

'Pat was taken as a loner by the powers in the Board of Cricket Control in India (BCCI). And let us face it he was basically a loner. He lost his father at age eleven, left home and went to school in England. New surroundings and all that. But the loner bit was misunderstood by the BCCI. They said he does not mix with the players. How could he, when he hardly knew any of the players? If I remember correctly, he came back to India in 1961, the same year he lost his eye, and when the MCC came visiting he was selected as vice-captain of the team. Nari (Contractor) was the captain. That was my first game with Pat, but I had met him before on our tour of England a couple of years earlier in 1959. He sat at my table at the welcome dinner for the Indian team at an Indian restaurant in London. He was introduced to me as a budding MCC cricketer. That is how I met Pat for the first time.'

In this question-answer format Bapu reminisces about Pat, who was a dear friend and also looked to the older man for advice.

'Bapu, what was your interaction with Pat when you met him as Vice-captain of the Indian team?'

'I had a very good friendship with him right from the beginning. He was a genuine cricketer and a genuine friend, let me be honest with you. Unfortunately people never understood him. His aloofness was taken as that "nawab" thing, as if he did not want to mix with others. He had hardly lived in India, so how could he socialize with us to that extent? He was courteous, decent to all of us, but reserved. I mean how could he socialize if he did not know the rest of the players?'

'You were on that tour of West Indies in 1962 when he became captain. What do you remember about that tour and his suddenly being named captain?'

'I remember everything about that fateful tour. Nari got hit badly and had to quit the tour. Pat was elevated as captain. Poor fellow did not even know the names of half the team. He came to my room at night and asked me, "Bapu, please mera ek kam to karo. Mere ko sab players ka naam to batao. [Bapu, do me a favour, tell me the names of all the players.]' I was a bit embarrassed as the vice-captain had also walked into my room. But I told him not to worry and that I would get all the players to the room for a meeting with him.

'I called them to the room. There were so many senior players—so very senior to Pat. There was Chandu Borde, Polly Umrigar, Jaisimha, Manjrekar, myself, and others, all seniors by years that he had to lead. I explained the problem and told them the poor fellow did not ask for captaincy. It was thrust on him due to circumstances beyond anyone's control. That he had grown up watching us all and hearing our names. How was he going to address us on the field, I asked—he could not call us all "sir". That would be against the etiquette of the game. So I said that, "if all of you agree and don't mind he will call us by our names." They were all seasoned cricketers and were nice to Pat, who himself was quite a jolly fellow. He showed his leadership qualities and every one fell into line.'

'Did he get friendly enough to mingle with the players?'

'No, that way he was different. Once the day's play was over, Pat was again a loner, and kept to himself. He had different habits. He had led his life like that. He could not get into "Indian culture" in just one tour. He needed time to settle down.'

'What about his handicap due to the eye injury?'

'One eye, one shoulder and one thigh. No many people know this, but he told me that at time of the accident he was thrown forward into the windscreen and damaged his right shoulder badly, and also his thigh. We all talk about the eye, but do you know that each time he threw the ball he used to get excruciating pain. This continued for almost two years after the accident. Yet he never showed any of it on his face.

'The way he came and played his first knock against Ted Dexter's team in Madras, scoring his Test 100 while facing Laker and Locke, the spin masters, was amazing. And what a 100. You could not say that he had lost an eye. He was so efficient and had mastered the problem so well.

'I told him, "Pat, today I have seen you play so superbly. I would have loved to see you play if you did not have this impairment—how did you manage all this?" He just smiled and said, "Bapu, I have worked hard to get over the problem and am confident that I will be able to play well with one eye." In all my first-class career of almost fifteen years, I have never seen a cricketer having so many handicaps and still going on to become a legend. Pat was simply unique.'

'You played a lot with him. Did you ever see fear in him when he faced the battery of fast bowlers all over the cricket world?'

'Never. He had no fear in him. He was such a bold man and led us with huge confidence. He was the one who made us understand and believe that we could face any foreign team and defeat them. It was Pat who gave that confidence to the Indian team. He was a fearless man and also a very jolly man, cracking jokes with people he got along with. So full of humour.'

'Did you ever talk to him about his impairment? And how

did he cope with it, especially while fielding?'

'Not much, but I did pursue it with him once and asked him how he coped with the problem. "I manage," he said "it is a gift of God". He started playing aggressive cricket. He had problems with flighted spin bowling but learnt to come down the track and attack. But he was not able to read the trajectory at times. But to be honest with you, he used to practice a lot at the nets. Much more than the others. I used to bowl many overs at the nets so that he got used to slow spin.

'Once on the field he was a real Tiger. He would tolerate no nonsense from any one, senior or not. In my room that day in West Indies, he told all of us. "No matter what, everyone has to show discipline. I will not tolerate any show of indiscipline. I have to do the job of captain, given to me by the BCCI*. I will do my best and so will all of you. I am a straightforward person and many of you are my seniors—I am open to any advice that you may want to give me. I will listen to you. After all you have played for India with distinction for many years." And he always took advice from Umrigar and Manjrekar. I think Pat commanded respect because he himself was highly disciplined on the field.

'As a fielder he was lightning fast, dynamic. He ran me out in a first-class match, brilliantly from mid-on. I was only half-way through. He could have been an athlete, what running he had—my god!'

'Lastly, what would consider to have been Tiger's best innings?"

'Well the image of Tiger, facing those demonic fast bowlers with no helmet, slanted cap over right eye, head at an angle to ensure he saw the ball with just one eye, will always remain with

*Board of Control for Cricket in India

me. But the knock he played at Melbourne against McKenzie on a green track was probably the best he played. I saw Don Bradman coming down to talk to him and tell him, "Young man, I wish I had some of the shots you played today. You were brilliant. Well played." And one shot of his is forever etched in my memory. When he scored his double century against MCC at Kotla in Delhi. He went down on one knee and hit the fast bowler for a six right over his head. The ball remained parallel to the ground at about 10 feet or so, till it crossed the boundary. Such force, such timing. It went almost 75 yards. Most fantastic shot I have seen.

'In the end all I will say is that the opposition was lucky he played with one eye. If he had both eyes he would have broken every record. He would have been a phenomenon. He was that good.'

Surely, Indian cricket was lucky that someone like Tiger Pataudi walked its pitches. And for his plethora of fans, the one question will always remain unanswered. What if he had the use of both eyes?

FARMAN BASHA
Pocket-sized Hurricane

Strength does not come from winning. Your struggles develop your strengths. When you go through hardships, and decide not to surrender, that is strength.'

~ARNOLD SCHWARZENEGGER~

Farman Basha may just be about five feet tall, but in that pint-sized body he carries a huge heart, an indomitable spirit and enough physical strength to shame a Goliath. A hugely successful power-lifter at both the national and international levels, he is one of the very few to have openly targeted the conduct of various authorities and sports officials. He has openly asked at the national level what help they provide paraplegic athletes who toil day and night for the glory of the country? These athletes train under the harshest of conditions with hardly any help of any kind just to see that tricolour fly proudly at international victory podiums.

Farman has raised these issues at international fora as well, notably at the 2012 London Paralympics, compelled by utter frustration and disgust. In London, Farman exposed horrendous facts such as actual helpers and coaches of the Indian para-athletes being totally sidelined, and in many cases not even being allowed to enter the Games Village; thereby forcing the hapless athletes to fend for themselves. The national media rightly called it a 'real shame for India'.

Farman had been expected to win if not the gold in the 48 kilograms category for India, then at least the bronze at the London Paralympics, but without his personal helper or his coach Satyanand, in whom he had immense faith, and who knew his physical strengths and weaknesses, he came a cropper, coming in at the fourth spot. Balachandra, the man suddenly deputed to be his coach at the Paralympics had never worked with Farman before. In its coverage of the situation at the 2012 London Games following Farman's very vocal protest, *Tehelka* interviewed Balachandra, who admitted, 'Satyanand understood Basha's body and its limits—he would stand on his back, pull his hands, stretch his dorsal muscles. I could not do that—I was afraid of injuring him.'

Farman, though fed up, is not about to quit. 'Giving up is not an option. I want to go to the next Paralympics and win a medal for my country. I am ready to shed blood for India.' The pint-sized hurricane is truly a man of courage. An Arjuna awardee, Asian Games silver medallist and world number four, he is still without a job despite trying desperately for years and living off the income of his wife. Nevertheless, he has never been one to surrender to the many problems he has faced and continues to face.

This is the unique story of his mammoth struggles and triumph.

The seventh of twelve children, Farman was born to Adam Saab Basha and Rahimunisa, on 25 March 1974 in the KR Puram area of Bangalore. With eleven other siblings, the house was always full of noise, games and excitement for the young lad. As Farman jokes, 'We were like an entire cricket team with an umpire to boot, a very self-contained family. Of course once I grew up and when played cricket, you can guess who was made the umpire most of the time.'

Father Adam Saab worked in the Indian Telephone Industry or ITI, as it was then known. With so many mouths to feed, the money earned by Adam Saab was naturally not enough and the family lived with lots of problems. Farman was the only one of the twelve children who was handicapped. When just about a year old he was afflicted by poliomyelitis, or polio as it is commonly called, in both legs. For the rest of his life he would have to walk with the help of callipers or use a wheelchair. The family was aghast. Mother Rahimunisa cried and wailed all the time, going to mazaars and dargahs close by, trying to get the Almighty to somehow make her son, her 'chand ka tukda', or 'little slice of the moon' as she called him, normal and able to walk and run like the rest of her brood.

Her teary-eyed yet solemn prayers went unanswered and she slowly had to accept the fact that little Farman would have a permanent physical impairment. With the family not having enough money to visit doctors and get him treated, Farman used to walk on his hands, pushing or dragging his lower body and feet forward.

'It was extremely difficult for all of us. I must mention here that though all my family helped me a lot, it was basically my mother who was really behind me like an angel. She would pick me up as if I were a small child, carry me on her shoulders to my school, bring me back from school and carry me to other places also. On my own I would crawl all over, using my hands to propel me around. Of course one good offshoot or positive aspect of all this crawling around was that my hands and shoulders became really strong. Till I reached the seventh standard, I was carried by my mother and, elsewhere, I crawled around like a cripple,' remembers Farman.

There were major problems faced by Farman and the family due to his disability, and the fact that neither parent was well-educated nor understood too much about how to help Farman, did not help matters at all. The fact that the parents were also constantly worried in equal measure about all the twelve children, ensured that young Farman was neglected at times. So though there were some attempts to visit local quacks or small clinics nearby, doctors of repute or bigger hospitals were unfortunately out of bounds. Farman therefore did not get callipers or crutches till quite late in life.

Some doctors who were approached by the family kept on postponing treatment, wanting Farman to become stronger and a little older. Therefore, it was only when Farman was almost twelve years old, that his parents got the much-needed operation done on his legs. The sides of both legs were opened and tubes put in to straighten the legs. Farman was on bed rest for almost three months thereafter, and his legs were strengthened with traction and weights so that after the recovery period he could get callipers installed and also start physiotherapy, which would help him walk with crutches. There are some twenty stitches on both legs showing how deep and long the cuts were.

After months of sessions with physiotherapists, Farman was able to walk a bit with the help of crutches and the callipers. From the eighth standard onwards he started going to school on his own, with his brothers. Rickshaws or school buses were out of question as there was no money to be 'wasted' on such ostentatious things. Ironically, therefore, going to school became an exercise that helped Farman strengthen his body as he propelled himself as fast as he could trying to keep pace with his siblings. Sports and games, of course, were out of question. 'Though the boys did not tease me as such or call me names such as 'cripple' or 'langda' (lame) since my elder brothers were around and they would protect me, yet the fact that I could not run or sprint like others made me question all sorts of gods.'

'Why was I singled out to be like this—why could not I soar like others, run around, fly kites or play games that other kids did in my colony. Games like gilli-danda, seven stones etc. I saw others having so much fun, while I just sat around doing nothing. I asked these questions at almost every mosque or temple that I would cross on the way to school or elsewhere. My mother would only say, "Farman, you are special. Allah has made you special, child, and He must have reasons for it. You do not have to question Him. You just wait and see, you will shine one day." I would cry sometimes and howl on some days. I just wanted to be normal and take part in games. But this was not to be. Family members tried to treat me as if nothing was wrong with me, but deep in my heart I knew that I was doomed to be like this all my life.'

The one exception to his otherwise dreary life was that he was drafted into playing the game of kabaddi at times in school, but only when his brothers were playing. He would sit and be a referee, but sometimes seeing the yearning in his eyes, Farman would be asked to join the team.

A smile creases his face when he remembers those days. 'Since I could not play standing—as I would fall down with the slightest of pushes—I was allowed to sit or crawl and play. I had really strong shoulders by that time, thanks to all the crawling around I had done as a small kid. I mean by the time I was fourteen years old, my shoulders were bulking out and my hand grip was really strong. In kabaddi once I caught hold of the opponent's leg, it was difficult for him to escape; I would not leave him. That gave me immense satisfaction and joy. I felt on top of the world, because I was contributing to my team's score.'

Life went on thus for Farman Basha and he finished his matriculation. Sports was not a priority, as by then he fully understood that the dreaded 'polio' would not allow him to run and be normal like others. Immediately after his board exams, however, came a turning point which was to slowly but surely propel him to stardom.

'My older brothers and their friends used to frequent a local health club or a gymnasium as people called them. It was a small shed but had enough weights to ensure that the patrons who came there went away each evening thinking they were Schwarzenegger in the making. There were huge mirrors all around where they would strike poses and try to see how big or muscular they had become, as if each session was turning them into a Hercules. I accompanied my oldest brother once and was mesmerized by the surroundings. I became an instant convert.'

Farman wanted to start lifting weights, but his brothers and his friends tried to dissuade him, saying that he was not strong enough and that he would topple over while attempting the lifts. He admits that his lower body was weak and also looked weak because of polio. A simple push on the chest would topple him over and he would hurt himself. Nevertheless, Farman was adamant and said he would try the bench-press, in other words would try to lift weights while lying down on the bench which also had a support to keep the bar and weights under control. Babu, a friend of his eldest brother, came around and decided to help Farman, showing him how to lift smaller dumbbells.

'I learnt slowly and my first priority was to keep my balance. Once that was under control I started lifting heavier weights, sitting on the bench. Then I wanted to lift the rod, which was heavier in comparison but again there was opposition. Someone said that I would die if the rod fell on me, and so on. But I was determined. Today I can lift all sorts of rods. But initially since my brothers and senior lifters would not allow me to lift the rod, I started sneaking in at timings I knew these guys would not be around. A couple of my friends helped me in this, standing around and helping me lift the rod, which weighed 20 kilograms. Word got around, however, that I had started lifting the rod with ease. My eldest brother gave me such a scolding, but eventually came around to the fact that I was good at this and I was enjoying lifting weights.'

Farman was by now besotted with this sport, though he did not know whether there were any competitions for the disabled. He recalls that some people made fun of his handicap when he joined the gym. 'These boys used to make snide remarks which hurt me immensely, but I did not allow all this to deter me. I had faced all this before, too, and I promised myself that I would excel in this sport.' Farman was just happy lifting heavier and heavier weights and showing off.

He started adding weights now on the rod and within a year, his tiny frame was lifting 60 kilograms which was as good as any 'abled' boy his age. He was now a star in this make-shift gym. The snide and hurtful remarks eased off and finally stopped as all members realized that here was a person who was going to be a champion of some sort. He was earning the respect of all his siblings and peers. But he wanted to create a name for himself, he wanted to take part in weight-lifting meets, but there was no one to guide him.

Then he learnt about Malathi Holla, a very famous paraplegic athlete from Bengaluru, who had made an international name for herself in athletics, wheelchair racing. Farman sought a meeting with her, requesting her to help him compete. Soon he entered local wheelchair and tricycle races, but realized that this was not his cup of tea. He tried shot-put, discus and javelin throws also, but just did not enjoy them. It seemed that track events were not for him. On his own, he started catching local buses and going to any power-lifting or body-building meets that he read about in the sports pages. These were difficult times for this youngster, as he had to do his studies, spend some four hours in the gym daily and then go gallivanting all over Bengaluru to attend competitions. At one of these meets he learnt that there were national championships for disabled weight lifters. This was music to his ears.

'There were no state-level championships in Karnataka in those years. In October 1997 I came to know that the National Paralympic Games were being held in Chennai. That was the turning point of my life. I spoke to my family and all of them encouraged me to go. I was lifting much above my body weight and everyone thought I stood a chance to win a medal. I did not disappoint my family and friends who sponsored my trip. I won the silver medal in the 48 kilograms category, lifting 75 kilograms against some really experienced lifters. The next year the south zone trials for the 1999 Asia Paralympic Games were to be held at Bangkok. Putting all my effort into training now, I realized that with extra effort I could make it to the national team. My siblings sacrificed food and meat for me, saying that I needed the strength—I can never forget that. In this sport you must have a good and correct diet. All their sacrifices, all their prayers paid off, as I won the gold—my first gold at the national level, in the 1998 championships.'

Such has been the stranglehold of this diminutive lifter on the national scene in his 48 kilograms category ever after, that he has won the gold at each and every National Games, including the National Powerlifting Championships for the Physically Challenged, the National Junior, and Senior Powerlifting Championships, the National Paralympic Games, the national selection trials for the Paralympics and for the Asia Paralympic Games among many others. From 1998 to 2013, there is not one title that he has not won in the country.

In short, Farman Basha has been simply unbeatable in India for an astonishing sixteen years. Such has been his ruthless domination over his sport. It would be hard to find a comparison among athletes in any other games, abled or disabled. He has been accorded the title of 'Strong Man of India' for many, many years.

The story of his domination at the national level does not end here, however. In 2006, just to see how he compared to 'abled' lifters in his weight category, Farman entered the National Bench Press Powerlifting Championship for abled lifters. While the 'abled' cannot take part in disabled meets, there was no rule that barred a disabled lifter from competing with abled lifters. Astonishingly, Farman lifted almost 20 kilograms more than his nearest rival to claim the gold. Sadly, according to Wikipedia, this feat of Farman's so shamed the Indian Powerlifting Federation and upset its officials so much that they immediately passed a rule banning the disabled from participating in their events.

Farman's international career started off with participating in the seventh Asia Paralympic Games in 1999 as mentioned above, where he finished in the fifth position. The year 2000 brought another turning point to his life when a girl called Antonita, an able-bodied athlete, fell in love with this simple man and proposed marriage. 'I used to see him going to the gym as I used to train at a ground nearby. I fell in love with his simplicity and the way he was focused on his career. We got married and have been blessed with a son, Sheikh Farhan,' says Antonita with pride. She was to play a major role in Farman's life and the first step was to come as early as the third Paralympic World Powerlifting Championship in 2002 in Kuala Lumpur, Malaysia, when Antonita was called upon to make that ultimate sacrifice to help the fledgling career of her husband. A sacrifice that typifies Indian womanhood, but also speaks of the horrible and demeaning way sports in India, in both abled and disabled categories, is administered.

Farman recalls, 'I was selected for the third Paralympic World Powerlifting Championships but just did not have money to pay for airfare, lodging and boarding. Even though I was selected to play for India at an official event, neither the state nor the central government were willing to bear our expenses. I ran from pillar to post, meeting officials, all of whom promised to help. But no help came from any quarter. Seeing my plight, Antonita decided to sell off all her jewellery. She invested in my future, but such is the way we disabled athletes are treated in the country, that till today I have not been able to buy back what she lost. She is the best thing that has happened to me. She has been a pillar of strength, support and inspiration to me ever since we met and married.'

The huge sacrifice by his wife Antonita, spurred Farman to train harder and do better in global competitions. He was determined that Antonita's selfless actions would not go in vain. He was selected for the 2004 Paralympic Games in Athens where he stood tenth. That same year, Farman cornered glory by winning a gold medal at the Dutch Open Powerlifting Championships in the Netherlands. This was first of the many medals and honours this diminutive but explosive paraplegic lifter won for his country.

The year 2005 saw him snatching the silver at the IPC Powerlifting Championships in Kuala Lumpur. In 2006 he was selected for the Melbourne Commonwealth Games where he stood tenth among thirty-two lifters in his weight category. The same year he was selected to represent India at the ninth Asia Paralympic Games. The year 2007 brought greater glory for Farman and India when he lifted his way to the much cherished gold at the International Wheelchair and Amputees Sports Federation (IWAS) World Games held in Chinese Taipei. Farman Basha had undoubtedly arrived on to the world stage. He had shown his mettle and his enormous determination and focus in being amongst the best sportsmen India has ever seen. A son that our country could be proud of.

He was now poised to enter into the realm of the legends. The years 2008 and 2009 were to prove globally what an extraordinary powerlifter he was. Without much formal training and hardly any financial rewards, he started excelling in the sport of his choice, propelled by sheer grit. 'For me the best moments of my life were when I wheeled myself into stadiums the world over, wearing India colours. Just touching the Indian flag embroidered on the shoulders of my official track suit gave me goose bumps. I wanted to bring as many medals and laurels as I could for my country.' He lifted heavy enough weights to end up fourth at the 2008 Paralympic Games in Beijing. And then the very next year he won gold again at the Bangalore IWAS World Games.

By this time Farman had become well known in the country and his exploits were picked up by the media, too. Finally, the government of India also took notice of his achievements and honoured him with the prestigious Arjuna Award. But he was not so lucky with the Karnataka government's Eklavya Award. That came only after the Arjuna and as an afterthought to avoid embarrassment and after much cajoling by some leading sportspersons of the state. The Eklavya was awarded to Farman in 2010, but the official citation said that it was for the year 2008.

Farman did not get a single rupee after getting to the fourth spot in the 2008 Beijing Paralympics, though, according to him, the able-bodied athletes achieving fourth position got monetary rewards. This despite the fact that the government of Karnataka had announced that any athlete selected from the state for the 2008 Olympics or Paralympics would receive a grant of ₹5 lakh. After returning from Beijing, Farman met the chief minister, other ministers and sundry officials, but even running from pillar to post did not get him the cheque. Farman was the only para-athlete selected for the national team from Karnataka.

'I was then approached by a middleman, a dalal, who told me that he would take half the cheque amount in cash to grease some palms, and assured me he would get the cheque to me. He saw my handicap, yet this demand was made to me. I will not take his name but look at the state of affairs in Indian sports. I spent almost four months chasing it but finally I got this grant. But, more importantly as far as I was concerned, the official order copy was given to me. The good thing that came out of this was that in 2012 all selected from Karnataka—and there were three of us—got the ₹5 lakh grant from the state government. This time too, the sports ministry was reluctant, but once my old order copy was placed in front of the Sports Secretary, there was no choice—the grant had to be given. We deserved that grant, as much as any able-bodied athlete representing Karnataka.'

In *Yuva Karnataka*, a state-government magazine, the then Sports Minister had also announced that any participant getting to fourth place in the Olympics would receive ₹15 lakh, a bronze medallist ₹25 lakh, and so on. In Farman's case, sadly, his fourth place at Bejing was overlooked and he did not get that reward. He has a copy of that *Yuva Karnataka* and he took it along to show to the concerned persons, but was shown the door every time. 'Such is the story of us differently abled athletes, who have brought glory to the country,' laments Farman. 'Imagine the great humiliation Devendra Jhajharia suffered when he came back with a gold medal from the Athens Paralympics with a world record gold medal in one-armed javelin throw. There was no one to receive him at the airport. No communication of encouragement, of applause or even support came his way. Many ministers in Delhi did not even know what the Paralympic movement is all about.'

But he never allowed such problems the lack of foresight, and, indeed, humiliation in many ways, to come in the way of his career. And so, though he could not win a medal at the 2010 Commonwealth Games in Delhi, he was back to his winning ways at the 2010 Asia Paralympics in Guangzhou, China where he lifted well enough to with the silver. At the IWAS Games in 2011 in Sharjah, United Arab Emirates (UAE), Farman had to be content with one more silver medal.

By now Farman had enough experience to make his tryst with the one thing that had eluded him, a medal that could change his destiny. A medal of any colour at the 2012 London Paralympics would have been the real cherry on the cake of his hugely successful career, as far as he was concerned. He was now thirty eight years old, but in real great shape and in prime of his power-lifting career. He was lifting up to 160 kilograms during practice sessions, much above the expected medal-winning lifts and Paralympics qualifying parameters of just 120–130 kilograms.

However, to his dismay and indeed to the dismay of legions of fans and sports lovers across the country, Farman went through hell and suffered much humiliation that not only cheated him and India out of the much expected medal, but made him vocal enough to list out complaints of a truly shocking nature in front of the national and international media. He brought out the sordid story of what was going on in the Games Village and how our para-athletes were cheated out of their helpers and coaches, so that relatives of officials could get into the national squad and visit the Olympic Village to enjoy a holiday at the expense of taxpayers.

'I have been through some unfortunate moments in my life. I have been hurt by snide remarks when I was young, alluding to my handicap. But I overcame all that. My wife had to sell her jewellery just so that I could be an international athlete, and I could do nothing about it. We were poor, but my career came first. I must say here that I thought of sports as a career only after going to that local gymnasium. Before that I knew I had no choice but to excel at studies so that I could get a job and contribute to my family, my society. But you know I could never get a job. Even today, I am an Arjuna Awardee, I have been world number four in Olympics, have won silver and gold medals in international meets, but I have no job. I wanted to be an engineer or a doctor as I thought education would be an escape route out of my misery, but financial constraints did not allow me to fulfil my dreams,' Farman told the *Hindustan Times* August 2008.

Eventually he settled for completing a diploma course in Electronics and Television Engineering, but however hard he tried he could not get a reasonable job. 'It was not long before I gave up, as all my hopes for a job were dashed.' He was also able to do train for a year as an apprentice in the engineering department of Bharat Electronics Ltd, but even that stint did not translate into a job. He had been trying desperately for a job, and actually lost out on couple of international events as he could not afford to pay for all expenses. In its report of 7 June 2004, 'Dreams Fading for Farman, but He Lives on Hope', the *Times of India* quoted Farman as saying, 'Though I have the qualifications needed for a job, people hesitate to recruit me seeing my physique. Despite reserved jobs for the physically challenged, I could not get a job.

When I applied for bank loans (to start a small business), my application was rejected due to lack of security. What could I do?'

Tormented for years by not having a job, and with his wife as the only earning member in the family, Farman has not had an easy life at all. But there is steel in the man. 'We have survived all this while with whatever Antonita earns. I could digest all this, after all what is life if there are no problems, no challenges, but what happened to me and my team-mates in London Paralympics was disgusting.'

After his performance at the 2008 Olympics, when he came up with a fourth-spot lift, Farman was named as the flag-bearer for the 2012 London Games. In practice sessions and training at the Sports Authority of India (SAI) facility in Bengaluru, under the watchful eye of his coach, the 'Strong Man' was easily lifting up to 165-170 kilograms and looked set to go as high as the silver medal. In fact, as far as the Indian contingent was concerned, Farman was the hot favourite for the Paralympic silver in his weight category.

'I was happy and honoured when was asked to be the flag-bearer for our team. But I backed out as my event was on the very first day and I wanted to concentrate and do my best to get medal for my country. I was taking rest. I thought that team management would ensure someone would bring me my food, as the eating area was almost 500 metres away and I did not want to wheel myself all the way there. There was no one left behind to look after me. I was totally alone in our living area. It was a big problem for me. I had to unnecessarily travel for almost a kilometre on my wheelchair, when I should have been resting. This upset me a lot. And of course there were other things also.'

For instance, before the games Farman had a six-month training stint along with others at SAI Bengaluru and he pushed himself to practice anywhere between four to six hours daily. But just a month before the games, the SAI training camp was abruptly terminated without any reason being given.

Undaunted, Farman continued with what he needed to do and applied for Antonita to accompany him to the 2012 Games as his helper. The government agreed that she was the right person and she was allowed officially to accompany Farman to London.

The current government rules and facilities allow, depending on the severity of the disability of a selected athlete, one helper along with a personal coach. The helper helps with personal chores like doing the athlete's laundry, escorting the athlete for meals, for taking him to and from training and, finally, escorting the athlete to the main arena where the championships take place. The helper takes the burden of chores off the athlete so that he may concentrate solely on trying to win glory for the country.

Ideally the helper should be a paramedic as well or someone from the close family of the athlete since they would know what exact help would be needed and when.

The accompanying coach generally must be someone who has been coaching the athlete for some time; should ideally be someone knowledgeable about the event and also one who has the athlete's confidence. The sports ministry very correctly bears the cost of such helpers and coaches and compulsorily therefore, this support staff gets to stay in the Games Village along with the athlete, otherwise the whole purpose is lost.

Now for years the Federation had been run by officials who overlooked government regulations and have taken their own family members and relatives, naming them as helpers, to various international events, while the athletes and taxpayers watched helplessly.

'These people would come for the opening ceremony, show

their faces for a day and then disappear for shopping and sightseeing, leaving us to our own devices. The only help we got was from the team manager who at least told us when the event would take place and how to go there. Nothing else. Without a helper we face major problems. In London I was so disheartened when Antonita was not allowed in the Games Village as my helper that at one stage I had tears in my eyes. I had come with dreams of winning a medal for my country and yet the Federation was playing games with us athletes. Should I be worrying about who will bring me my food, wheel me around, clean my clothes, help me do my training properly, or should I concentrate on getting glory for India? I was so incensed that I blew up and informed the media about what was going on. I wanted the country to see how we, the best of Indian athletes, were being treated.'

Farman is happy that another Indian participant Girisha was able to win a medal in the high jump. Girisha, also hailing from Karnataka, won India's lone medal and incidentally was not in the first selected team. He was drafted in after another jumper could not pass the doping test. Girisha made most of this opportunity to corner glory for the country. But, the fact that Farman lost out on a medal made him bitter.

'My coach, who had accompanied the team to London, was not given the Games Village entry pass. I had trained with him for six months and he knew my strengths and weaknesses inside out. But he was not allowed as our officials and team management had their own person, whom I had not trained under in my entire life, to enter and stay in the village. I could have done with a helper as this coach could also have helped as an escort for me. But they cheated me and did not allow him in. That is the main reason why I lost out on my dream of winning an Olympic medal for my country. One of the senior officials of the Paralympic Committee of India (PCI) was named as the coach. I came to know of this even before we left for London and somehow I knew this was going to happen. I pleaded that my coach be allowed into the Village and I would certainly win a medal.'

Continues Farman, 'One of the officials even asked me, "Why should we bother about your medal? Are we going to get anything out of it?" I told the PCI Secretary about this and he just ignored me. In fact one another senior office-bearer told me that if I persisted on 'pressurising PCI', I may be dropped from the squad. "Who do you think you are, taking up cudgels with the Secretary or Joint Secretary of PCI. We can finish your career." I had no choice but to keep quiet before leaving for London, where in fact we reached fifteen days before the Games started. The squad had my personal coach Sadanand—paid for by the ministry. And the other coach was also present with whom I had not trained and did not get along with. What was more important for team management was to see whom I was comfortable with. But despite being in London, my coach was not given an entry pass and therefore could not help me at all. This was a severe disadvantage for me on the psychological and emotional level.'

The Hindu reported on 3 September 2012 that Farman Basha had lashed out at the Federation and the PCI. He was quoted in the newspaper, saying, 'I do not have an escort here and even my coach is not allowed to stay with me. I have been in London since August 11, and Federation representatives promised that all arrangements will be made, but nothing has been taken care of. My escort is supposed to take me to the dining area which is half a kilometre away, but the escort is not available. There is only one escort for all of us (there were ten para-athletes sent by India). It is very difficult for us to move around in wheelchairs. I was confident of a medal but now all my training has gone in vain.'

The *Times of India*, Bengaluru, reported on 6 September 2012 that India's physically challenged power-lifter Farman Basha lashed out at the PCI for using the free facilities meant for athletes and for their support staff during the ongoing London Paralympics. Basha said in his letter that his wife Antonita, who was his legal escort, and personal coach Sadanand Malshetty were not allowed to enter the Games Village despite having an official permit.

Blogger Nishita Jha, in *Tehelka* (31 August 2102), went hammer and tongs at the PCI. She did not mince words in a piece titled, 'What Can Anyone Say to a Person Who Finishes Fifth?' She wrote that at the SAI's Bengaluru gymnasium, Basha, the Indian contingent's senior-most athlete was lifting 165 kilograms—nearly thrice his body weight—on most days, and 170 kilograms on exceptionally good training days. Coaches and teammates were already congratulating him, for his performance during training assured him at least a bronze, if not a silver, medal at the London Paralympics. But in the fifteen days that Basha had been in London, his performance underwent a steady decline. 'I have no hopes. No one here cares about a medal,' Farman said. He was proven right. In the powerlifting event, Basha lifted a mere 155 kilograms, his personal worst, and finished fifth.

Continued Jha, 'One reason that surely affected his performance negatively is the absence of his coach. Basha, who had trained under weightlifting coach Satyanand for the past six months, was making do for the past fortnight with coach Vijay Balachandra, who was assigned to him once he arrived at the Games Village. Though Balachandra tried his best he could not do much. (Basha was so upset he could not lift more than 158 in all the days he was in London). In absence of coach Satyanand, Basha spent first week without any training at all. "They told me to eat, sleep and enjoy London," he says. In the second week, he was assigned a general coach who was responsible for training Farman along with ten other athletes of various disciplines, entirely different from Farman's. When Basha wanted and demanded answers from PCI, he was warned of speaking against the press. Another athlete, Amit Kumar Saroha, a paraplegic discus thrower, threatened to boycott his event if his coach Naval Singh, present in London but not allowed in the village, was kept out of the Games Village.'

Further, wrote Jha, 'The reason coaches have not been given proper accreditation to enter the village, athletes believe, is because the PCI wishes to give government officials the treatment and accommodation which should have been reserved for the Paralympic contingent. Speaking on the condition of anonymity to *Tehelka,* a senior source from PCI admitted that no other country had such an official-to-athlete ratio as skewed as India's. The ratio of officials, which includes coaches and escorts, to athletes is supposed to be 6:1. But we were told that we had to include certain government officials and their relatives in the total tally, even at the cost of coaches. The source however added that "the athletes should not get involved in politics—they should focus on winning medals". On the night of the opening ceremony, one athlete Jaideep Singh admitted he was not on the field along with others because he was yet to receive his official blazer and training kit. Said Singh, "We would not worry about politics and focus on our event if we did not have to beg the committee (PCI) for kits, shoes, blazers, and yes, a coach."

Nishita Jha concluded by noting that 'the hapless Vijay Balachandra, who was supposed to help Farman Basha, looked resigned to his fate. Said Balachandra, "Satyanand understood Basha's body and its limits—he would stand on his back, pull his hands, stretch his dorsal muscles. I could not do that—I was afraid of injuring him." '

Farman says he simply wants to forget London. How can we ensure that the future of Indian sports persons becomes better, he asks? 'We represent India because we work so hard in our lives. The officials simply do not understand that they exist because of us and not vice-versa.' In the Indian context, however, it seems that the all-powerful officials are a law unto themselves. They treat athletes like slaves. No one bothers about them. The athlete may have a career for few years, but take any sports federation and one can find the same faces running the show without a break for decades and more. The likes of Farman Basha are sadly dispensable. That is why sports officials of the country are not bothered that Farman, now forty years old, an Arjuna Awardee, an IWAS Games World Champion, a National Champion for more than a decade, ranked fourth and fifth in two consecutive Paralympic Games, is still without a job. Is that not a matter of shame for the entire country? Should not all of us feel embarrassed about this? We would not be surprised if the sports officials of this country had no idea about the plight of this great athlete.

The story of London Paralympics does not finish here. It is important to see further how our hardworking para-athletes were humiliated and deprived of help that the government of India had sanctioned as their right. That is why we quote here in detail what Nandini Kumar wrote in her *Bangalore Mirror* report which was published during the event.

'Indian sports is never devoid of controversies when it comes to self-seeking officials. At the London Paralympics, PCI officials, without bothering about the needs of our differently abled sportsmen, have left the escorts and coaches in London city while they are enjoying comforts of the Games Village. Imagine a wheelchair athlete left all to himself ahead of his event, without any training and without any escort. How will he go to the toilet, or get dressed? [Instead of seeing to the needs of the athletes] It seems all [the officials] are on a trip here with family members. And it is very saddening our basic needs are not taken care of [Farman is quoted as saying].'

Continues Nandini, 'At major events like these it is essential to have escorts to help the wheelchair athletes, take care of their needs and help them move around. Unfortunately the place of escorts and coaches has been taken over by the kith and kin of PCI officials, who have nothing to do with sports. The PCI President here has made an appearance with his wife. The treasurer of PCI has arrived here with his wife and daughter. The General Secretary of the PCI is showing his son Amar Singh as an official. Treasurer Gurcharan Singh's daughter is travelling as assistant to Secretary Ratan Singh while Amar Singh has been named as attachment to the team.' According to Nandini, and as is quoted further in the report, Ratan Singh was agitated when asked about all this. 'Surprisingly, when the team list was sent to the sports ministry for clearance, PCI had mentioned 10 athletes, five escorts and six coaches. None of the officials who gate-crashed have been mentioned in the list. Of the escorts and coaches only two named were allowed in with daily entry passes.... Clearly the Games are meant for everyone else who does not belong here.'

Finally former ace athlete Ashwini Nachappa and founder member of Clean Sports India, is quoted as saying, 'These guys are running a family business, and therefore I am not surprised with whatever is going on in the London para games. These are athletes who need special attention. How can they perform, unless we provide them with the support required?'

Farman, however, feels that things will not change easily. It is shameful the way we are treated, he says. In London, even though the government sanctions an amount for daily expenses, the athletes had to beg for their daily allowances. 'They would give us three or four pounds, when they could have given us at least, say, fifty pounds and taken account of the same after a week or so. But we had to beg every day. Further, even though I could not train in the first week, once I started training no one would stay with me and bring me back to where we were staying. In fact the coach assigned to me left me high and dry a couple of times and I had to tell the Secretary PCI what was happening. He told me, "Stay cool Farman, just enjoy your stay." I went to London to get my rightful medal and not for a holiday. The officials never understand these things, the hunger for a medal, the burning desire in us to bring glory for the country.'

One irony in this whole sordid chapter is that the government of India sanctioned and allowed Farman's helper and coach to accompany him to London, with expenses to be paid by the sports ministry. But that, too, after Farman threatened to boycott the Games if at least his coach was not allowed in the contingent. In fact even though he was not allowed to train at SAI-Bengaluru for one last month before the Games—yes, he had to shift to his old gymnasium and train there, much to his annoyance—he was in great shape and mentally positive as finally the coach and helper got their visas and official financial allowances. But what happened in London? The coach and helper had to twiddle their thumbs, enjoy a holiday when all they desperately wanted was to help Farman win a medal.

His wife has faced all problems and obstacles along with him and with a smile. 'Life is so much more than all this. I am happy that Farman is a part of my life. He has given me such joy and happiness and the will to see life in its perspectives. We had major problems getting married as we belonged to different religions, but we together overcame everything. I have never seen a person more simple or with more determination than him. He has achieved so much in his career, but he never boasts about anything. We are struggling, yes. It is such a shame that despite being a top sportsman of India, winner of Arjuna and Eklavya Awards, undisputed national champion for more than fifteen years, Asian Games medallist, ranked fourth and fifth in two consecutive paralympic games, an IWAS Games world champion, and so much more—yet he has never been given a job. It is such a shame. Farman does not say much about this but I know it is eating him inside. But I will try to keep his dreams of winning one Paralympic medal. I owe him that much,' she says with tears in her eyes.

The powerlifting legend however has now gone beyond the London Games. He has seen the ugly side of life from close quarters. He has turned into an optimist and is looking more at the future. And he knows there are enough good people in the world to tilt the balance of life. He feels very happy describing the one other messiah in his life, Rizwan.

Rizwan is the owner of Emphar Holdings, a property developers firm in Bengaluru. Says Farman, 'He is truly a messiah in my life. He has been so generous and so giving. After reading an article in *Times of India* in 2004, which reported my financial and other problems, he contacted me and since then has stood like a pillar behind me. Without ever asking for anything in return, not even publicity, for his incredible deed. He has donated my expenses of going to the Paralympics and other events and his charity has run into lakhs of rupees. Even now I get a monthly sum from Emphar for my diet. He does not even want me to wear the logo of his company on my apparel. He says "You are trying to bring glory to India—towards that, my contribution is so small." What can I say about this great man?' Farman is truly blessed to have people like Rizwan and Antonita in his life.

Farman feels it is important not to lose confidence or mental strength in life. 'The abled and disabled are all the same. The abled are also disabled in some ways. If abled/normal people are not satisfied in life, they are disabled mentally. No one is born perfect or leads a perfect life', says Farman. 'Some people are fair and some are dark, some have illness and disease, some are suspicious of everything—some are depressed. These factors lead to disability. Who is truly happy?' asks Farman. The moment one compares oneself to another, one finds oneself inferior in some way or the other.

Has he any message to give to rest of his countrymen?

'I have learnt to be patient. I have learnt not to lose my mental strength, my optimism. I have learnt not to give up on my goals. This job thing for example—I have been struggling since the last twenty years or so. I have met every chief minister, so many ministers and top officials in Karnataka. All promises were made, but nothing happened. The media has highlighted my plight, all newspapers and TV channels have carried this story. Nothing has happened. Jobs have gone to able-bodied athletes, not to us disabled players. I do not know what happens to so-called job quotas for the disabled. Maybe it was in my destiny. But I am a trier. I will always have faith in myself. Having faith and belief in yourself is so important. I know one day the Almighty will bestow reason upon all such people who are in a position to offer me a job. On my own, I will keep on trying. My last wish as far as my sports career is concerned is to get a medal for India at the next Paralympics [the 2016 Rio Games].'

Farman however has heaps of praise for erstwhile sports minister, Ajay Maken. He has seen many ministers in his twenty years in sports, but never someone more helpful, more willing to listen to the problems of para-athletes and wanting genuinely to help out, as Maken. Today all cash awards are equal. Girisha therefore got the huge award of ₹30 lakh for winning the silver medal at the London Paralympic Games in the high jump event. Maken is also the first sports minister who came to see the Paralympic Games in London and promised that all selected would get a job at the SAI, within a year. Unfortunately before the order could be implemented Ajay Maken had to leave the sports ministry. The new minister is seized of the issue and Farman is sure that some day soon he will get that much-needed job.

The man however is always thinking of helping fellow athletes. He always speaks out his mind, not bothered about the consequences. He has been highlighting the issue of having specialized coaches for para-athletes. 'I would like to see the day when we get dedicated coaches for likes of us. Coaches who understand our problems, our special needs. That is why it is important that we get jobs in SAI so that the next generation of para-athletes is well looked after.'

There is no doubt that Farman Basha is unique in many ways. A differently abled athlete par excellence. One who has fought against and braved life even though the dice rolled out wrongly for him. The PCI and sundry officials may not like his outbursts, but then he has helped cleanse the system in his own way. We as a country have much to thank him for, much to learn from him. We may not be able to help him get a job and we may wallow in our own shame that we could not do much for a person such as Farman who has done so much for India. Indeed, to paraphrase John F. Kennedy's immortal words: 'Ask not what and how much Farman Basha has done for the country, ask what the country could have done for him.'

RAJARAM GHAG
Conqueror of the Seas

Whatever you do, or dream you can, begin it. Boldness has genius and power and magic in it.

~JOHANN WOLFGANG GOETHE~

On 22 August 1988 one man set out to change the course of his destiny. One man set out to show one and all that he would conquer the Mount Everest of long-distance swimming, the English Channel. Having suffered the taunts of people for a long time because of being physically handicapped, India's long-distance swimming sensation Rajaram Ghag battled the giant waves and the devious currents of the treacherous Channel.

The year was 1961; a tiny baby boy was born in Kapre village located in the picturesque district of Ratnagiri. The joyous occasion soon turned to despair for the young parents as they realized their son was born with a deformity, both his legs were joined together. 'Everyone has a common perception that I was born with polio, but that is not the case. My legs were joined together at birth. Relatives tell me that my mother started crying in shock when she saw me, thinking that she was being punished for some sort of a bad deed by god,' says Rajaram Ghag.

With many relatives suggesting that urgent medical care was required for the newborn, the family shifted to Bombay. Thus began Rajaram's tryst with Mumbai's Wadia hospital after only a week of his birth.'I had to undergo eighteen operations so that my legs could have some mobility. I can now walk on my own with the aid of callipers but I am also wheelchair-bound sometimes.'

After overcoming the initial shock of giving birth to a disabled son, Laxmibai became Rajaram's fiercest supporter. The family lived in central Mumbai's Kalachowkie area (once the bustling commercial hub of the metropolis), which was approximately two to three kilometres away from Wadala Hospital. With Rajaram's father, Nayaran Ghag, taking up a menial job as the bus conductor with the Brihanmumbai Electric Supply and Transport Undertaking (earlier known as the Bombay Electric Supply and Transport Company or BEST), the family hardly had any money for the young boy's travel to the hospital. But the determined mother did not let the paucity of funds deter her and carried young Rajaram on her back every day in the harsh sun, walking nearly six kilometres to and fro from the hospital.

After eighteen major operations and countless visits to doctors and hospitals, the eight-year old boy learnt how to walk with the aid of callipers. However, while the hospital visits ensured that he walked, they also ensured that his studies suffered. In order to divert his attention to education, Rajaram was promptly enrolled by his parents in the SSC Day School in Agripada, a special educational institution meant only for disabled children so that they could achieve decent and dignified life.

'Let me tell you one thing, many crippled people have some sort of anger towards the society. This anger seems to fester in people like us because we cannot run like normal people, basically cannot live a normal life like able-bodied people. As I recollect my childhood today at the age of fifty-two, I feel that everybody has a certain degree of anger, but disabled people are angrier than others at society.'

Young Rajaram was angry with the world because of his problems and frustrations—though the operations had separated his legs, he still had to crawl on all fours to get about. At the age of eight or nine, when he was enrolled as a student in the first standard at the SSC Day School in Agripada, all his classmates were five to six years of age. His younger classmates bore the brunt of his anger, the swimming sensation recalls, because he was ashamed of his advanced age and his limitations as compared to them.

'As an eight-year-old studying with five-year-old children, I felt that I had no future. I guess I felt a little ashamed to be in the first standard. So I started bullying and beating up all the younger children in my class.'

As Rajaram went about his usual business of bullying younger children, he was spotted by the principal, Kamal Pandey. So incensed was she with what she saw, that the principal picked up a duster and flung it at Rajaram. The furious child, not to be outdone, picked up the duster and flung it back at her, hitting her in the process.

The infuriated principal called Rajaram's parents and told them that their unruly child was better suited to a boarding school, where he could be disciplined better. 'My mother did not agree at all to send me to the boarding school. But my second-oldest brother Vishnu, took the hard decision to send me away as he felt this was the only way to discipline me.'

And so the unruly boy was sent to the government-run Shaskiya Apangh Balak school in Miraj, a small town in southern Maharashtra. Young Rajaram was again admitted to the first standard and it was in Miraj that he stood on his own feet for the first time with the aid of callipers. 'Actually, I was initially accepted in the second standard in Miraj, but due to the operations that I endured there, I could not really focus on my studies. So I was sent back to first standard.'

'I have some great memories of Miraj,' he recalls. 'I studied there from the first to the fourth standard. Prior to coming to Miraj, I could not even stand, I used to crawl on my hands to ferry myself, you know, like a monkey. An American doctor attached to the Mission Hospital in Miraj operated on me twice more. I walked for the first time on my own two feet with the aid of callipers. I cannot event describe the moment when I stood on my own two feet for the first time.'

It was also in Miraj that Rajaram first started eating non-vegetarian food, something that would help him later in his swimming career. In fact, all the students were fed non-vegetarian food for adequate protein intake on Wednesdays, Fridays and Sundays, with the other days being vegetarian days.

However, Rajaram's reputation as a bully was very well known among fellow students, teachers and the hostel wardens. Known as 'Bambai ka Gunda' or the 'Thug from Bombay', he was routinely beaten by his teachers to bring him under control.

'I was always a very mischievous student at Miraj. I could never understand why I was being beaten by the wardens. But looking back today, I am actually grateful that they straightened me out. I now value the discipline that they imparted and it has helped me reach where I am today.'

One particular teacher at Miraj who was fondly called Kale Nana by the students, helped Rajaram develop an affinity for sports. Since he was not only physically older but also stronger than his classmates, Kale Nana always made Rajaram play in the weaker team during the games hour.

'We played games like kabaddi and lagori during our physical education hour at Miraj. I would always get beaten by him during lagori. We played with a makeshift ball which was essentially a sock filled with mud and big stones. I always ended up getting bruised by the end of the game as Kale Nana only targeted me from the team.'

Rajaram never cried or got cowed down by the beating during physical education hour; in fact he would pick up the ball and hurl it back at Kale Nana with all his might, with the intention of causing him some pain. Being high-spirited, Rajaram even told Kale Nana that when he grew up he would come back to thrash him. Despite being beaten black and blue, Rajaram began to develop a liking for sports after playing games ranging from kabaddi, to kho kho, atta patta and, of course, lagori.

He however, has one complaint. 'Despite everything I learnt there, I always felt that the teachers were not really equipped or trained. I will give you a simple example. If a teacher is supposed to teach a particular language then she is supposed to be proficient in it. My fifth grade English teacher did not know the language, yet she was the one person who taught English to the handicapped students. Looking back, I feel that if I had also been given proper educational facilities, then today I would also be proficient in English."

In 1975, after completing the fourth standard, Rajaram made his way back to Bombay. After living amongst fellow handicapped students for four years, the youngster knew that in order to gain a bigger perspective in life, he needed to rub shoulders with normal people. Having already been through so many hardships in life, the ambitious boy wanted to study in an English-medium school. There were two English-medium schools in Wadala at that time, Shirodkar High School in Parel and Aryan Bhatt, both of which were fairly famous. Young Rajaram had high hopes and dreams of donning the uniform and becoming a student at Shirodkar High School. However, the boy's dreams were shattered as both schools rejected his admission on the grounds that he was physically disabled.

And so a dismayed Rajaram had to take admission in the SSC Day School once again and it was here that his tryst with swimming began. 'All the physically handicapped students were taken for swimming at the YMCA once a week for two hours from 11 a.m. to 1 p.m. by Dr Nanavati. He came over and asked me if I knew how to swim. Prior to this, I had not swum and had not even seen a pool. When I saw the expanse of the blue-green water in the pool, and after seeing all the young kids diving in the water, I also felt inspired. I felt that even I could swim, but little did I know that the children were trained.'

Dr Nanavati asked young Rajaram if he knew the basics of swimming, to which the young boy replied in the affirmative. And so he dived into the pool, thinking that it would be easy. 'Once I hit the water, I did not know how to keep myself afloat and so I started drowning. Dr Nanavati had to rescue me and drag me out of the water.'

The kind doctor made young Rajaram sit down and asked him to observe the other children, in order to understand the technique. After a while, he made the young boy enter the pool again, but this time with a float tied around his waist.

Dr Nanavati made him take two rounds of the pool to help build his confidence. During the third round, the doctor removed the float and Rajaram, who could only swim by flapping his arms, had absolutely no inkling. Without the support of the float, Rajaram flailed but with Dr Nanavati's support he completed the last twenty-metre stretch of the pool.

Emboldened by the success of his student, Dr Nanavati told

Rajaram to complete another lap of the pool without the support of the float. The young boy completed the round of the pool, thus learning how to swim around the age of twelve or thirteen and was undoubtedly elated. Seeing the young boy's enthusiasm, Dr Nanavati started training him for competitions. Rajaram's first competition (a meet meant only for the physically challenged) was held at the Kamgar Stadium at Elphinstone.

'I was used to swimming 25 metres at the YMCA pool which was comparatively smaller. After realizing that I had to swim 50 metres Kamgar Stadium, I did not know what to do and broke into a cold sweat even before the race.'

Dr Nanavati calmed the nerves of the young boy who felt that he would not only be unable to complete the event but would also drown in the process. Rajaram had simply refused to swim without a float in this meet. After repeated assurances from his mentor, the physically afflicted young boy stepped up to the plate and emerged in first place in the race and received, as the prize, a tin of Bournvita, a trophy that the champion swimmer still values. 'Those days, we never received any medals or any trophies. I have not forgotten that Bournvita prize that I received and I guess that Bournvita-power has propelled me to achieve everything that I have achieved in life,' says Rajaram with a smile.

Little did Dr Nanavati know that his protégé would rewrite the annals of not only Indian, but also world swimming history in the future. Meanwhile, never the best at his studies, young Rajaram somehow managed to scrape through his fifth standard exams at the SSC Day School, and once again tried to get admission in Shirodkar High School. He was once again rejected by the principal and the management. But luckily for Rajaram, two local toughs affiliated to a regional political party took notice of his plight.

'Sometimes bad people can also have a heart and can help change the lives of people in distress. Bandu Shingare and Bhai Shingare who were famous as local toughs in Lalbaug came in as angels and really helped me.'

The Shingare brothers paid a personal visit to the principal of Shirodkar High School. Mr Beri, the principal, tried to reason with them—if the crippled boy was admitted, who would take responsibility of his safety? The brothers told him in no uncertain terms that if Rajaram was not given admission they would get the school closed. Principal Beri promptly altered his stance and Rajaram was soon living his childhood dream, donning the colors of the Shirodkar High School.

Rajaram studied at Shirodkar High School for four years, until he completed the tenth standard. For all those four years, Principal Beri was the last person to leave the premises everyday, ensuring that the young boy had safely left the premises.

'My class was on the fourth floor of the building so I used to climb the stairs daily with my callipers to get there. I feel if a teacher like Principal Beri had come into my life earlier and encouraged me then I would have been able to achieve much more.'

The physical education teacher, Mr Abha Naik, was not only a good kabaddi coach but was also a keen sports enthusiast. The teacher ensured that the physically challenged boy was included in various activities as a drill instructor or even as a referee during games like kabaddi and kho kho. 'On sensing my keen enthusiasm for sports, Abha sir asked me if I liked any game. I told him that I had just learnt swimming and wanted to pursue it and requested an hour and a half off from school to go for my training.'

With the threat of the Shingare brothers loudly resonating in Principal Beri's ears, he promptly complied and the young boy resumed his swimming at Kamgar Stadium. In 1978, Rajaram suffered yet another setback as his training pool was shut down by the authorities due to some problems in the water. So the keen young swimmer had to stop swimming for a little while again as the only pool available was at the erstwhile Shivaji Park in Dadar.

'We used to stay near Gandhi Hospital at the BEST Quarters in Lalbaug. My father was a bus conductor so he was given a small residential room on the first floor because of my physical disability. We could not live in a chawl because I was unable to go to the bathroom as in most chawls there are only common ones which are located a distance away and are used by everyone in the vicinity. In Mumbai itself, which is considered to be the financial capital of India, there is no infrastructure for the disabled. There are no bathrooms which we can use when we travel, there are hardly any ramps and so a wheelchair cannot be taken easily anywhere. It is like the physically challenged are living in a prison in their own country. Nobody even bothers to see how we are living or even help us in this country says.' Rajaram in anguish.

Shivaji Park was approximately located four to five kilometres away from Rajaram's house. While his father worked as a bus conductor in BEST, the meagre income was not really sufficient for the large family. In fact, the young boy only owned one school uniform which he used to wash every day when he returned from school, only to wear it the next day.

While his father was against his swimming initially, Rajaram's two oldest brothers, Vishnu and Shridhar supported his endeavour as they felt that swimming would help him strengthen his otherwise weak body. But when the young boy applied for his swimming membership at the Shivaji Park pool, the coaches there refused to teach him the basics of the sport.

Undeterred, Rajaram applied for the student discount at the public pool as his school had given him a certificate stating that he was a student of the Shirodkar High School. While the membership fee for regular members was ₹12 per annum, students were asked to pay only ₹5 to use the pool.

'Somehow my older brothers and my mother got together and collected ₹5 for my membership. But the bus ticket was 5 paise one way on the direct bus that went via Lalbaug to Shivaji Park. My mother did not have enough confidence in me at that time. She felt that I could not travel for such a long distance alone in the bus.'

In order to test his independence and confidence, Laxmibai Ghag gave her son 10 paise and told him travel to Shivaji Park alone in the bus and collect the sand from the beach in Dadar. After a couple of hours Rajaram returned home triumphantly with the jar of sand, thus convincing her of his love for the sport.

With his family now firmly standing behind him, Rajaram started swimming regularly at Shivaji Park on Saturdays, Sundays and on all national holidays. Rajaram was allowed to swim unhindered for two to three hours instead of the regular one hour, as the Shivaji Park personnel never set a time limit for him like they did for other members. The head coach at Shivaji Park was a Parsi gentleman by the name of Percy Hakim, who would instruct all the other young students except Rajaram.

'Nobody was bothered that a young handicapped boy would come to the pool regularly, remove his callipers and swim haphazardly. Percy Hakim and his assistants would give instructions to every child in the pool but completely ignore me. Of course it really hurts when someone discriminates against you. Sometimes I would sit and wonder why these so-called great coaches of Mumbai were ignoring me, but then I always knew the answer. It was only because I was handicapped.'

Undeterred albeit a little hurt, Rajaram practiced on his own and would emerge from the pool thoroughly exhausted after one-and- a-half hours. At that time, the teenager only competed in the physically handicapped races and would always emerge first. After winning almost every meet for the handicapped, Rajaram began to focus on competing against able-bodied people.

News about Rajaram wanting to compete in normal races soon reached the ears of Percy Hakim and other private coaches, all of whom only discouraged him. 'I think it is very important to have detractors in your life. When all these people refused to coach me, I focused on developing my own strokes. My arms had become very powerful as I could only use them to swim. I am still angry and hurt as to why I was discriminated against by these people. I still talk to all these people with respect, but if people like Percy had given me some training or corrected my strokes at that point in time, then I would have achieved much more.'

Despite humiliation, the teenager approached Mr Danke, a private coach and asked him for help. In turn, Mr Danke asked the young boy, 'What can you do, since you cannot dive or even swim properly because you are crippled?' Humiliated and dejected, Rajaram would sit by the poolside for hours wondering why he was such a pariah in the eyes of all the instructors. He would also observe acclaimed deaf, mute and partially blind swimmer Taranath Shenoy's technique. The differently abled swimmer had emerged as a star on the Indian swimming scene after swimming in the English Channel three times successfully.

After all the humiliation endured by Rajaram, it seemed that lady luck finally smiled on him as Taranath Shenoy gestured to the teenager to get off the bench and swim with him in the pool. 'I was so fascinated by Taranath's swimming technique that I would observe him for hours. When Taranath told me to join him in the pool, it was the ultimate silver lining for me at that point in time. He did not really coach me in any way, but he was kind enough to encourage me. After a couple of days, I even began to understand his signs and gestures.'

The star swimmer would make Rajaram take a head start in the pool and then try to catch him, thereby working on his speed. Though initially he liked it, Rajaram was intelligent enough to understand that his own speed would not develop if he continued to play second fiddle to Taranath Shenoy. And soon enough, Rajaram started working to develop his own speed with the star swimmer.

A girl called Sangeeta Patil was being coached by her father around the same time in Shivaji Park. Sangeeta's father always used to glare angrily at Rajaram whenever the teenager would swim in the pool. 'Sangeeta and I were roughly the same age. The water at Shivaji Park was a translucent blue and one could see everything through it. Her father probably thought that I was trying to ogle his daughter. He asked me one day as to why I was keeping pace with his daughter in the pool once Taranath would move on ahead.'

The teenage boy told Sangeeta Patil's father that he was merely trying to develop his speed and strokes in the pool. Once the girl's father understood that Rajaram was not a threat to his daughter, he told Rajaram to submerge and float his body a little more while swimming in order to gain more speed. This proved to be a turning point for Rajaram and he started focusing more on developing his own strokes and speed. He stopped swimming with both Sangeeta Patil and Taranath Shenoy and started practicing alone.

In order to develop his strokes accurately, Rajaram would routinely observe many stalwarts of the sport. 'Milind Soman [who later became a supermodel and film star] was the national champion in the breaststroke category. Nobody was able to break his record at least for fifteen years. I used to emulate his flawless technique and practice the breaststroke with him. Thus I began to observe all the masters of various strokes.'

Similarly, Rajaram observed Vishwanath Takle, a swimmer who was the national champion in the butterfly category. Any swimmer who wishes to master this difficult stroke needs to build a lot of muscle power in their legs. This was certainly a challenge for Rajaram as his legs did move at all. The champion swimmer told Rajaram that he would guide him in mastering the stroke. But he first requested Rajaram to try and swim only the butterfly stroke for fifteen days and thus Rajaram mastered the dreaded butterfly stroke, which was quite a feat for someone like him.

Meanwhile, a window of opportunity suddenly opened for Rajaram on World Disabled Day in 1981 as many government institutions decided to recruit handicapped sports on persons their payrolls. Rajaram was one of the lucky few that got a job with Western Railways. A huge financial burden had been lifted off his family, thus allowing Rajaram to concentrate on his swimming.

Now realizing that he would not be able to compete in the sprint swimming category with the able-bodied, Rajaram started focusing on the distance swimming scene in Mumbai. 'After learning all the strokes, I started participating in the Shivaji Park Home Gala with all the able-bodied people. I always stood fifth or sixth but always ensured that I would never finish last. In 1984, I felt that I was ready to take on long-distance swimming scene in India.'

In 1984, Rajaram Ghag sent his entry for the famous Sunk Rock meet, which takes place from Gateway of India to Sunk Rock which is some five kilometers away. In a huge setback, his entry was rejected on account of his disability. 'It was truly a frustrating moment for me. Mr Adi Bharucha was a famous waterpolo player who participated in the Olympic Games, probably felt that I did not deserve to swim in the competition. Maybe god had sent Mr Bharucha to torture me for the better as it was this rejection that spurred me on to show people that disabled people could also become world beaters,' recalls Rajaram.

At that time, the press had also caught a whiff of this story and began reporting on the injustice meted out to Rajaram with great gusto. A press conference was also called but the organizers remained undeterred and did not allow Rajaram to participate.

Despite regular setbacks, Rajaram continued to participate in the Shivaji Park Home Gala, a race that stretched from Shivaji Park to the Sea Rock Hotel in Bandra and back. Every year at least 300 people participated in the Home Gala race and everyone had to finish swimming the distance within the one-hour time limit. 'I still remember it was my first long-distance swimming competition in 1984. I managed to finish the entire distance in an hour and twenty-six minutes. Despite the time-limit given, not many able-bodied people were able to finish the race in an hour. Champion swimmer Anita Sood also took longer than an hour to complete the meet. I finished twenty-sixth out of the 300 people that participated.'

Anita Sood's mother who saw Rajaram's inspiring swim made an emotional announcement during the prize distribution ceremony, thereby interrupting it. She told the audience present that for the first time in the history of this competition a physically disabled man had not only participated but also completed it. She also said that she wanted to award Rajaram for his inspiring performance. 'I was the first person that was given a prize during the presentation ceremony. She gave me a cap, a pool buoy, swimming goggles and a kicking board to help with my practice.

Prior to this grand gesture, I never swam with cap and goggles as my financial condition was not very great,' says Rajaram.

An elated Rajaram thanked her for all the gifts but asked her what he would do with the kicking board. Anita Sood's mother told him that he had to learn how to kick in order to become a complete swimmer. Though Rajaram never learned to kick while swimming, his body started floating properly in the water after a lot of practice with the kicking board.

After garnering success in the Home Gala, Rajaram re-entered the Sunk Rock meet in 1985. Once again he was barred from participating in the race on account of being disabled. This time around, M.R. Rao, a reporter from the *Times of India,* wrote article after article questioning Rajaram's disqualification from the Sunk Rock race.

But nothing happened despite the appeal by the press. At that time, Mr Salunkhe who was appointed the director of sports by the government of Maharashtra was also witness to the injustice that was being meted out to the handicapped swimmer. 'I fought like a lion with Mr Salunkhe, even abusing him in the process. I did not know he was such a senior officer. He took me to the side after the race started and first told me to get a grip on my now famous temper. The officer also promised to help me out and ensure my participation in the next race that was thirty-three kilometres long.'

A livid Rajaram still smouldered with anger and told Mr Salunkhe that if he was not allowed to participate in a five-kilometre race, then how could the officer ensure his participation in the longer one? The officer told him to concentrate only on his practice for the race. Mr Salunkhe also told him that he would be checking up on Rajaram's practice to ensure that he would attain the optimal fitness required for such a long and arduous race.

Trusting Mr Salunkhe to keep his word, Rajaram requested the municipality management at Shivaji Park to keep the pool open for him to practice till 9 p.m. The management complied, thus standing firmly behind their star champion. And so Rajaram began practicing day and night for the biggest race of his life. It was this race that would decide his future as a serious swimmer and if he failed to finish it then his career was as good as over.

The All India Sea Swimming Competition is a thirty-three-kilometre-long annual competition that is swum from Dadar to Malad and back. All participants are given a time limit of twelve hours to finish the race. Despite vehement objections of the swimming fraternity, Mr Salunkhe remained firm on letting Rajaram participate in this invitational event. Following many rounds of meetings and negotiations between Mr Salunkhe and the Swimming Federation, Rajaram was sent the letter of invitation for the competition. Despite overcoming a huge hurdle in terms of participation in a major race, Rajaram remained a worried man as he required a coach for this ultimate test. Many organizers allowed competitors to have their coaches guide them to completion, with the coach and the lifeguard travelling in a boat next to their competitor.

'Desperate, I asked Percy Hakim to become my coach. Instead of encouraging me, he said if normal people cannot complete such a big distance then how will you finish the race?' Hearing these words, Rajaram started practicing like a man possessed. He realized that he would have to pass this test with flying colours if he had to shut his detractors up. He resolved not to swim in front of the Shivaji Park chief coach and started swimming at the Mafatlal Boat Club at Girgaum Chowpatty, and Kamgar Stadium instead.

One day, Mr Salunkhe came to meet Rajaram during practice

and asked him to discuss couple of things with him before his make or break race. 'Salunkhe saab first asked me if I needed any extra facilities for the race. I shook my head. Seemingly happy with my answer he then explained that he had put his pride on the line to ensure my participation. I promised to keep his pride intact and finish the race at any cost. But he kept tabs on me to see if I was working hard enough.'

Desperate in his quest for success in his maiden distance-swimming meet, Rajaram put himself through a punishing schedule. He would leave his house in Ghatkoper by 4.30 a.m. by train to reach the pool and start training half an hour later. He would swim for three hours from 5 a.m. to 9 a.m. continuously, getting out only to change and rush for office. After working for seven to eight hours at his office which is located at the famous Western Railway headquarters, the budding legend would pack his bags and head out once again, practicing another two- and- a-half to three hours, finishing only at around 8.30 or 9 p.m. After a gruelling session, he would then walk two to three kilometres to the Dadar railway station on his callipers from the pool, reaching home only at 10 p.m.

Soon enough, after two months, the day arrived and it was time for Rajaram to prove his mettle. Everyone, including the organizers of the race and mediapersons, asked him if he needed any extra facilities to which he replied in the negative. However, Rajaram was missing a vital link for the race, as coach Percy Hakim was still refusing to help him out. Finally, the organizers and some other swimmers firmly told the Shivaji Park head coach to help out Rajaram as he was after all a 'Shivaji Park' boy.

Under immense pressure from the swimming fraternity, Percy Hakim was forced to relent and accept the offer of becoming Rajaram Ghag's coach for the important race. Participants for this ultra-long race were also allowed to avail the services of a lifeguard along with that of a coach. It certainly seemed that lady luck was also smiling down on the swimmer as a gentleman called M.R. Dalal, who was incidentally also the Indian Navy coach for swimming, was appointed Rajaram's lifeguard.

The diminutive and lightly built navy coach quietly approached Rajaram and told him that whenever he felt like giving up, Mr Dalal would either guide him to completion or to the safety of the shores. But he remained firm on one thing, that Rajaram would have to put in 100 per cent effort in completing race or else Mr Dalal would not help him out.

Recalling the sequence of events, Rajaram says, 'I told Mr Dalal not to worry because I would complete this race 100 per cent as it was a do- or- die race for me. I also told him that I couldn't trust Percy who was always trying to push me one step back. I firmly told Mr Dalal not to leave me in this race alone and to be my guide and mentor.'

With the race about to begin, all the swimmers were standing in a line, Rajaram asked the organizers to leave him till the water as he could not run like other swimmers. The organizers promptly complied with Rajaram's request but told him that he could not start till the other swimmers had touched the waters. Stalwarts of distance swimming like Anita Sood and Taranath Shenoy were also participating in this prestigious race.

'Salunkhe saab had once asked about the duration that I would take to complete this mammoth distance. I only told him one thing, that if Taranath Shenoy takes eight to eight- and- a-half hours to complete the race then I would take ten hours. I told him that I would take two hours more than Taranath because of my physical handicap.'

The time limit was twelve hours. As expected, coach Percy

fell seasick mid-way and had to be taken ashore. The young swimmer had no idea and was informed of the developments by his lifeguard. A visibly relaxed Rajaram did not take coach Percy's abandonment to his heart and instead focused on the race and finished the mammoth distance in the time limit, twelve hours. The elated lifeguard and Mr Salunkhe—who had put his name on the line for Rajaram—bear-hugged the exhausted swimmer. Of the twenty-three swimmers that were invited to participate in the long-distance swimming meet, only ten finished, with Rajaram finishing tenth. He had not only succeeded in finishing the distance but had also defeated thirteen other able-bodied swimmers who were unable to finish the race.

'The next leg of the same race was in Gujarat. I sent my entry form but I did not mention that I was disabled as I was competing with able-bodied people. So when I reached there they revoked my entry saying that I did not mention my visible handicap.' With the organizers refusing to budge from their stand, Rajaram was offered a position of a coach for an unknown participant called Deepak Paleja. A day before the race, all the coaches were taken for a survey of the route by boat and following the boat was a huge shark. Rajaram thanked his stars that he was not going to step into the water on race day.

'In competitive swimming you will find that some people become coaches despite not knowing how to swim and never having stepped into the water. Deepak Paleja's actual coach was an individual known as Mr Dholakia who was sitting in the boat with a lifejacket. I asked him why he was so scared. He then told me that he did not know how to swim and never entered the water as a swimmer!'

Legendary swimmer Taranath Shenoy finished first and Deepak Paleja was second. This was Rajaram's first attempt at coaching and he enjoyed the experience so much that he would go on to coach six Chatrapati Award winners in the state later on in his life.

In 1987, Rajaram returned to the city and told his brother Harishchandra that he wanted to attempt the thirty-five kilometre long Dharamtar-Mumbai circuit. Dharamtar is a small but a busy port near the picturesque Alibaug district of Maharashtra. Swimmers usually attempt to swim this distance from November to January as both the weather and water are cool then. With the Veraval Churva long-distance swimming competition culminating the season in Feburary, there were no races for Rajaram to compete in in the month of March, when most weather changes take place in India. The swimmer told his brother that since his time was being wasted, he might as well attempt to swim the distance between Dharamtar and Mumbai.

'I told my brother to hire a boat as soon as possible for my attempt to swim the distance. A big boat would cost anywhere between ₹15,000 to ₹20,000, a huge amount during those days. So my brother approached his friend, a certain individual whose name was Kohli, who lent him a padav. This is a large, open-bottomed, high-sided, local fishing boat. We finalized the deal for ₹400 with a promise of refuelling the padav.'

Rajaram feels he should have finished in eight hours but it took him fourteen hours and twenty-three minutes to swim the distance, with the current changing twice during his attempt. Despite taking a longer time to finish the Dharamtal-Mumbai swim, Rajaram attempted two more races in 1987. The first race was an invitation to swim eighty-one kilometer in the Ganga River from Kolkata. It took Rajaram eleven hours and fifty-five minutes to finish. The second race was the Veraal Chaurval circuit in Gujarat in which Rajaram emerged sixth out of twenty-seven participants.

In the 1980s, the English Channel was considered the Olympics for long-distance swimmers. Crossing the English Channel meant that a swimmer had attained legendary status in their country. Swimmers like Taranath Shenoy and Anita Sood had crossed this formidable stretch of water, thereby attaining legendary status in the annals of Indian swimming. The first Indian who crossed the Channel was Mihir Sen in 1958, thereby acquiring cult status in the field of Indian sports.

'In those days, the English Channel was the biggest water body any swimmer could cross. I had finished all the distance-swimming competitions in India successfully but I was lacking an international experience. Even a swimmer like Taranath had stumbled in his first attempt in 1982. Hence the thought of attempting to cross the Channel came to my mind.'

The year was 1987 and all the distance-swimming competitions had ended in India for the year. Conquering the English Channel was firmly on the minds of Team Rajaram, and to turn this dream into a reality, Harishchandra went to talk to people who had already crossed the Channel, in order to find the route. However, nobody came forward to give any information. Only one man came forward and decided to help young Rajaram out, Vinod Guruji, the man whom the legendary Taranath Shenoy regarded as a 'guru'. Along with him, the youngest Channel swimmer of that time, Aarti Pradhan, too came to Rajaran's aid and gave him some guidance.

'Though the English Channel is only twenty-one kilometres long, it is really treacherous—not only because of the currents but also due to the height of the waves, that can actually come up to the fifth floor of any high-rise building in Mumbai.' Both Vinod Guruji and Aarti Pradhan clearly told Rajaram and his brother that expenses were going to be steep and that they would need at least ₹2 lakh for this endeavour, a princely sum in those days.

'In 1987, my brother had already become a member of the Lions Club of Midtown. So when I told him about the cash crunch, he immediately contacted them for financial assistance. My brother told me firmly to focus on my practice for the Channel swim and that he would handle the rest. I was totally focussed on my practice and had absolutely no clue as to what Lions Club was.'

The Lions Club of Midtown decided to help out the differently abled swimmer in his endeavour and made an announcement for the same but did not disclose the amount. Someone in Rajaram's camp decided to tell his story to the media and so renowned reporter Madhav Gadkari of *Loksatta* wrote about the young swimmer's endeavour. After the article appeared in the major Marathi newspaper, the Public Relations Officer of Air India, Mr Dabolkar wrote a letter in Marathi to Rajaram, informing him that two return tickets were available to him for free for the event.

With a quarter of the battle won, Rajaram and his brother went to meet him at the majestic Air India building at Nariman Point. While Rajaram who was on his first visit to Mumbai's tallest building at that time, was lost in its wonders, Mr Dabolkar told his guests that the national airline would provide him with a free airline ticket for as long as he worked there. Harishchandra informed the Lions Club of the joyous news. In response to their earlier advertisement, a very wealthy donor called Ibrahim Kaskar decided to donate ₹40,000 to help Rajaram navigate the Channel and bring glory to India.

'I absolutely had no clue that Ibrahim Kaskar was the dreaded don Dawood Ibrahim. I mean sometime criminals, too, have a heart and can help good causes. This had happened for the second time in my life.'

In order to achieve his dream, Rajaram did everything that he could possibly do. Apart from the money donated by Ibrahim Kaskar, the Lions club of Midtown was gracious enough to give Rajaram's brother an additional amount of ₹90,000 in cash. However, they were still falling short of funds, and Rajaram decided to take out a bank loan to go to England. The brothers were able to collect a lakh plus ₹80,000 overall for this endeavour.

'Everybody told me different things. Some people told me to put on more weight as cold hits the human body from the legs and my legs were useless. So I increased my weight to 100 kilograms. I would swim at least six to seven hours a day and on Saturdays and Sundays, I would also practice at night, as the water was much cooler.'

While his employers, the Western Railways, extended their support, allowing him to leave early from work at 2 p.m., Rajaram only left his office building after the completion of all his work. He followed a punishing schedule in order to achieve his dream. He would practice his swimming techniques from 10 p.m. to 4 a.m. in the morning, all alone. Sometimes, his friends and brothers would also accompany him to the pool, and while they would hit the sack, Rajaram would still swim alone.

Before leaving for England, Rajaram and Harishchandra wrote a letter to famed Channel Coach, Carey Dickson, who was incidentally also Taranath Shenoy's coach. However she refused to coach him in his attempt. 'We were very surprised, but Vinod Guruji told us that Carey Dickson would not even acknowledge me till I landed in Dover. He asked me to take a Nataraj idol for her as a token. But my brother bought two idols for her.'

So Team Rajaram landed in England on 1 August 1988. After landing at Heathrow Airport, the brothers had to take the train to Dover, where the English Channel touches British shores. The champion swimmer had not used a wheelchair and could walk around only with the aid of crutches but he could not step on the escalator that was taking him to the station.

'I saw an escalator for the first time in my life and did not know how to get on it. Meanwhile, my brother was already hauling four suitcases containing not only clothes but also items like rice and daal. My brother and I were both in a fix as to how to get on the escalator with me and the four bags. On seeing our predicament, a kind policeman came to our aid and took us down the escalator and to the station. This was the first time I saw how respectfully disabled people were treated in England as compared to India where hardly anybody bothers about us.'

Rajaram, who was on his maiden trip abroad, felt that musicians were employed to welcome tourists who arrived in Englad. Upon seeing a fairly well-dressed man playing a guitar, he asked his brother if this was the welcome band for them. His brother then kindly informed him, the gentleman in question was a busker who was begging for some money by playing a guitar.

Before leaving Mumbai, Vinod Guruji had told Rajaram that many Indians who had gone to cross the Channel had behaved badly with the English coaches when it came to of issues money. He also told him that many coaches would refuse to help him on account of their behaviour. Upon arrival at Dover, Rajaram's brother went to meet the highly esteemed coach, Carey Dickson who flatly refused to entertain them. But Harishchandra decided to give her the Nataraj idol regardless of her refusal. A change of heart followed and the coach told Rajaram's brother to have him ready by 9 a.m. next day or else she would leave.

Rajaram's brother had firmly drilled into his head that 'first impression was the last impression,' and so they stood in the cold at the gate at 8.30 a.m., waiting to be picked up by Carey

Dickson in her car. 'Carey told me that my body was too bulky and that I would have to lose some weight. She asked me what my weight was and I told her I weighed 100 kilograms. She told me that so much weight was unnecessary and was not required at all for the swim.'

The coach told Rajaram to get in the water and get out in half an hour, as it was too cold. Rajaram then jumped into the cold water without applying any grease, and the water was so cold that he felt as though hundreds of needles had pierced him at the same time. Rajaram was unable to swim fast in the ice-cold water and his speed became less than half of what he would swim in India. Half an hour later, a shivering Rajaram emerged from the water and was given half a cup of black tea, some of which he dropped due to his shivering. He was also given half a banana and half a cake to get some much needed energy and was sent back into the chilly water.

'An hour later I emerged from the water again and Carey asked me how I was feeling. I told that the water was too cold and that I was shivering quite badly on the first day. Then I saw a young boy who was shivering even more than I was. I promptly told my coach that I wanted to get back and swim in the water for another hour. Little did she know that I had realized that it was much colder outside than in the water,' chuckles Rajaram at the memory.

An hour later, Rajaram met twelve-year-old Abhishek Rao who had already been training for two months with Carey. Despite being so young, Abhishek was so fast in the water that Rajaram could hardly match his speed on the first day.

He started training with Abhishek and soon enough regained enough speed to beat him easily in the water. Twelve arduous days later, it was Rajaram's birthday on 12 August and he wanted to attempt his swim on that special day. But his coach flatly refused, saying that he was too bulky. Carey put Rajaram through such a gruelling schedule that he lost twenty kilograms in fifteen days. 'Carey Dickson would give me a half cup of black tea, half a banana and half a cake after every hour of swimming. But then she made me swim for six hours every day. She would train the other Indians for only two hours but make me train for six whole hours. I told my brother to ask her as to why she was training me so harshly. My brother was too scared of her as she had a very short temper.'

One day, Harishchandra finally managed to ask the short-tempered coach the big question. Carey told them that she wanted to see for how long Rajaram's legs could bear the cold water, since they were not movable. But one fine day, the coach made Rajaram swim for nine hours straight and on seeing him swim for that long, she decided that 22 August 1988 would be the D-Day.

On 21 August, Carey and her husband took a couple of swimmers who wanted to attempt to cross the Channel. An unnamed swimmer went first for his solo event from England to France, which resulted in a failure. The coach's husband then got a Chinese relay team that was attempting to cross the Channel from the French side, and that too resulted in a dud due to the prevailing harsh conditions. And soon enough it was Rajaram's turn to conquer the challenge presented by the English Channel.

'There were eleven of us in the line up, out of which we were two Indians. They asked me if I was ready, I replied in the affirmative and all of us jumped into the water. It took me twelve hours and forty minutes to cross the Channel because of my own stupidity. I had reached the half-way mark when my body became really warm. I could only see the blue expanse of water all around. It felt as if I was stuck swimming in the same place as whenever

I would turn around I could only see the white cliffs of Dover.'

Harishchandra would give him black coffee to drink every hour to combat the chilly water. He wanted to drink a cold drink as his body had become really warm. Everybody told him not to drink the cold beverage as it would slow him down but Rajaram refused to swim further until he was given his drink.

'My body's temperature fell drastically due to the cold drink and I became really slow. The cold slowly crept through my feet into my body, but I somehow managed to cross the Channel. The first paraplegic was a Japanese swimmer (whose name I do not remember) who had crossed the Channel successfully in 1952. I narrowly missed the world record set by him by five minutes,' rues Rajaram.

On 22 August 1987 Rajaram became the first Asian and second paraplegic swimmer in the world to successfully cross the English Channel in twelve hours and thirty-five-minutes. What Rajaram has achieved is so mind-boggling that it is nothing short of a superhuman effort. Imagine facing waves as high as a five-storey building, changing currents that are pulling in the opposite directions and swimming against them without the aid of your legs. Rajaram Ghag is no less than a modern superman to have successfully swum the English Channel and that too without the aid of his legs, relying solely on his arms. His achievement is no less than Nick Wallenda, the daredevil who walked a tightrope over the mighty Niagara Falls. His feat can also be compared with the achievements of Oscar Pistorious, the blade runner who broke all barriers of convention and qualified for the 400 metres semi-finals in the 2012 London Olympics.

When Rajaram stepped on to the shore at Calais, France, the sun was just setting and the moon was rising in the sky, and the champion swimmer bowed down in respect to both. With his entourage calling him back to the boat, Rajaram decided to swim back, but could not see the boat due to the huge waves. Carey Dickson and her husband had to come to the shore in a smaller boat to fetch Rajaram. Once he reached the big boat, he was rushed to the heater room where he dozed off to sleep for the next two days.

'Initially, I did want to travel and discover England but I was informed of an extremely tragic news when I woke up. On 23 August, a beautiful young Brazilian swimmer, Renata Agondi who practiced with me for ten days, had died during her attempt. After hearing the tragic news, I decided to return to Mumbai immediately.'

Rajaram returned home to a hero's welcome by his well-wishers. He received a much-awaited promotion from his employers, the Western Railways. However, he was not made an officer which should have been the case, considering his incredible achievement.

After coming back from England, Rajaram represented India at the FESPIC Games for the Disabled in 1989 in Japan. A total of five Indian differently-abled athletes had gone on participate in Osaka. Of these five athletes, three were swimmers, and only Rajaram managed to win one silver and two gold medals in the 50 metres Freestyle, 50 metres Backstroke and 50 metres Breaststroke categories.

'After winning three medals at the FESPIC Games, I thought that I should try out for the Paralympic Games. The office of the Paralympic Committee of India in the year 1989–90 was situated in Kolkata. A certain differently abled gentleman called Mr Tapan Dhan was the President of the committee. Sometimes you know, disabled people do not want their kind to succeed and they go out of their way to put a fellow disabled person down. The typical crab mentality exists in our world also. ₹40,000 were demanded from me in exchange for my participation at the Paralympic Games.'

Corruption had reared its ugly head in sports but his upbringing and his integrity did not allow him to succumb to such demands. An anguished Rajaram had to let his dream of wearing the India colours in the Paralympic Games die. But the champion valiantly fought back and represented India in the 1994 and 1999 FESPIC Games held in China and Thailand respectively.

'Disabled sportspeople may have become world beaters and may have achieved many accolades but in India, we are not given any respect. Only since 1992, disabled athletes have been getting Arjuna Award regularly. However the process seems to be dubious. Some athletes who have been given the prestigious award have never set foot in an international competition. They have been selected for some international event, travelled with team but have never competed. Many a times before 1992, many disabled athletes had to fund themselves as compared to able-bodied athletes whose expenses were always borne by the government. In contrast the disabled athletes were left to fend for themselves.'

Despite becoming the first Asian and only the second paraplegic man to conquer one of the most difficult straits of water in the world, Rajaram has not yet received his dues. His achievements have not been honoured with any award, be it the Arjuna Award, and not even a flat, which the Maharashtra state government awards to sportspersons only, has been granted to him.

In 1990, Rajaram had given an application to the Maharashtra state government for a flat in the sports quota. He met the then chief minister, Sharad Pawar, who recommended that a flat measuring 550 square feet in area be given to the wheelchair-bound champion. 'I went back to Mr Sharad Pawar with another request, asking him for a flat measuring 700 to 800 square feet in area so that I could move more easily with my wheelchair in my house. The flat was sanctioned almost immediately by Mr Pawar but, till today, I have never seen that flat. I met a number of politicians like Sushil Kumar Shinde and Vilasrao Deshmukh but to no avail. Nothing ever came out of it.'

Rajaram firmly believes that physically challenged people must move hell and heaven to achieve their dreams. He also feels that most differently abled individuals, be it physically or even the mentally challenged, should take up swimming to strengthen their body.

'Despite all my achievements, I have looked back at my life and wondered what else could I have done to gain more recognition. I may have crossed the English Channel and won medals for India but my achievements have not been recognized. I have not been given any awards or certificates by the government. It is just as if no one cares about physically challenged sportspersons in India. We are all world-beaters in our own right but we are made to feel like dirt in our own country. This should change.'

After conquering the English Channel, Rajaram went on to coach eight Chatrapati Award winners like para badminton player Satya Prakash Tiwari, para swimmer Manoj Khaire, para rifle shooter and swimmer Shankar Phansekur, to name a few. Rajaram Ghag is now a full-time coach and is committed to helping out and changing the lives of other differently abled people.

DEVENDRA JHAJHARIA
A Real Indian Hero

Courage, is finding the inner strength and bravery required, when confronting danger, difficulty or opposition. Courage is the energy current behind all great actions and the spark that ignites the initial baby steps of growth. It resides deep within each one of us, ready to be accessed in those moments when you need to forge ahead or break through seemingly insurmountable barriers. Courage is that intangible force that propels you forward on your journey.

~CHERIE CARTER-SCOT~

Hardly ever in the annals of Indian sports, since Independence or earlier, has there been a sportsman who has dominated his sport as totally as Devendra Jhajharia has. In fact it may not be possible to find a parallel at all. And here we are referring to the likes of Dhyan Chand, Milkha Singh, Sachin Tendulkar, Prakash Padukone, Vishwanath Anand and Leander Paes among the 'abled' sportsmen of India; and Murlikant Petkar, Rajeev Bagga and others among the luminaries of para sports of India.

Jhajharia, at time of writing this book, is the only Indian to have won a World Championship gold in the one-armed javelin throw, with a world record, in July 2013 at the the France World Para-Athletics Championships. It is only because of him that the tricolour was proudly unfurled for the very first and only time so far, at the main athletics stadium of any world championships, with the national anthem playing in the background.

It is only because of this exceptional athlete that the same scenario was played out in the 2004 Athens Paralympics, when he comfortably won the gold medal in the javelin throw in the F 46 category, which emphasizes his disability. Here, too, he broke the existing Olympics record. He won his first international medal, a gold, at the 2002 FESPIC Games in Korea, setting an Asian record.

Devendra Jhajharia today holds the Asian, the Olympics and the world record in the sport which he loves to dominate. He has broken his own world record four times, and though he missed the 2008 and 2012 Paralympics, both the world and Olympic records still stand in his name.

He was just eight years old when, while playing with his gang of friends, he happened to touch a live electric cable with his left hand and received a shock of 11,000 volts. He was badly burnt, lost consciousness, was almost given up for dead, and even with medical help, when he came to his senses a day later he found to his horror that his left hand had been amputated, as had two small toes of his right leg.

People called him viklang, disabled. He hated that. Born a fighter, he realized that sports was a way out of the depression that was seizing him, his thinking, and came out trumps, beating all odds, to become a true icon. He had had to fight all the way to ensure that his rights were not trampled upon, and to ensure that he got the recognition he truly deserves. His entire journey to this iconic status has been simply a matter of proving that despite his handicap, he could be and indeed was, better than others—that is us able-bodied. Yet, despite having brought untold laurels for the country in world of para-sports, Devendra Jhajharia is still a class four employee of the Indian Railways.

Devendra Jhajharia was born into a farmer's family on 18 June 1981 in a village called Jaipuria Khalsa in the Churu district Rajasthan. The heat in deep summer can cross 50 degrees Celsius and on winter nights fall to a freezing low of minus 5 degrees. There was no electricity in Devendra's village, though high tension cables snaked high up, passing on poles just outside the village, carrying power to the urban areas of Rajasthan. In sum, the village of Jaipuria Khalsa was not an easy place to live in, nor to make a living in, and the Jhajharia family, being educationally and financially weak, faced immense hardships.

Nevertheless, the harsh climate and harsher reality made for strong bodies and minds. Father Ram Singh and Devendra's older brothers worked day and night to get the family two square meals a day. The cruel earth was hard to till, and every day was full of back-breaking tasks. Ladies in the family, including mother Jevini Devi, trekked some half a kilometre, sometimes ten times a day, to pull heavy buckets of water from the village well.

Devendra, as the youngest of seven siblings, was pampered by mother Jevini Devi and by his older siblings. He was usually able to get away from the household chores that others were made to do. Allowed to have his way often, he spent his free time playing with the local village boys. He was a real shararti, naughty, boy, as the household referred to him with affection. Young Devendra was not pressurized to study books. Games and fooling around with his friends was what he really liked.

As a youngster, while the entire family, nay, the entire village was hard at work every day, Devendra and his friends, all between seven and nine years of age, were worried about what new game to play the next day after the local school got over.

'It was a real carefree time for me. I clearly remember those days,' says Devendra, with a twinkle in his eyes. 'I was always outside playing some game or the other. School was basically a bit of rest for us. Games would include kabbadi, football, gilli-danda, kite flying, etc. We were poor but my mother always saw to it that I had enough milk to drink. Our fields were not very big, but my father ensured that though there were no luxuries or fancy clothes at home, we had enough to eat. And I remember that we always had two or three cows at home and I also helped in milking them from a young age. Sometimes I would go to help my father or take his lunch. But whether it was high summer or bitter cold, games were always a priority and enjoyable.'

Most families in the village had at least one member working as a soldier in the armed forces. Says Devendra, it was like a religion. National feelings and duty were sacrosanct. Throughout the year the kids would see soldiers in uniform, either going to their regiments or coming back on leave. Each one of these boys wanted nothing more than being a soldier someday, including the precocious Devendra. 'Like all the boys I also wanted to be a soldier one day and fight on the front against the enemy. We saluted the soldiers whenever we saw them. This was a life I wanted when I grew up. But for now the most important thing was to go out and show the boys what I could do on the playing fields.'

It was during one such game that to hide from his friends he climbed a tree with thick foliage and grabbed a high-tension wire, which was charged with 11,000 volts of electricity. As the current coursed through his body, he fell almost fifteen feet, stunned and unconscious. Young friends gathered around not knowing what to do, till sense prevailed and one of them ran to get Ram Singh. The tearful and horrified family rushed Devendra to a local hospital, where the first thing local doctors did was to amputate his charred and blackened left hand.

He was in a very serious condition and after a couple of days, the family took him to a bigger hospital, the SMS hospital in Jaipur. 'I had become very weak and was not eating anything. Whatever I ate, I vomited. In fact the doctor told my father that though I was lucky to be alive, and would be so weak all my life that it might be difficult to keep me alive! For next few months I was just a skeleton, as my body refused to react to any sort of medicine and rejected most food. My mother tells me that all I did was stare into space. In fact I lost my mental balance for some time. But our scriptures say that even the gods bow before the love of parents. It took all my mother's affection and father's care to slowly bring me around and, after a couple of months, I started to improve and slowly regained strength in my body. My mind became strong and I wanted to go out and play again with my friends. I had lost some six months of schooling by now. I accepted everything because mother called it fate. But what society did to me, hurt me more than what the 11,000 volts of electricity could do.'

Still a child, young Devendra was shunned initially by his friends. They called him viklang and kamzor (handicapped and weak), and refused to play with him. He felt like an outcast and was humiliated. Were these the same boys who had been close friends just a few months ago? In all fairness, these boys were children themselves and were surely parroting what they had heard at home from their elders. It was just society baring its ugly fangs, enveloped in its own cocoon of ignorance and myopia, as it has been for centuries.

Not knowing what handicapped meant, he ran with eyes brimming with tears into the safety of his mother's arms. She soothed him and told him not to worry and stay mentally strong. 'I felt really bad when my friends called me weak. I knew I had lost an arm, but then, was the accident my fault? It could have happened to anyone. I did not go out of the house for a few days, just contemplating what to do. Another thing that used to upset me a lot was when the village ladies would come to meet my mother, and their conversation would inevitably turn to my disability. They would sympathize with my mother as I was viklang and a weakling. They would speak out aloud that I could do nothing in the future and implied that my life was doomed. She always cried after they left, wondering who would look after me when I grew up.'

Time as usual, healed the bitterness and soon enough Devendra was accepted by his young friends and once again became an integral part of their gang. He became mentally aggressive and swore to himself that he would play as hard as the other boys. Come what may, he did not want to be called a weakling. So he gave as good as he got in kabbadi, football or whichever game was being played.

As time passed Devendra became tougher and stronger. By the time he reached the seventh standard, he was *the* well-known footballer in his village and in surrounding areas. He played left-back and was the one boy that opponents feared in a tackle. He realized again that sports was the way for him. He also realized that he needed to have greater stamina and strength than the other boys. On his own, therefore, he started running and jogging, and also started chopping wood with an axe which was quite heavy, but which started building up and strengthening his right arm and shoulder.

By the time he reached the tenth standard he was shifted to a school in nearby Ratanpura village, and there he saw that the school encouraged sports, specifically athletics, with emphasis on running, jumps and throws. For young Devendra, the school was heaven and, he was soon in the thick of everything.

'I went up to a PT teacher who was teaching shot-put throws to a group and asked if I could join. They all said I could but pointed to my left shoulder and implied that I was bound to fail. Even the teacher had a faint smile of sarcasm on his face. But my very first throw was much further than their best. This created a sensation and I was adopted by the teacher who could not believe what he had seen. I had become mentally strong also—with just one goal—to show everyone that despite my handicap, I was not going to be cowed down or accept defeat. I did not want people calling me weak, as this had a negative effect on my mother. I wanted to prove that I could be better than the able-bodied. The very next day at the school-team selections for the district school championships I threw the javelin farther than most, and was selected to play for the school in both the shot-put and the javelin events.'

The rest, as the cliché goes, is history. Devendra Jhajharia never looked back, and though he did win national and international titles and medals in other throws, it was the javelin, or bhaala as he calls it, that became his favourite throw. At Ratanpura he threw the 'junior' javelin a distance of 47.5 metres and was placed second.* In the same year, 1995, he gotmanaged the fourth position in the javelin event at the State School Championships. The next year he won the State Championships, something he was to repeat at both junior and senior levels for years.

By now he was seriously into this sport and had fashioned himself a javelin of bamboo with a spear attached to the tip to

*Meant for children under sixteen, this javelin weighs 600 grams.

give it some semblance of the actual thing. Though he still did not have any expert guiding him, Devendra was happy with his running, chopping wood and throwing the bhaala hundreds of times every week, and dominating the Rajasthan State Athletics scene in his event. He was competing and regularly defeating his able-bodied opponents.

It was around the end of 1999 that he learnt of the National Para Games, and that the year-2000 edition was to be held in Bengaluru. He decided to take part in it, following his first All India Inter-University Championships. By this time Devendra had moved on to enrol at Mohta College in Sadarpur Rajgarh, a tehsil near his village and had broken the record at his own university even though they used an aluminium javelin, which he did not much care for. Yet he easily won the gold with a 61 metre heave.

He was given the highly sophisticated javelin used internationally for the very first time in the Inter-University Championships in Gwalior. Unable to grip it properly, though, he ended up a distant seventh in the field of some forty athletes. But he was noticed as he was the only disabled athlete in the fray. He threw an impressive 61 metres, but was outclassed in the event. Made with a special type of steel, the javelin was expensive, at almost ₹20,000, and he had no means financially or otherwise to procure one of these. But destiny was going to change as far as he was concerned.

Despite the fact that there was no para-athletic team from Rajasthan, and without much knowledge of the National Para Games, Devendra and one more athlete decided to come down to Bengaluru. The journey to the stadium was a nightmare which still haunts him. 'I did not know any English and no one spoke Hindi in Bengaluru. We reached the city and then it took us three hours to reach Kanteerva Stadium by autorickshaw. We had exhausted all our resources and it was late in evening. We took shelter in a Ganesh temple outside the stadium for two nights and even though the priest offered us food, we declined. It was a very embarrassing time for us. We found out that though there was a one-armed javelin throw competition, we could not take part as Rajasthan did not have a para-sports association and had not sent any entry. But Lord Ganesh smiled upon us and I met some athletes from Hisar, in Haryana. They talked to their manager and he agreed to make us part of his entourage, on the condition that I try my best to get a medal. I told him I would win the gold—nothing less.' And he did.

Devendra was now a national champion. He repeated this feat the next year, winning the 2001 title. In between, on the advice of one of the athletes from Hisar, a town that happens to be just a hundred kilometres away from Jaipuria Khalsa, his father Ram Singh wrote a letter to a very benevolent and helpful non-resident Indian (NRI), Mr Ram Swaroop Arya, requesting help to buy the ₹20,000 steel-tempered javelin. Mr Arya lived in America but was always looking to help Indians in need, especially in sports. Much to the surprise and delight of the Jhajharia family, Mr Arya immediately got him the javelin. This helped Devendra hugely as he was now able to practice with the right equipment.

The javelin expert was now on a roll. After winning the 2001 National Para title he was selected to represent India at the 2002 Far East South Pacific (FESPIC) Games at Busan, Korea. The only question was how to get there, because the government of India did not fund para-athletes*. The athletes and the Paralympic Committee of India (PCI) were thus left to their own devices. The PCI was not of much help in any case. It wrote to Devendra

*The government of India began funding para-athletes only from 2006 onward.

informing him that he had been selected and would be required to deposit ₹75,000 towards all his expenses, including air-fare, boarding, lodging, and other expenses.

Stumped and not knowing what else to do, he turned to the state government, which informed him of rules which said that the selected athlete must first compete and then claim reimbursement. Devendra found this very silly. 'I am approaching you since I do not have the resources to go—I cannot afford it. If I cannot go, then obviously I cannot come back and claim a refund. This was bizarre. The government rules existed only to make fools of us. I wanted to train and bring India a gold, but there was no one to listen to me and I did not want to waste time going round in circles. I got Ram Swaroop Arya's phone number from my friends in Hisar and described the situation to him. I also told him I was confident of winning the gold and faxed him the selection letter.'

Devendra reveres Mr Arya. He did not disappoint the young javelin thrower who had dreams in his eyes. The amount was dispatched promptly and Devendra flew to Busan where destiny awaited him with open arms.

This was his first international event where, in the very first attempt he threw some 52 metres. 'One official from our team told me that Asian record was 56.27 metres, which I should aim for. My second attempt was a good 57.15 metres and I was in the gold position already with a new Asian record. There was lot of applause and local Korean officials shook my hand. One of them, knowing I did not understand English, wrote on my hand that the world record was 59.38 metres, very much achievable by me. I tried, but 57.15 metres remained my best throw, the major reason being that I did not have spike-studded shoes for my run-in. I had ordinary canvas shoes. We never trained in India with spikes. They not only ensure that you get more speed in the run-in, you also never slip as your feet are firmly grounded due to the spikes at front. This helps to have a better control. I vowed to buy the spikes and train in them as soon as I returned to India.'

Upon return the team was felicitated by then prime minister Atal Behari Vajpayee, who announced cash awards to all medallists. Devendra received a cheque for ₹5 lakh—a much needed amount if he was to continue his sports career. Incidentally, after the prime minister announced the cash award in front of media, the government of Rajsthan contacted Devendra and offered him a further ₹75,000 as the refund of his expenses to Busan. He was now ready to see the tricolour flutter proudly all over the world. The next stop was the British Open, an invitational international para-athletics event held in Birmingham in 2003.

His sight was now firmly set on the world record. He trained really hard in his village prior to departure with only one goal in mind. At Birmingham, the second throw saw him conquer the world with a heave of 59.77 metres, easily breaking the 59.38 metres record which had lasted for six years. He also won a gold medal in the triple jump, which is an optional combination event with the javelin, and also the gold in the shot-put throw. Devendra was now a hero among Indian para-athletes and was so impressive that a couple of British officials asked him to stay back in the United Kingdom (UK) and start representing them after two years. They also offered financial compensation. 'But I refused. India is my country, I told them, and I love my country and will play only for India. It does not matter if we are rich or poor, we are still Indians and I want to do my country proud.'

By that time the Athens Paralympic Games were round the corner, and very much on Devendra's radar. He started training in earnest with just one goal again—to win gold at the Games. In between, he competed in the 2003 All India University

Championships and this time claimed the third spot in the 'open' category. This boosted his morale. One dampener was to still haunt him for some time. Neither the state nor the central government recognized the Para Games or the para-athletes. The cash award from Vajpayee, after the gold at Busan, was a one-off, which he had announced from the Prime Minister's Fund. And though Devendra was clear in his mind that the focus was to remain on the Athens Games, he still felt troubled by the non-recognition from the authorities. A clash of sorts was brewing. By this time, he had joined the Railways as a class-four employee, the best that could be offered to him under the existing guidelines. He was offered the job after throwing 66 metres at the Inter University meet where he had snatched the bronze medal from a big field of able-bodied athletes.

Athens beckoned. He was going as a world record holder. Rajasthan Sports Minister Younis Khan saw him off saying that he expected a medal. Devendra replied that nothing less than a gold medal would satisfy him or his family. 'If you get a gold for India and Rajasthan, we will give you a felicitation that will be remembered for some time to come,' said the minister.

Devendra was the flag bearer of the Indian squad at the opening ceremony. 'I remember I had tears in my eyes as I walked around the main stadium, proud to be an Indian. Waving our flag, one thought struck me—the tricolour had never been unfurled at the main stadium of any Olympics—for the abled or the disbled, as national flags are unfurled only at winning the gold. And no one from India had ever won the gold in any athletic competition ever*.'

---

*Murlikant Rajaram Petkar had won the 1972 Heidelburg Paralympic gold in swimming and received the medal at the swimming stadium, not the main stadium.

Devendra swore to himself that he would ensure the tricolour was unfurled at the main stadium, and the world would applaud. There were twenty-eight other throwers. And in the very first throw of 58 metres, the Indian ace broke the existing Olympic record of 55.67 metres. 'In my next four throws I broke my own world record three times and my last throw as 62.15 meters, remains the world record even today. I must say here that apart from winning the gold and seeing our flag being unfurled, one other great moment for me was when President Kalam sent me a congratulatory message and spoke to me when I was still in Athens. So did our nation's Sports Minister Sunil Dutt and my state's sport minister, Younis Khan. Upon return I was given a great reception in Delhi. In Jaipur Younis Khan, true to his word, announced an award of ₹11 lakh at a grand reception. The same year the state government announced the Maharana Pratap Award and I was the first disabled sportsman to get it.'

The government of India also announced the coveted Arjuna Award for Devendra in 2005. However he faced a lot of difficulty in getting the ₹30 lakh cash-prize that was awarded to Olympics gold medal winners, and which should have come to him automatically. It took six years of pursuing for him to finally get the amount in 2010. Though resigned and quiet about it now, Devendra was bitter about the entire process early on. The media also supported him in a big way.

Sandipan Sharma wrote in the *Indian Express* on 9 March 2005 that at the Government of India's awards night to felicitate international-level Indian award winners, Devendra Jhajharia was conspicuous by his absence. Sharma wrote, 'The only Indian to have won a gold at an "Olympic" was missing. While Sports Minister Sunil Dutt feted winners of even the ten-pin bowling competition, the one-armed javelin gold medallist Devendra

Jhajharia was completely ignored. Jhajharia had also created a world record when he hurled the missile at 62.15 metres. Before him no Indian had ever won a medal in athletics at that level. Said Jhajharia, "I was expecting a call from the ministry for the awards function, but they did not call, they did not recognize my achievement at all." PCI official Raghunath said that "Sports Minister had promised cash awards on par with winners of Olympic medals. We do not know why the promise was not kept and why the gold medallist was not invited." Pointedly, Raghunath said it was a shame that the government did not encourage people who triumph internationally in spite of their handicaps.'

The article further stated that Devendra's father Ram Singh was upset that his son had been ignored. The article, quoted his father, as saying 'Devendra is only a class four employee of the Railways. Our resources are very limited. The government says they will give special attention to people with handicaps. Look at how my son is being treated. The Rajasthan Government announced cash and a flat in Jaipur. But after all these months we have no word on the flat.'

Devendra is philosophical about the whole thing. 'I told the media and the government, I have done my job, got the gold for India. Now you do your job and give me the promised award. Sunil Dutt was sympathetic and did mention that my achievement was more than any able bodied sportsperson and recommended that I be treated at par. But since the government did not recognize para-sports, they could not give us awards. I fought against this for many years. Many ministers came and went but finally, in 2010, I did get the recognition I deserved along with so many of my fellow para-athletes.'

The real irony was that till the 2004 Athens para-games, the government of India did not even pay the air-fares and other expenses of such athletes. Shamefully, Devendra Jhajharia the first Indian to win a track-and-field gold at any Olympics, paid his own expenses all the way through. However it was Sunil Dutt who put things right and thereafter the para team for the very first time had all its expenses paid while participating in the 2006 Asia Paralympic Games in Malaysia.

'We must recognize their achievements, especially that of Devendra Jhajharia who has broken the world record many times and claimed the gold,' wrote Sunil Dutt in 2005 before demitting office. This process finally ended when KPS Gill handed over the cheque of ₹30 lakh to an emotional Devendra. 'My fight, my struggle was not for the cash award—it was for recognition of all para-athletes, who have over and over again proven they are as good as their abled brothers. Why was such discrimination practiced against us? That was the crux of the question facing us.'

Devendra Jhajharia continued to win the national para title every year and soon the 2006 Asia Paralympic Games were upon the scene. He focused on breaking the world record of 62.15 metres, which in any was in his name. Heavy rain showers prohibited the breaking of the world record, but he did throw a respectable 60.92 metres to break his own Asian record. He was now twenty-five years old, at the very pinnacle of his remarkable career.

The next year, in 2007, the International Wheelchair and Amputees Sports Federation (IWAS) World Games were held in Taiwan, Chinese Taipei, some two months after he got married. He had a shoulder injury and could manage only a silver, with a 55 metre throw. Many people laughed and told him that his marriage had distracted him. Even his wife joked that society would fling mud at her, since he had lost the gold medal for the very first time in his international career. 'But I told her not to worry. Forget society, this husband of yours promises you a gold in the very next tournament, just to snub these so-called friends of ours,' chuckles Devendra, recalling his conversation with his wife. He redeemed that pledge and won the gold in the 2009 IWAS Games in Bangalore with a 57.15 metre throw. He also won a silver in the discus throw.

Devendra then was struck down by a major knee injury, which slowed him down a bit. His career also went adrift for a few years when, after the 2006 Asia Paralympic Games, the International Paralympic Committee (IPC) omitted the one-armed javelin event category F 46 from its programme for the 2008 and 2012 Olympics and the Asian committee therefore omitted it from the 2010 Asia Paralympic Games. So barring the IWAS in 2007 and 2009, Devendra Jhajharia did not have any international competition to compete in.

The Indian Committee did appoint him as coach for the London Games, but since his knee injury had not yet healed, he did not accept the assignment and refused to go with the squad. 'I did not think it right on my part to accept the job as I was injured myself. I told IPC to take someone else to help the squad.' However, Devendra made the mistake of training while the injury was yet to fully heal and this compounded the problem, though only for a short while.

By the end of 2012 he was feeling much better. Devendra found out that the F 46 category was very much a part of the 2013 IPC World Athletics Championships, an event as important as the Paralympics itself. With the world record still intact and in his name, he stood a very good chance of being the first Indian to win a gold at Lyons, France, where the event was to be held in July 2013 even though he had not competed internationally for almost five years. With six months in hand, and as much motivation as earlier, he started training in earnest to reach his peak form by the time the championships came along.

Incidentally this was his first IPC World Championships. In 2011 the Indian body had 'forgotten' to enter a team at the Championships being held in Christchurch, New Zealand. In 2007 and in 2009 an Indian team wasn't sent due to infighting within the IPC.

Prior to the World Championships, Devendra had to qualify, which he did at the German Open with a 55 metres throw in May 2013. He also wanted to get into the competitive mode once again. He managed to attain the world number one ranking in Germany. That same year he had shown his fitness by claiming the gold in the shot-put, discus and javelin throw events at the National Championships.

In France, he led the field of eleven throwers, with a heave of 54.71 metres. But it was his effort of 57.04 metres that sealed the gold and a new championship record. 'This was a culmination of equal measures of disappointment, hard work and pain, spread over several years, for Jhajharia,' wrote Mihir Vaswada in the *Indian Express* on 23 July 2013. He also quoted Devendra as saying, 'I had only this World Championships to look forward to and participate in, after so many years. Obviously the morale was down. For any sportsperson it is important to compete regularly at the highest levels.'

Today there is no one in the country from any sporting discipline who can claim to be good enough to rub shoulders with this mighty athlete. He holds the world record, the gold in World Championships, the Paralympic gold and record, and the Asian Games gold and record. In sheer achievement no one can touch him. He is also ranked world number one. The government could have announced the Rajeev Gandhi Khel Ratna award in

2013, the timing was right, but somehow he was missed out. Vaswada hopes that at least in 2014, the country will rise to the occasion and recognize the huge and unparalleled achievements this man has garnered.

Vaswada further writes that Jhajharia used the latest technology to compile videos of the best javelin throwers in the world to ensure his own technique kept on improving. He quotes the ace athlete, 'What happened in these intervening years was not in my control. I knew I would again get a chance some day to prove myself and it came with these World Championships. I kept myself motivated and did not allow negative thoughts to creep in. I will confess that by my own standards, I did not have great throws in first few attempts. But I did not give up and broke the championship record with my last throw. I may not be physically fit, as compared to an able-bodied, but I have made myself very strong mentally—perhaps more than able-bodied. And I think this is my biggest strength.'

Today this valiant Indian has laid low the ghost that haunted him early on. No one refers to him as weak or handicapped any more. Yes the horrific accident when he was just eight years old has left a scar in his life. He lost his left arm and over the years he has managed to accept his problem. 'I am handicapped and I accept that. But I am not weakened by it and I am not weak. I have proved that over and over again. I am satisfied with the way my life has turned out to be and I look forward to the next challenge. The next Paralympics in Rio, Brazil in 2016, is my one big target. God willing I will again get the gold for India. And before that I will get a chance to break my world record at the 2014 Asia Paralympic Games.'

His dream of becoming a soldier was shattered when he lost his arm. But then in his own way he has fought and taken on the world on his terms and emerged triumphant. He has made the country proud. There are some regrets yes, and he is out there fighting for his fellow para-athletes, who have got the short end of the stick. 'I am happy with the way Indian Railways has treated me. Today I am respected in the Railways but my status is still that of a class-four employee. But in a way I am happy as I have also received many rewards from the Railways, including a cheque for ₹5 lakh on winning the World Championships.' However what continues to sadden him is that 'so many of us have no jobs.'

The last sports minister had announced grade-one public sector jobs for all Olympians, but sadly says Devendra, those promises have not been met. 'Players like Farman Pasha, fourth in Olympics and Girisha, who won a silver at London, have no jobs. This is very sad. If we can't get our top athletes that recognition and respect, then how we can show the way to the new generation of sportsmen.'

It is not just our elected representatives, the state or central government ministers who should be held responsible, feels Devendra. After all, as he says, the government is but a facet of society. Representatives are elected from amongst the general public and will reflect what society at large feels. Can he suggest some ways to suggest how a change in our mindset can be brought about? Can sports be a way out of difficult circumstances, as it has been for him and several others?

'From my experience I can say that playing sports is one way out. The handicapped person can show his strength, his commitment to society through sports. Personally I feel that for handicapped children sports must be made compulsory. They will learn so many things like fair play, competition, how to overcome failure—they will have a purpose to live.'

Devendra also feels that the way society looks at the

handicapped people must change. This is very important. 'Society must change its outlook. The government cannot do everything. Society must give us a level playing field in everything and also give us recognition. Most handicapped people can contribute if allowed. I will give you one example of how the handicapped are looked at abroad. In France after I won the gold medal, one mother brought her handicapped seven-year-old to me. She was accompanied by a few friends. She stopped and introduced me to her son in French. She explained to me what she was doing. She told her son to one day be a world champion like me. She was trying to motivate him and also tell him at same time that having a handicap was not the end of the world.'

'Here in our country,' adds the champion, 'the first thing done is to tell the handicapped member of the family to sit at home and do nothing. The family members themselves make our lives more miserable. Abroad, the handicapped are out and working. They have special toilets, special buses, ramps for wheelchairs—all over. Do we see anything like that here in India? I am telling you the bitter facts. The parents are the first to make a handicapped child stay at home as they are afraid to hear the barbs of the society. The outer world is even more cruel, implying that a handicapped person has no place outside the house. He, or she, will suffer, along with the family members. I have seen it so often. So, I feel that forget the government, let us first change the way society looks at us handicapped people.' He feels that once society changes, the government will also change its outlook.

He says that a para-sports facility must be available in every school and there should be at least two championships or events annually, so that society at large sees their spirit, and the children are able to confidently face the outside world. It is only after the handicapped are brought into the open and accepted as equal citizens, will society change, Devendra feels. If society and the government work in tandem, the private sector will also be motivated to come out and offer jobs to the handicapped, he feels.

He says that anyone could suffer the misfortune of having an accident and becoming handicapped. In any case, all of us will become handicapped in a way, after we cross seventy years of age, he philosophizes. 'As it is, 6 to 7 per cent of Indians have a physical disability of some kind or the other. That is a huge number. If we add to that huge figure the 70-plus age group, we may well have almost 20 to 25 per cent citizens who need special care. Our society must think on this with utmost seriousness. We need the changes now, so that we see the result in next five years or so.'

Talking specifically on para-sports, he reflects on how each and every stadium he has visited a broad, has in-built facilities for para-athletes. There are wheelchair toilets, wheelchair water drinking areas, changing areas, and so on. 'We have nothing like that in this country, simply because we have never given this a serious thought.' The great para-athletes in Indian have made it themselves without any facilities. 'Abroad, the paras have more facilities than do abled athletes. They have coaches, trainers and helpers, dieticians who help out—in short there is a full system available. The able-bodied may be made to struggle, but in my view, no para-athlete is made to suffer. And the problem is that we handicapped do not have a religion, caste or creed. We are nobody's vote bank. If we were, and imagine how many crores we are in India, then surely the government and society would have looked upon us differently. We are isolated.'

Devendra Jhajharia is very grounded and very pro-India in his outlook. As far as training is concerned he has benefitted immensely by using local systems. No far-fetched ideas or swanky gyms for him. Getting up at 4 a.m. every day, winter or summer, he is out for a long cross-country run, alternating with speed runs and sprints. Special care is given to strengthening the thighs and calves. 'High speed, jump and sudden stop are the keys for throwing well. So the legs have to be very strong. For this I repeatedly run up small hillocks. For shoulder and arm strength I chop wood and also stretch a cycle tube. This helps in getting the right trajectory when I throw the javelin up in the air. I do not like to workout in gyms as I feel no need. We all can evolve our own system. Training in my village has made me an Olympian and a world champion. I train about five to six hours daily when preparing for a big meet. So the system is good.'

He emphasizes that there are no short cuts for success. One has to sweat it out, handicapped or not. Excellence in sport cannot be achieved by sitting on our haunches, adds Devendra. He also swears by milk—drinking two litres daily along with sweet lime juice, daily intake of almonds and local chana (gram). He is quite satisfied with what he has achieved so far. Yet there are times when the anger against an unjust government and society surfaces. For example when he returned from the World Championships in July 2013, he told *DNA*, 'I did not get even a congratulatory message after I won the World Championships, unlike in 2004 when I won the Olympics. This is the tragedy of para-athletes in India. Generally, the sports ministry is quick to congratulate Olympic or World Championship medallists. But after so many days I am yet to get a call from the government. I am an Olympic Gold medallist and a world champion, but still a grade four employee. It is a tragedy, but a fact of life. The sports ministry had promised a grade one job in SAI to any Indian winning an Olympic or world championships medal, (in fact the minister said that just representing India at these events would be good enough), but the promises have not been kept. There is discrimination between abled and disabled athletes in India. This should be wiped out. We too have won medals and brought glory to the motherland. There is no approved policy for us. While the abled Olympians get jobs—we get nothing'

Devendra Jhajharia has come a long way from the little eight-year-old who suffered an amputation. It could have ruined him mentally. He almost died after that horrendous accidental electrocution. While growing up he was made to feel different from other children. He was called weak and handicapped—words that he came to hate. Today he has proven them all wrong. He has, one javelin throw after another, proved to the world that he is better than most of us.

He has a really thought provoking answer to this last question put to him—Is showing sympathy to a handicapped person an answer to their problems?

'No, we do not need sympathy, or any show of it. You do not solve a problem for a wheelchair-bound person by picking him up and then depositing him on top of a staircase. That is not a solution to his permanent problem. Why not make a ramp for him, so he can face the problem of climbing the height himself. He needs that freedom, but the society must provide the facility. We are part of you, whether you like it or not. That is all we ask for. Give us a level playing field and then see what we are made of.'

Devendra Jhajharia was honoured last year with the Padma Shri by the government of India. In a statement after receiving the award he touched another raw and emotional nerve. Something we, the so-called able-bodied, would do well to dwell upon. 'The honour given to me by the people of this country, is an honour for all those parents and caregivers of children or family members who are born handicapped, or unfortunately are in that state due to disease or injury. These parents and caregivers fight all sorts of obstacles and embarrassments, poverty and exclusion from society, to try give as normal a life as they can to the handicapped. How difficult it must be for them, when they do not know what tomorrow will bring for people under their constant care They are as much victims as the invalid himself. They too deserve help and affection of the society at large.'

We Indians must indeed be thankful that someone as iconic as Devendra Jhajharia has walked amidst us and touched us with his greatness.

MALATHI HOLLA
Queen of Her Chariot

We are the music-makers,
And we are the dreamers of dreams,
Wandering by lone sea-breakers,
And sitting by desolate streams.
World-losers and world-forsakers,
Upon whom the pale moon gleams;
Yet we are the movers and shakers,
Of the world forever, it seems.

~ARTHUR O'SHAUGHNESSY~

On 6 July 1958, a young mother, Padmavati Holla, gave birth to her fourth child, a girl, in a nondescript village called Dasra Canara in South Canara district near the picturesque city of Mangalore. This, the chief port city of Karnataka, is located close to the Udipi district which is not only famous for its food but also for its inhabitants, who are called the Shettys.

Father Krishnamurthy Holla's joy knew no bounds as he announced the latest addition to the family to all his relatives. The newborn baby girl was named Malathi. True to the tradition of the Udipi district, the young couple did the only work they knew, the Udipi restaurant business that saw them migrating from the sleepy village to the state capital, Bengaluru, in search of better prospects.

Malathi reminiscences, 'I was born a very normal child. My parents used to say that I had actually started walking when I was only nine months old. I believe it was very difficult to hold me down as all I wanted to do was walk, run and play. Since I was the baby of the family, everyone wanted to hold me and mollycoddle me. I was actually a pampered child.'

Just as things were progressing joyfully in the Holla household, tragedy struck. Fourteen-month-old Malathi was struck down by a fever. Many tests later, Padmavati and Krishnamurthy Holla's worst fears were realized as Malathi was found to have been infected by the dreaded polio virus. Life changed drastically, not only for the young child, but also for her family.

'The virus affected my body right up to my neck. Only my neck was functioning properly till I was five and, other than that, my entire body was paralysed. I also lost the function of everything, including my eyes and my tongue. I was completely bedridden till the age of five.'

Young Malathi's parents were not too financially well-off as they were still getting their bearings. Determined to provide a decent life for her daughter, Padmavati Holla used to carry her, changing two buses en route, to the government-run Victoria Hospital in Bengaluru, so that Malathi could get treatment for her affliction. 'Victoria Hospital was government-run, so the treatment for me was free. In those days, the only treatment that was recommended by doctors was physiotherapy and electric shock. Electric shocks were basically given to shock the paralysed muscles into some action. Two years of my mother's struggles helped make the upper part of my body functional.' Two years of electric shocks had jolted and lifted the paralysis from the young girl's upper body. Unfortunately Malathi's lower body had been badly ravaged by polio and no amount of electric shocks could jolt it into action. The gritty youngster had to undergo two operations in Victoria Hospital and it was here that one of the doctors offered a ray of hope.

A doctor treating the young child forced Krishnamurthy and Padmavati to think about the kind of life their daughter would lead if she were alone. He told them that Malathi should lead her life unaffected even if her parents were to die tomorrow. This statement forced her parents to make one of the biggest sacrifices of their life as they got her admitted to a rehabilitation centre in Chennai. In 1963, young Malathi was admitted to the Iswari Prasad Dattatrey Rehabilitation Centre in Chennai. Here, Malathi met many other children who were suffering from similar and even worse conditions than her.

'For fifteen long years, I was brought up amongst 150 or so children at the Centre in Chennai. From the age of five years till I turned almost twenty, I lived at its hospital. Along with treating polio, the hospital authorities also educated all the children living there. I finished my tenth standard in Chennai and eventually underwent almost nineteen surgeries to enable my upper body to function properly.'

Malathi's condition was called Post Polio Residual Paralysis or PPRP in medical parlance. It is a nerve contracture where a given nerve gets contracted in a given place of a human body and can only be released through surgery. Being a young child, Malathi was very naughty and did not have a full understanding of the seriousness of polio. By her own admission, the differently abled athlete remembers going to the operation theatre for major operations and then just getting out of the theatre for the heck of it. Being an active child with constraints, she was quite prone to fracturing her hands or legs. So, nineteen surgeries had to be carried out not only to correct PPRP but also to correct her fractured limbs. Once a year, the differently abled athlete would visit her family in Bengaluru but her heart was always left behind with some of her friends who were languishing at the rehabilitation centre in Chennai.

'I would visit my house for a month in Bengaluru but I was always very keen to go back. There were some children who were languishing there for the longest time as their parents probably thought that their responsibility was over once their child was admitted to the rehab centre. Such parents do not come to visit their children but only keep sending their monthly fees. Such children usually had nowhere to go and would only stay at the hospital. With all this going on in the back of my mind, I was always very keen to get back to Chennai even when I was visiting Bengaluru.

'The doctors wanted to strengthen our shoulders and, in order to do that, we had to compensate in some way for our legs. I used to walk with the help of callipers and crutches, but I always felt that I was being punished somehow. So actually, the exercises were quite therapeutic but we always thought that we were being punished for some mischief we had done. I used to hide myself in the washroom to escape the exercises but would always be dragged out the next day and be given double punishment for my deed. Now looking back I realize that those years made up the golden period of my life. In fact, whatever I am today and everything I have achieved today is because of those extra punishments.'

The silver lining for the children at the rehabilitation centre was provided by sports competitions organized by various non-governmental organizations (NGOs) on 3 December, International Day of People with Disability. The afflicted children would compete fiercely with one another to come first. In fact, Malathi was so competitive that she always stood first and won a prize. She always competed in the 50 metres wheelchair and crutch races (where a participant has to run 50 metres using a crutch), winning both easily. The winning participants were seldom awarded any medals but were given more useful items like tiffin boxes and geometry sets.

'I never used to miss my family but only missed my father who would come to visit me once or twice a month. He would arrive on Saturday, stay in a small hotel, meet me and leave on Sunday evening. I never missed the rest of my family as they seldom visited. My mother was a very emotional lady who would faint on seeing the plight of children who were worse than me.'

Malathi would seldom spend time at home during her visits to Bengaluru. Her brothers were so overjoyed that they would carry her around and show her things that she would have missed. Padmavati was not so carried away with Malathi's visits and would delouse her daughter's hair as the young girl's thick hair was always infested with lice.

The long years at the rehabilitation centre also taught Malathi not to be a fussy eater. The quality of food that was given to the young children was not up to the mark and usually had worms. Malathi would just set the worms to one side of her plate and eat the rest of the food without batting an eyelid.

'I am not a fussy eater as I have eaten the worst quality of food for fifteen years in Chennai. We could not even blanch or just throw away bad food as nothing would be given to us to eat as a form of punishment the next day. Even today all my junior athletes sometimes laugh at me when they see me eating, as I eat simple food, maybe just a handful of rice and some rasam. For fifteen years in Chennai, I did not see proper vegetables; it was only after I came back to Bengaluru did I realize what vegetables were.'

After completing the tenth standard, Malathi returned to her family in Bengaluru. The seventeen-year-old had scored a distinction in her tenth standard board exams and was looking forward to a bright future. In fact, the gritty teenager aspired to become a doctor. She recalls how she used to threaten her doctors with amputation once she became a doctor, to pay them back for the pain they caused her and her friends after each operation. She still remembers cursing the doctors after each operation due to the huge amount of physical pain she suffered during her stay at the centre in Chennai.

'My inspiration to become a doctor was a polio-inflicted spastic inmate called Rajni who also lived at the centre in Chennai. I met her when I was about seven or eight years old, and she was ten years older than me at that time. When faced with the monthly female menstruation cycle, she did not know what was happening to her and did not know what to do. Such was her plight that she could not even tell the attendants to prepare her for her problem. I would see her dragging herself and trying to ask someone to help her. Finally the attendants would understand and prepare her for the menstruation cycle.'

Rajni's plight had such a lasting impact on Malathi's mind that she learnt how to prepare her for the monthly cycle. In fact if the attendant would ever get late in helping Rajni, the young girl would take over that role and help change Rajni's clothes and give her cloth pads to soak up the blood. In fact, Rajni's plight still haunts her to this day.

'I relocated to Bengaluru in 1973 and joined a pre-university course (PUC) at the Maharani Lakshmi Ammanni College her admission form had been given in by an NGO. My second day at college coincided with the National Sports Day for the Handicapped, which was being celebrated at college. A local NGO had organized various sporting events for handicapped children sponsored by various NGOs across the country.'

As luck would have it, Malathi's old teammates were coming to Bengaluru to take part in that event. They requested her to team up with them so that they could win some events. Since the youngster was not representing any NGO, she decided to wear the colours of her old team. With no wheelchair at her disposal, Malathi was forced to borrow one from Shehnaz Kirmani, the national champion in wheelchair racing. The budding athlete won the gold medal in the 60 metres obstacle and the 50 metres wheelchair races. Malathi was also awarded the silver medal in the javelin throw and the shot-put categories, coming in second behind Shehnaz Kirmani.

'Seeing my performance and the strength in my shoulders, Shehnaz encouraged me. She told me that I certainly had the scope to improve in sports. At that time I did not quite understand her as I knew only two languages, Tamil and Kannada. Later Mrs Laxmi Nizamuddin [whose NGO had organized this meet] encouraged me and said that her NGO would register me and that I had to start representing them in tournaments.'

A new partnership was forged and Malathi started playing for the National Society for Equal Opportunities for the Handicapped's (NASEOH's) Karnataka branch. Till 1981 the budding sportswoman represented the NGO and Karnataka in all state and national games across the country. It was, in fact, Mrs Laxmi Nizamuddin, the NASEOH head, who had given Malathi's admission form to the Maharani College in Bengaluru.

While her wish of attending college was granted, Malathi was finding it increasingly difficult to attend classes as they were all situated on the third floor. By the time she would climb three floors on her calipers and crutches, holding books in her hand, the lecture would be over. For the first few days of college, Malathi Holla was unable to attend any lectures.

'Initially I came back with many dreams and ambitions but slowly they just faded away and reality began to sink in. For fifteen years I was queen of the hospital, I never knew the meaning of an inferiority complex but when I came here, my entire body was filled with complexes.' After attending or rather trying to attend her classes for a few of days, Malathi told her father that she wanted to discontinue education. Her uneducated but worldly-wise father patiently listened to her problems and advised her to accept her world and herself as she was, with her disability. He also advised her to demand her rights from others to overcome her problems.

Malathi approached her college principal the very next day, who patiently listened to her problems and transferred all of the youngster's classes to the ground floor. This incident proved to be the turning point for Malathi, who decided to do something worthwhile with her life. The budding champion thoroughly enjoyed college life while continuing sports alongside and was soon ranked national number two in her disability class in the country. Destiny, however, was soon to take another turn.

Malathi recalls that she was in her second year B.A. when, 'Someone advised my father to approach corporate houses for a job for me that very day, as everyone was celebrating World Disabled Day. At that time, one of the prime nationalized banks, Syndicate Bank, had a branch close to our house and my father had a bit of hold in their head office. So he collected all my sports certificates and they were impressed enough to give me a job. In fact, I even got to select the branch that I wanted to work at.' Malathi then took the heart-breaking decision to quit studying and to complete her graduation privately. The budding champion's sporting career started professionally soon after, as she had to represent her new employers who went all out to support her.

In 1981, Malathi got a chance to represent her bank and Karnataka state at a national event held in Ahmedabad. The budding champion had undergone her twenty-sixth surgery just a month earlier. As luck would have it, Malathi was the only athlete registered in her category. The organizers informed her that she would have to withdraw from the event because at least four registered athletes were required to participate. Malathi, not ready to take no for an answer, announced that she would participate in the men's category. The organizers were dumbstruck, as was her brother who had accompanied her, but it was the only solution that Malathi could see. 'We had come such a long way from Bengaluru to Ahmedabad and it did not make any sense to return home without participation. I did not know the rules and had no clue about my competitors. Everyone started laughing at me when I informed everyone of my decision to participate in the 100 metres wheelchair race.' However, seeing Malathi's enthusiasm, the organizers granted her she was given a 15 metres handicap by the organizers, which meant that while the others would have to complete 100 metres, she would only have to run 85 metres.

Reaching the starting line, Malathi glanced at her fellow competitors. It was a sight that made her pray to the Almighty; all the men were tough, war-wounded defence services personnel. Her heart sank for a moment as she wondered if she had made the right decision to compete with men, but she calmed herself down. She had absolutely no delusions or expectations of winning anyway, she only prayed not to be the athlete who finished last. The race began, she just closed her eyes and began wheeling herself and lo and behold, she finished first, ahead of all the servicemen.

'This race gave me a lot of confidence and led me to realize that physical strength is not important at all; only mental strength is important in a human being. This was a big stepping stone in my life. After this incident I started moulding myself into a professional athlete who knew no bounds. I have not looked back since that day.'

In that year, 1981, she competed in the 100 and 200 metres wheelchair dashes, and in the shot-put and javelin throw categories. Within a short span of time Malathi Holla became a force to reckon with in Indian para-sports. In 1988 she went international at the Paralympic Games in Seoul. A state body affiliated to the Indian Olympic Committee (IOC), had recommended her name and the elated national champion entered the 100 and 200 metres wheelchair races.

'We were a contingent of about four athletes. There were only two or three days left for departure, and our visas had yet to be cleared. So the contingent went to Shastri Bhavan where noted politician Margaret Alva, then minister of state for sports, had her office. Since she too hailed from Karnataka, the others pushed me to request her to release our visa forms. She was probably in a really bad mood and asked me angrily, "Who do you think you are? You think you are P.T. Usha? When she is coming back empty-handed, what do you think you guys are going to go and do there?" I got a little upset and told her very calmly, "P.T. Usha is P.T. Usha, Malathi Holla is Malathi Holla. P.T. Usha cannot sit on a wheelchair and push for 100 metres and Malathi Holla cannot run on her feet for 200 metres. Instead of comparing us, you should clear my papers as I might just reach the finals and come back. You cannot predict the future." So Margaret Alva promptly released our forms and the Indian Paralympics contingent managed to reach Seoul just in time.'

Nevertheless, this Indian contingent was probably the least

prepared among the participating teams. 'We did not have anyone to guide us or coach us and we certainly did not know the rules and regulations. We did not even have the proper wheelchairs. I had always considered myself the queen of para-sports in India, but my confidence was severely shaken with what I saw in South Korea. The way international para-athletes conducted themselves, the way they trained, and even their warm-up routine was a novelty for me. I never knew one had to warm up before the actual event,' recalls Malathi.

As for the wheelchair, she says, 'Luckily, my brother had escorted me and he rented a wheelchair for me for 50 dollars a day. We had only carried 500 dollars for our entire stay.' It took Malathi two days to adjust to the lightness of the racer-wheelchair which meant that she could not make it for the 100 metres race. On the bright side, she qualified for the 200 metres wheelchair finals, but finished last. She finished the race in 56.10 seconds, a timing that nobody has yet been yet able to beat in India. Though she did not win a medal, the race did give her a lot of confidence and she knew that she had a purpose in her life, that she would make her mark in the international arena.

The following year, in 1989, Malathi was selected to represent India at the prestigious World Masters in Denmark. In order to avoid the mistakes made in Seoul, Malathi and her entourage arrived in Denmark four days prior to the event so that she could practice on the racer chair. The practice paid off and Malathi won four gold medals in the 100 and 200 metres wheelchair races, and in the shot-put and javelin throw events. Despite achieving immense success, Malathi decided not to compete in wheelchair-racing events any more, as renting a special wheelchair and then getting used to it was not very easy for each event.

On a visit to Pune, legendary swimmer Anthony Pereira

advised the differently abled athlete to seize the full advantage of her strong shoulders and take up discus-throwing in place of track events. Paying heed to the legend's advice, Malathi added one more event to her repertoire, the discus throw, which was to become one of her favourite events.

After her immense victory in Denmark, Malathi's international career began full swing. In 1991, the differently abled athlete participated at the World Masters in Australia and bagged three gold medals in the javelin-throw, shot-put and discus-throw events. In fact, she even set a record in all three events in her class and category, as her attempts in all events were the longest throws ever attempted by an Indian woman. Malathi's record stands unbroken even today. In 1994, Malathi bagged a silver medal at the Asia Paralympic Games held in China.

By now she felt confident that she had achieved enough to be considered for the government's highest award in Indian sport, the Arjuna Award. Never one to let the grass grow under her feet, Malathi had always expected to be honoured by the government of India by the Arjuna Award, which is exclusively awarded to sportspersons on account of their achievement. So in 1994, Malathi made a trip to the sports ministry in Delhi to give submit her papers for consideration for the prestigious award. In 1979, two differently abled sportspersons, Taranath Shenoy and Shehnaz Kirmani, had been given this prestigious award. However, thereafter, the sports ministry in its wisdom had brought in an amendment stating that physically challenged athletes were not to be considered for the award. Therefore when Malathi reached Shastri Bhavan, where the ministry was housed, she was told that there was no amendment to give the Arjuna Award to differently abled sportspersons.

Malathi was furious and says, 'In 1979 Taranath Shenoy and

ShehnazKirmani were given this prestigious award but the sports ministry had brought in an amendment saying that the physically challenged athletes were not to be considered for this award. I was so angry when I heard the official tell me that physically challenged athletes could not be considered for the Arjuna Award. I also felt really hurt, when I heard this statement as we the disabled athletes also bring laurels to the country in our own way. I had to argue with them till the officials had no choice but to accept my papers and change the amendment. Now, at least one or two disabled athletes are considered for the Arjuna Award every year.' As the officials must have realized, Malathi was a force to reckon with, both on and off the field.

The year 1994 marked another personal victory for Malathi. Though now a manager with Syndicate Bank, Malathi used to commute the long distance to work and back by autorickshaw which was working out to be quite expensive. Travelling by bus was, of course, out of the question. One day, during the course of a conversation, a colleague informed Malathi that the Rs 1,60,000 duty on the purchase of a car had been exempted, nationwide, for differently abled people. However, it was the finance minister's office in Delhi which would grant the necessary sanctions. The elated Malathi immediately set off on an arduous, forty-six-hour journey by rail to the capital, undaunted by the fact that she would not be able to use the bathroom while on the train. A local member of Parliament (MP) from Bengaluru who knew Malathi had arranged to meet her in Delhi and had arranged a pass for her so that she could visit parliament and meet the then finance minister, Dr Manmohan Singh, to get the duty exemption sanctioned.

Upon arrival, the differently abled athlete and the MP were taken up a flight of stairs to the visitor's lounge, which was situated on the first floor. The Parliament was in session and during a break, Dr Manmohan Singh arrived, along with Arjun Singh, to meet her in a conference room that was located close to the Ministers' Lounge. Since Malathi was standing on crutches, she was offered a chair as a courtesy by the ministers. Malathi recalls wryly, 'Both the honourable ministers were in a really bad mood. I was showing them my certificates and medals that detailed my achievements in the international arena, but they seemed unimpressed. In fact, Dr Manmohan Singh asked me, "How do we believe that you are Malathi Holla and how do we believe that all these certificates belong to you?" I replied in the exact same tone of his voice, 'How do I believe that you are Dr Manmohan Singh?'"

The astounded finance minister asked her what she meant. Malathi responded by asking him why she would undertake a harrowing forty-six-hour-long train journey, during which she had to control her bladder and face a lot of mental trauma, just to cheat the ministry. The stunned finance minister told Malathi that the central duty exemption papers would be waiting for her at home when she got back to Bengaluru. Dr Manmohan Singh kept his word. Malathi says, 'I arrived in Bengaluru on my birthday and the papers were waiting for me. I had opened the door for other disabled people. Now any disabled person who wants to buy a customized car can apply for the central duty exemption papers in Delhi,' says a gushing Malathi.

Malathi's sporting victories continued unabated, too. She won the silver medal for the discus throw at the 1998 Bangkok Asian Games. In 2001, the government of India bestowed its third highest award given to civilians, the Padma Shri, on her. The differently abled athlete was training for the Asian Games in Pune whenre she received a call informing her of the news that she was being considered for the prestigious award on account of her achievements by the Indian government. 'I was surprised to know that I was being considered for the Padma Shri. I was not sure if I would even get the award. But the next day, when my name was splashed all over the media I was in shock. That day I truly felt that despite all the trials and tribulations, I had truly achieved the goal that I had set for myself.'

In 2002, Malathi was named captain of the Indian contingent to the Busan Asian Games and given the ultimate honour of being the nation's flag bearer at the opening ceremony. In 2003, 2004 and 2005, she participated in the Open Championships held Belgium, Birmingham and Manchester respectively. She once again proved her mettle and picked up gold and silver medals. Malathi also got an opportunity to participate in the 2006 Commonwealth Paralympic Games where, despite suffering a serious injury, she emerged fourth. She also managed to land two silver medals in the discus-throw and shot-put events at the 2006 Asian Paralympic Games in Kuala Lumpur.

In her personal life, too, Malathi Holla took the same undaunted approach, hoping to realize her cherished girlhood dream of being a wife and a proud mother. But somewhere down the line in life, her experiences with men changed her attitude towards settling down as a married woman. As quoted in the book, *A Different Spirit*, written by Anantha Krishnan, Malathi has said that two incidents had a lasting impact, changing her attitude towards marriage. The first occurred in Chennai at the Mahavidyalaya when Ratnakumari, whom Malathi had befriended, told Malathi her own harrowing story.

An amputee, Ratnakumari had been duped by her husband who had taken all her money and run off. Owing to her own disability, Malathi felt that an incident like this could also occur with her. The second incident was what she calls the 'Kumar' episode, which occurred later in life. Much before that, however, one Mr Thirugnyanam, an administrative officer at the rehabilitation in Chennai, started writing love letters to the youngster who replied back in equal earnest. The man, who was ten to fifteen years her elder, would write poetic letters in Tamil, telling her how beautiful she was and how her beauty and her jovial nature had attracted him to her. Floored, Malathi would also reply in the same rein. One day, the warden caught the pair exchanging letters and the tryst came to an abrupt end.

Then, in 1981, Malathi met Kevin Fernandez, a technician with Martha's Hospital in Bengaluru. The athlete, who would frequent the hospital to get her callipers checked every three weeks, soon developed a friendship with the technician. Before she even knew it, friendship blossomed into love and Kevin started courting her. With a sporting career and a bank job in place, Malathi, at this point in her life, wanted to get married and settle down. It was not that she specifically wanted to marry Kevin, but she did want to settle down. And so the pair went out for movies, for dinners and even exchanged rings in front of friends. But this relationship too came to an abrupt when Kevin wrote a letter to Malathi after three years, telling her that they could not get married as they belonged to different religions and that his family would never agree to the marriage. A sad Malathi had no choice but to move on.

Then came the 'Kumar incident'. Malathi met Kumar at a seminar at the Yavanika Auditorium in Bengaluru on 4 March 1992. She was the celebrated para-athlete who was making her mark internationally, and he was the fan who wanted her autograph. After that first meeting, Kumar and Malathi would chat on the phone and he even came to visit her in office on a couple of occasions. When Malathi had to attend a national event with the Karnataka team, she asked Kumar to become the team escort. He readily agreed. Malathi taught him to use a wheelchair and he soon became an expert in gauging the requirements of the differently abled athletes. From helping the athletes to arranging their accommodation, and local transport with a view to their comfort and convenience Kumar perfectly understood the needs of these athletes.

Over time and over many such trips Malathi grew to trust Kumar and they grew closer. Within a year and a half of meeting her, Kumar asked Malathi to marry him. Every love story has its struggles and this one was no different. Malathi was a Kannadiga girl and Kumar was a Tamil boy—her parents would never agree to this match. The feisty girl duly informed Kumar of this complication.

As quoted in *A Different Spirit,* Malathi also told Kumar, 'Just seeing me like this is fine. All that people see is us sitting on wheelchairs like dolls. No one knows the pain behind that. If you want to marry someone like me then you should know the struggles that we go through in life. See us when we crawl on the wet floor to use the toilet, how we struggle when we shift ourselves from the ground to the wheelchair. Only if you understand all the pain and suffering we go through, can you even start thinking of marrying someone like me.'

Kumar took another three months to understand all of Malathi's problems and it took her almost a year to say 'yes' to his proposal. Kumar spoke to her family and took their permission to marry her too. Having cleared all the obstacles at her end, Malathi was flummoxed when Kumar kept putting off talking to his family. Soon after, Kumar's second sister got married and after her wedding he started avoiding Malathi. His phone calls became less frequent and he also did not meet her often.

After four years of courtship, Malathi and her brother finally confronted Kumar and asked him what his intentions were. He was very evasive and told them that he would be ready for marriage in 'two or ten years' time'. The siblings were disgusted. As quoted in *A Different Spirit*, Malathi told Kumar, 'May god bless you. You may not think that you have cheated me but god knows the truth. You will never again be happy in your life because god knows how much pain you have given me.' Her brother told Kumar, 'If this is your attitude, I can only thank god that it happened before the marriage and not afterwards. If this would have happened after marriage, my sister would have been neither here nor there.'

After a couple of years, Kumar invited Malathi and other differently abled athletes to his wedding in Bengaluru. While she attended the wedding and congratulated him, Malathi could not even eat or even drink a sip of water at the reception.

After the 'Kumar' incident, Malathi decided that marriage was not meant for her. Many men have proposed marriage to her even after Kumar, but she has declined them. She feels that she is not strong enough to give her heart away yet again.

With over 300 gold medals and numerous prestigious awards in her kitty, Malathi Holla has always wanted to give back to society. Her good friend and fellow differently abled swimmer Krishna Reddy, has helped her realize her dream of working with disabled people and assisting them in coping with their problems. Her fondest dream finally came true on 5 February 2004 when, with his help, the Mathru Foundation was registered.

The Foundation aims to reach disabled children in rural areas, especially those whose families are financially disadvantaged and cannot afford the cost of the rehabilitation of their children. 'Mr Krishna Reddy said that we should adopt two differently abled children and teach them everything that we knew so that these children could do something with their life. He agreed to throw his support behind me and together we started our NGO. We turned our attention to the rural areas and adopted two children who were neglected by their own family. Today I am proud to say that I am to mother of seventeen children.'

Through the Mathru Foundation, the distinguished athletes have decided to provide basic educational and medical facilities to the disabled children. The Foundation also offers unconditional support to these individuals until they are able to become independent and earn their own money.

Malathi Holla has conquered seemingly insurmountable physical, emotional, psychological and financial odds and has achieved everything that she set out to do. She has given a face and, more importantly, an identity to the differently abled athletic community in India. After winning many accolades in all spheres of life, Malathi wants to share a word of wisdom with the other budding differently abled athletes in the country.

'There are so many unsung hero and heroines in this country but their own complexes (that come along with being disabled) prevent them from truly shining in this world. A minute part of our body is paralysed but our confidence is not paralysed, our determination is not paralysed, our self-belief is not paralysed and, most importantly, our dreams and aims are not paralysed. Nothing is impossible for the disabled people. You have to accept yourself as you are and you also need to accept your failures. My father has taught me that we can turn our failures into achievements, only if we accept them.'

She hopes that her story will inspire and help many other differently abled champions from India.

ACKNOWLEDGEMENTS

It has not been easy to write *Courage beyond Compare* as a lot of emotion was attached to it. The stories of each and every one of the ten persons highlighted were overwhelming. We were given insight to astonishing human behaviour and the insensitivity of our elected officials and those in authority, who could have easily changed, or even just followed, rules and helped the differently abled sportspeople.

We must therefore acknowledge the people who have been extremely helpful in bringing this book out. First and foremost we thank Kapish Mehra and his team at Rupa Publications India. He agreed from day one that this book needed to be published as it can be an eye-opener and highly motivational to all.

Sharmila Tagore was extremely charming while giving us insights into her late husband's life. Former cricketers Yajurvendra Singh and Saba Karim, as well as the great old man of Indian cricket, Bapu Nadkarni, have to be thanked profusely for allowing us to interview them, helping us to understand what a great sportsman Tiger Pataudi was. Continuing on the Pataudi chapter, we thank Dr Ranjit Maniar for giving hours of his valuable time to help us understand how Tiger actually went on to play so well in spite of his handicap.

Prakash Padukone is such a legend and yet so humble. The great shuttler readily agreed to write the wonderful foreword. We also thank P. Gopi Chand and Ayaz Memon for their contribution and encouragement. Thanks also to budding film director, Rikhil

Bahadur, for taking some lovely photographs for the book. Profuse thanks are also due to Getty Images. They know why. All pictures in the book are courtesy either the authors or the sportspeople themselves, except when otherwise mentioned.

The families of Farman Basha, Murlikant Petkar, Satya Prakash Tewari, Rajaram Ghag, Taranath Shenoy, Devendra Jhajharia, Rajeev Bagga—all of them set aside much time to relate stories and anecdotes. It was not easy for them to relive the experience all over again. Many thanks to the paraplegic soldiers at the Army's paraplegic rehabilitation centre at Khadki in Pune who gave us details about Nir Bahadur Gurung. Malti Holla, the only female subject in our book, was so articulate and clear in her thoughts and speech, so forceful and confident in her demeanour—we hold her in high esteem.

Finally we must acknowledge the caregivers, whose astounding contribution and help in a differently abled person's life is grossly overlooked. To paraphrase Rajaram Ghag's statement in his chapter, it is not only the person in question who leads a caged life. The caregiver too is caged during the lifetime of the differently abled.

Antonita, Farman Basha's wife, Satya Prakash Tewari's father, Rajaram Ghag's wife and mother, Taranath Shenoy's wife and his entire family, Rajeev Bagga's siblings and parents who went all out to make his life comfortable so he could concentrate on badminton. These were whom we met. Of course every 'differently abled' has to have a caregiver.

And yes, Mrs Rani Sharma, mother to author Sanjay Sharma and grandmother to Medini. Her husband lost a leg to cancer, but the couple lived together to complete golden jubilee wedding anniversary and few years more. All because of the great care she gave. We salute and acknowledge her and everyone else.

A WORD OF GRATITUDE

Badminton has given me a unique life. Not just for the fitness I enjoy or the honour of playing for India for many years, but for some wonderful lifelong friends over the decades.

Some of these friends have played against me and during such matches we have been at each other's throat. But once the matches are over, we are thick as blood brothers. This is what makes sports so wonderful.

Some of them have stood by me when I was writing this book and encouraged me in every way. They were there solidly behind me when things looked bleak. They backed the cause wholeheartedly. I cannot thank them enough. Without their unstinting support, this book would have remained an unfulfilled dream. Their help and generosity allowed us to travel many times to Bangalore, Jaipur, Delhi, Sangli, Pune and to other places in search of my subjects and to research their achievements. And to take months off from other work to concentrate on writing this book.

I must mention these friends from Bombay Gymkhana, that wonderful club in Mumbai.

Kartik Jajal, Lalit Daga, Amol Shah, Mayank Mehta, Achutan Siddhartha, Shailesh Daga, Ayaz Bilawala, Ravi Kumar, Bliss Pharma, Pradip Mafatlal. Most special thanks to Gautam Ashra, who stood like a rock behind the project. And Kiran Kaushik, who made the book release function a reality in a memorable way.

I thank, from depths of my heart, my wife, my life—Deepti.

She has been a great companion for almost thirty-two years, suffering my eccentricities and idiosyncrasies, sometimes with a frown, but mostly with a smile.

And my never-ending love affair with the two most precious girls in my life—my daughters Medini and Shachi.

Finally, many thanks to actor, Salman Khan, for all his help. He has a heart of gold.

Sanjay Sharma
Mumbai

DEDICATION

I first met Late Aditya Birlaji, doyen of Indian industry, sometime in 1984, after playing the National Badminton Championships in Pune. I had done well and was known in the sports circles of Mumbai. My first meeting with Adityaji was by chance at the badminton courts of the Cricket Club of India.

He was a keen follower of sports and quite a good badminton player. He was very humble and very down to earth. A man who was very soft-spoken, very intellectual and worldly wise, and someone who always put you at ease. He followed badminton regularly and was a big fan of the legendary Prakash Padukone.

And he was a wonderful host. When he came to know I lived near his residence on Malabar Hill, Mumbai, he called me over for breakfast a few times and we talked a lot about sports in general and badminton in particular, in his wonderful house.

Adityaji was snatched away from us at a very young age but his memories remain with us. And his large heartedness was well known when he was alive through the philanthropy and charity he personally indulged in but never talked about. After his most sad and untimely demise, the Aditya Vikram Birla Memorial Trust was set up by the Birla Family.

The Trust continues to do yeoman service to society by donating crores of rupees to needy causes annually. For the handicapped, there are huge provisions for help with motorized vehicles and other facilities. Donations from the Trust have also helped in eradicating polio in a big way.

The Trust is a multifaceted organization engaged in various charitable activities in India and overseas. It is actively associated in rural development projects and assists the underprivileged strata of society in education and medical relief.

It funds the Indian National Theater, a seventy-year-old organization, in conducting research in folk arts, especially in Maharashtra and Gujarat. The trust also provides seed capital to young and needy entrepreneurs so that they can achieve self-reliance.

Amongst many other activities, the Trust also donates substantially to the ISKON Food Relief Foundation.

We dedicate this book to Aditya Birlaji and to the Aditya Vikram Birla Memorial Trust.

Sanjay Sharma
Medini Sharma

Printed in Poland
by Amazon Fulfillment
Poland Sp. z o.o., Wrocław